'Kenny tells his amazing story with heartfelt honesty. A compelling read'                                     Alan Peary, *Rugby World*

'Laugh-out-loud good and the triumphs and tragedies of Logan's life on and off the field are told with searing honesty. Not your average sportsman's autobiography'                              *Observer*

'An engaging autobiography . . . offering an extra dimension with the story of his dyslexia'                              *Guardian*

'An emotional ride with the goalkicking Scot, who hid his dyslexia for three decades'                                     *Rugby World*

'A better read than the tabloid headlines suggested, with Logan's typical blunt honesty making it a refreshingly candid account of professional sport'                                     *Scotsman*

'Kenny writes movingly about IVF treatment'        *Sunday Express*

**Kenny Logan** is Scottish rugby's most capped winger with 70 caps. He played in three World Cups and numerous Five and Six nations campaigns for his country. After winning the Scottish league Championship with his local team, Stirling County, in 1997 he transferred to Wasps where he won three Premiership titles, two English Cups, a European Challenge Cup and the Heineken Cup. He appeared in *Strictly Come Dancing* and is now heavily involved in charity work. He lives in London with his wife, the sports presenter Gabby Logan, and their twins.

**Michael Aylwin**, who worked with Kenny on the writing of this book, has been a sportswriter since 1996, and a rugby writer at the *Observer* since 2000, with whom he has covered two World Cups. His account of the two years he spent with the Saracens squad, *The Red and the Black*, was published in 1999.

# KENNY LOGAN

## JUST for KICKS

### The Autobiography

with Michael Aylwin

headline

First published in 2009
by HEADLINE PUBLISHING GROUP

First published in paperback in 2010
by HEADLINE PUBLISHING GROUP

1

Cataloguing in Publication Data is available from the British Library

ISBN 978 0 7553 1970 1

Typeset in Adobe Garamond by Ellipsis Books Limited, Glasgow

Statistics compiled by John Griffiths

Printed and bound in Great Britain by
Clays Ltd, St Ives Plc

Headline's policy is to use papers that are natural, renewable
and recyclable products and made from wood grown in sustainable forests.
The logging and manufacturing processes are expected to conform
to the environmental regulations of the country of origin.

HEADLINE PUBLISHING GROUP
An Hachette UK Company
338 Euston Road
London NW1 3BH

www.headline.co.uk
www.hachette.co.uk

To Dad and Hamish

# Contents

# Acknowledgements

It would take another book to thank all the people I want to. So let's start with a big thank you to everyone. You know who you are.

Some special mentions, though. To begin at the beginning, thanks go to Mum. You've been a rock from the start, there's no one better in a crisis, and I know Dad would be proud of how you've handled things since he's been gone. To my brothers, James and Andrew, we've had our run-ins (what else are brothers for?), but we've always come back for more.

A huge thank you to my cousins across the field – John, our beloved Hamish, Ally and Kelso, as well as Uncle Archie and Aunt Margaret. I spent so much of my childhood with you, and so much of me has grown from that. So too to Jas Logan and Muff Scobie, more cousins who have had such an influence on me, and to Hendy and Margaret and Tommy Brewster and his family.

Robbie, you've been the best best mate a man could ask for. You were always my biggest supporter and my harshest critic –

and that's saying something. Thanks, too, to your mum and dad, Jenny and Iain, and to your sister, Nicola, for doing so much to help me through my early years.

Norrie Bairner was crucial then too. Thanks to you for crossing the picket line, when other teachers were striking, so that we kids could still play sport. It ended up being pretty important to me, I'd say.

I'm nervous about picking out even a few people from my rugby career, because where do you stop? Thanks to all the staff and my team-mates at Stirling County, Wasps and Scotland. That's a lot of people. But here goes with some special mentions: Sandy Bryce for the early years; Richie Dixon for his help both with Stirling and Scotland; Jim Telfer for being the most brilliantly loveable and hate-able guy in the world; Ian McGeechan for his wisdom and listening; Nigel Melville for helping me settle in London; Gareth Rees for keeping me together through some dark times; Kevin Lidlow and Mark Bitcon for just keeping me together; Shaun Edwards for, well, everything. And then there are all those I took to the field with, some of whom are still such good mates, long after we finished: Shawsy, Kingy, Scrivs, Greeny, Lol, Big Gav, Brush, Gregor, Taity, the McKenzie brothers… Stop it. We could be here for ever.

Thanks to Gabby's parents, Terry and Christine – Terry for his wicked humour and advice from a lifetime in sport; Christine for her support and high spirits. And, Auntie Jayne, you've been the fourth grandparent the kids never had.

Ola and James Jordan have taught me new skills I never thought I'd have (but lay off the Grey Goose, James), as have Ed Percival and John Vincent.

Writing this book has been a big journey for me and one I couldn't have considered taking just a few years ago. Thanks to Jonathan Conway of Mulcahy Conway Associates and Matt Jones of Benchmark Sport for setting up all the handshakes. Thanks to David Wilson of Headline for agreeing to publish it and to Rhea Halford for her time and patience editing it. Graham Law, Jim Mailer and the Stirling Observer have all provided information and photographs. My business partner, Paul Sefton, and our PAs, Philippa and Bernie, have kept things going while I've been wrestling with words and proofs, as have Maria and Paula. And big thanks to my ghostwriter, Mike, for all the hours on the couch and at your screen. I hope Vanessa and young Max recognise you with that beard you've grown.

Lastly and most of all, thanks to Gabby. I've been flying ever since you walked into my life. You made me face up to my biggest fear and overcome it. You've given us a couple of stars in Reuben and Lois. The future's looking bright for all of us.

# Prologue

'Here, have a read of this. Tell me what you think.'

It was a simple suggestion by the gorgeous blonde who had walked into my life only three weeks earlier. She pushed a tabloid newspaper in my direction, but little did she know she was setting me an impossible challenge. The paper sat in front of me, open at a page that featured a big picture of her. I recognised that much. If only I could make out any of the words.

Here I was, a twenty-six-year-old man with a job to die for and a reputation for confidence and banter. But I was carrying a secret that had dogged me throughout my life. A fear of being found out turned that life into a long and exhausting exercise in avoidance and cover-up. Almost all the things I had going for me were actually little more than defence mechanisms, called up to hide the flaw that, as far as I was concerned, made me inferior to every man, woman and child I ever met.

I couldn't read or write.

The woman standing over me had a law degree and a

blossoming media career. She was smart, successful and beautiful, and already I had fallen in love with her. But at that particular moment I couldn't see how our relationship was going to make it into its second month. She was onto me.

This was a secret I'd kept for nearly thirty years. My brothers must have known about it, but we never discussed it. Same with my friends at school. I'd played rugby with some of the best players in the world, in the most elite environments, which meant I had spent hundreds, maybe thousands, of hours in the company of big hairy men, baring our souls and analysing our strengths and weaknesses. Here we were at the top of our chosen field and none of them had any idea that I didn't even know my vowels. They hadn't noticed that whenever there were pens and pieces of paper waiting for us in the team-meeting room, Kenny wasn't there. They certainly didn't know I was hiding in the toilets all the while.

From the moment I met Gabby I knew my life had changed. She can read better than anyone I've ever known. And I don't mean just books. Gabby sussed me out almost immediately. Not only that, but she could see what dyslexia had done to me and what it might still go on to do. She pushed and pushed and pushed until I'd faced up to my condition, the guilty secret and bane of my life, and done something about it. That something ended up being a programme for treating dyslexia that has transformed my life. I finally learnt those vowels, aged thirty. Anything seemed possible.

Some of the best years of my rugby career followed. It's unusual for a winger to improve in his thirties, when his pace and power may not be what they once were, but it was as if my brain had become unlocked. I could see new things on the field. I could concentrate better and remember calls. I became more measured and mature.

It dawned on me that I was actually learning. This was what it was like. When I was at school I suffered from this feeling of shock and terror that never went away. My time there was simply a matter of crisis management and damage limitation. I found it demoralising and exhausting, and if it hadn't been for the fact that I was from a family of good, honest farmers and that I then went on to prove myself a good rugby player, I don't know where I would have ended up.

But I've always found a way through – to the tryline, to the bar, to getting the girl, to being able to read and write. And now I'm married to the person I adore more than I ever thought you could adore anyone. We have two beautiful kids, a boy and a girl, both born the same day, both with their lives ahead of them. Everything's worked out perfectly. I'm happier now than I've ever been.

Just don't ask me how it happened. Any of it – the tries, the caps, the cups, the triumphs, the disasters, the dancing, the reading, the writing, the wife, the kids. All I can try to do is sit down and describe *what* happened. And even that would have been beyond me a few years ago.

# I

# School's Out

The clearest memory I have of my time at school is the moment I walked away from it. I remember that long, dark corridor I strode along with windowless double doors at the end, my head burning with frustration, embarrassment and exhilaration at what I was doing. For the first time in a school environment I knew that what I was doing was exactly right. Ten out of ten at last.

I slammed my hands against the doors like a cowboy in the Wild West and they flew open. The light outside blinded me, the sun was so bright, and I flinched, but I carried on walking. I didn't look back once, not even when I remembered I'd left my bag in the exam room. It was 1988, I was sixteen, and I was walking away from my first and, as it turned out, last shot at a qualification.

That's how my schooldays ended, and it was a liberation. For nearly ten years I'd suffered tension in my stomach every day at school, I found it so stressful. It was as if I was going to a job interview five times a week, that feeling when you're about to meet someone really important, and you're scared, worried you might say the wrong thing. I've had nerves in other situations since then. Before a big game you get nervous, but they're good nerves – they put you on the balls of your feet and make you feel as if you could fly if you had to. Those school nerves, though, dragged me down. It was like being in shock.

The whole time at school I'd just wanted to be normal. When you're a child, all you're doing is trying to get through. You're not thinking, 'Oh God, I'm different. I'm not working normally. I can't read or write.' School can be cruel – kids don't mean to be, but they're vicious. It's, 'You stink,' or 'You're fat.' In my case it was, 'You're stupid, you can't read.' I used to try to ignore it, but it was impossible, and I would get so upset and embarrassed. I look back now and I can't believe I stuck it out. If I have problems with something these days, I'll address them, but I didn't have the tools to do that as a lad. So I just took it all on the chin and suffered in silence.

However hard things got, though, I would always turn up and face the music. I never once plugged school, as we used to call it. I missed a fair bit, because my nerves made me ill, but I was always taught to face up to things, which is what I tried to do.

So, every time I went into the classroom, I took a big, deep breath and sat there, scared out of my mind. I couldn't wait for the bell to go, or to get myself thrown out for being naughty, which at least relieved the pressure.

It wasn't so bad early on, because at primary school everyone's a wee bit slow, trying to get to grips with new things, but that confusion I'd felt at the start when I was confronted with letters and words never went away. By the end of primary school I was feeling inadequate – by the time I got to high school I just felt stupid.

Concentration was another serious problem. I couldn't concentrate at all. I was always looking out the window, distracted by the smallest things. Words were coming into my head at all angles and from all sources and I just couldn't process any of them. They fell straight through my brain, which was like a sieve.

Teachers would say, 'Kenny, you can't even copy from the blackboard. You must concentrate,' And I would try so hard. Hundreds of times I said to myself, 'Right, I'm really going to concentrate today.' I would look at the first word, and I would check it and check it, letter by letter, and then I would hear noises from somewhere else, and I would start to fall behind and my writing would falter. I would check it again, hear more noises, and then it was, 'I've finished, Miss.' But I'd only done two words. And I'd usually spelt them wrongly. I had problems realising where I'd got to in a word, so that I would rewrite individual letters, not realising I'd already written them. Instead of writing 'history', for example, I might write 'histostory'.

No one discussed my problems with me, not my family, not

my teachers, not my friends. I don't blame anyone for it, certainly not my family. Why should anyone have thought I had a problem? People just thought I wasn't the brightest. I was outgoing and keen to get involved in anything. I thrived on the sports field, not just in rugby, but football, athletics, golf – I loved playing them all. In my teens I was offered trials by Dundee and Hearts but the dates clashed with rugby, which was the sport I preferred – and the advice of my cousin and mentor, Hamish, was always ringing in my ears. 'Och,' he used to say to me, 'you're not a hard man if you play football.'

I never had any problem making friends, either, and on my father's farm I was in my element – there might even have been the odd sign of intelligence there because I picked up practical things quickly. So I know it would have been difficult for anyone to see past all that, but there was a little kid inside who just wasn't growing up with the rest of me. He was desperate for help but didn't know how to ask for it. He didn't even understand that what he was going through wasn't right.

———————

The place where I was really happy growing up was at home on the family farm. There, my problems were irrelevant. Everything came naturally, from jumping in the lorry with my cousins to mucking out pens. At the age of six I could drive a tractor. I was lifting bales at seven or eight. Reading and writing didn't get a look-in.

Our farm, or farms when you consider the two neighbouring

ones were run by my uncle and his sons, stretched over six hundred acres at the foot of the Ochil Hills, near Stirling. The Wallace Monument stood high over us on Abbey Craig. It's known as Braveheart country nowadays, but even before Mel Gibson we were proud of the land.

It was an amazing place to grow up, flat farming country as far as you could see in one direction and the higher ground rising up around us in the other. Off to the left was Dumyat, a rocky hill at the edge of the Ochils. It has some of the best views in Scotland – the Forth Valley, Edinburgh, Stirling and the Wallace Monument – and I was always told that it was actually up there, not on Abbey Craig, that Wallace watched events unfold before coming down to give the English a bit of a doing at Stirling Bridge. We were nestled in between Dumyat and the monument, which rose up out of the woods on the slopes of the craig. It was there that I proposed to Gabby.

Compared to its stunning surroundings, our farmhouse was grim. It looked as if it had been built of old stone and crap cement, then rendered over and painted grey to blend in with the other farm buildings. At the front there was a little porch that looked ready to blow over in the wind. There was no central heating, so I put on more clothes to go to bed than I wore during the day. 'Can't we get some central heating, Dad?' I would beg. 'Ach, son, you're soft!' Well, I was more than happy to be soft! Sometimes when I got up in the morning, the curtains would be stuck to the windows with frost. The glass was as thin as paper. My father was always buying new tractors for the farm. 'How about some new windows for the house, John?' my mother would say.

The place was heated by coal fires and we had an Aga, so we were always chopping wood. We had four bedrooms with one bathroom upstairs, and a shower downstairs – but that was only because we'd built a tiny extension. I helped Dad knock the wall down for it and managed to drive the sharp end of a claw hammer into the top of my head.

My lovely mad old aunt Rita, who was known as Bonzo, had a section of the house to herself. She only used the downstairs, but for some reason wouldn't let us use her upstairs, even though we were overflowing in our section. My brothers and I would alternate sharing a room. For a while I even shared with my dad, because he got up so early my mum wanted her own room.

I was happy there, though. I had a focus on the farm that I didn't have at school. I knew my path and felt a different energy. It was like when I was on the rugby field – it was my domain, I knew what I was doing, I could see things clearly. When I came up with ideas about what we should do on the farm, my dad would say that it wouldn't work, but within a year we'd be doing it. He wasn't good with practical matters. My brothers and my cousins and I, we were all good with our hands, creative with them, but none of that was for my dad. He was only concerned with his animals, and he understood them like no one else. It was almost mystical.

Dad was one of the most respected farmers in the country. Everyone called him Uncle John. You ask any farmer of a certain age in Scotland about John Logan, they'll tell you he was one of the nicest farmers they've ever known and one of the most honest, too. His herd of cattle was renowned throughout Scotland, even

9

throughout the world. He kept Holstein-Friesians, award-winning ones, and people came just to see them. There were always school visits, with my dad showing the kids around, but even his peers would come to have a look. We'd be working on the farm and a bus would turn up. 'Who are these blokes?' I'd ask. They were usually farmers who had come to see his herd. Some of them had travelled from overseas.

Farmers did that kind of thing. Dad was so devoted to his farming that my parents went as far as to visit a farm in Devon for their honeymoon. Maybe partly because of this obsession, Dad didn't marry until he was forty. When I was born, which was on 3 April 1972 in Stirling Royal Infirmary, he was fifty-five. I see it as a mistake to have left it so late, but Mum, who was fifteen years younger than he was and a farmer's daughter from Lockerbie, says that it just came naturally to him that way.

By the time I was a teenager and old enough to be looking for trouble, my dad was in his sixties and my mum in her early fifties. My brothers were off discovering girls. James is seven years older than I am, and Andrew five years older. It was just the wrong age difference – too big for me to be of any interest to them and too small for them to be mature enough to want to look after me. They didn't want me hanging around. A little brother wasn't cool.

So, as I grew up, I spent most of my time with my cousins – Hamish, John, Ally and Kelso. They were older than my brothers, but younger than my parents, and had no problem with me tagging along, riding in the tractor, going away with them in the lorry. They were at an age where it was quite fun to have a little feller to keep them company.

I was very close to my dad, but he was more like a granddad to me. If I had a father figure, it would be Hamish, my eldest cousin, who was seventeen years older than me. They lived a mile down the road from us, my uncle Archie, who was my dad's younger brother, Auntie Margaret and the four boys. I used to cycle round to theirs or run over the fields, and I spent so much time with them that they were like my immediate family in the early years.

When I was about twelve, just as my problems at school were becoming serious, the families decided to split up the three farms. The youngsters were all getting older, and there were too many people wanting to work, so each of the three farms took a portion of the land and became loosely independent. I didn't understand what was happening and thought it meant I wouldn't be able to see my cousins any more. I was so upset I cried my eyes out for days. It turned out that it didn't make any difference, but it showed how important they had become to me.

And still no one ever talked about school, which was fine by me. I think maybe my mother feels a bit guilty about it now, but I would never blame either of my parents for not trying to tackle my problems with reading. I never wanted to talk about it because it stirred up so many emotions that I'd kept hidden. It's only in the last few years that I've learnt to discuss the subject.

My father was a very well-educated man. He had been Dux of his school, which means he was top of the class. None of that made me any more inclined to approach him. At that age I didn't want to let him down, or even show him any signs of weakness. Besides, he was a reserved man – a gentleman from another era

– and he probably wouldn't have felt comfortable if I'd unloaded all my insecurities on him. There was barely the time for it anyway. He went to bed at nine and got up at four every day of his working life – even when he fell ill towards the end of it.

I would occasionally ask my mum what a word said, and she would tell me, but I don't think she had a great time at school, either, so we never took it any further. She had been a matron, but she has never liked to discuss her own school life. She can get emotional when she doesn't want to talk about something, and I honestly don't know much about her childhood because she has never told me. I do know that she was very sporty. She was a fast runner and has always loved horses – even now, well into her seventies, she rides – and she still has plenty of get up and go. In a crisis, she was the one we all turned to. She is so supportive, and if something needs doing, she wants to do it right away. In that respect, I can see a lot of her in me. I can see a lot of my dad, too. They both taught me the value of honesty and integrity, and I've tried to follow that.

I remember one time a local man was keen to buy some of my father's land so he could build a house on it, but he needed planning permission. He offered to pay £2,000 a year for five years while he tried to get it. My dad had actually tried himself and knew it couldn't be done, so he told this guy not to waste his money. I was about fifteen and I said to Dad, 'Why don't you just take the money? If he doesn't get planning permission, that's his problem.'

'That house might be their dream,' he replied, 'and they're not going to get planning permission for it. You don't ruin a person's dream and take their money while you're doing it.'

His manner was understated, and he was a quiet man, which is not something I've inherited. At a young age, I was messing around with words I didn't understand. We had a horse called Sammy.

'Dad,' I said to him once while he was reading his paper. 'Sammy's a fucker.'

Dad ignored me. I repeated it, but still no reaction. The next day I came in and said, 'Dad, Sammy's my friend.' He dropped his paper immediately and said, 'That's more like it, son.'

I think he understood me, although I was very different from him in a lot of ways – I was more outgoing and flamboyant, like Hamish. And I did get into a lot of trouble, not just at school.

I was often bored on the farm, because I had no one my age to play with. One day I was so bored that I blew up a van. It belonged to Burt Adams, who was a slater by trade and a dear friend of my father's. Every now and then he used to buy a knackered old combi van, same type, same colour, and strip off parts as and when he needed them for the van he actually drove around in, which was always falling apart. He kept his substitute one on an old road behind our farm. I was wandering past it with a box of matches and decided there and then to blow it up, basically for something to do. Although no one rated me much in the classroom, I knew that petrol plus matches equals bad. So I lit one, dropped it in the tank and legged it.

What followed was just like in a Bond film. The doors flew off and the van leapt into the air. I kept running, all the way home. Unfortunately, Burt just happened to drive along the road in time to see his van go up and my little arse fast retreating into the distance. I was covered from head to toe in dust from the explosion when I ran into the house, gasping with shock at what I'd done. My dad was there but, before he had time to say anything, in ran Burt shouting that his van had exploded and that he'd seen me running away from it. I denied all knowledge, of course, but I was all over the place and covered in dust so I never stood much of a chance of getting away with it.

Dad never bollocked me. I got a long talk about safety and why I shouldn't have done it, but there was always sympathy and understanding in everything he did. That's all a kid really needs, I believe, for a sound upbringing, and, however horrific my time at school, it was always offset by my happiness at home on the farm. It was the perfect place to escape.

But no child can ever really escape school. Most kids have some kind of problem while they're there. There's a lot of pressure, whether it's pressure to be clever, good at sport, popular – boiled down, it's the need to be cool in some way, and if you're not you can suffer terrible alienation. I was all right in a lot of those ways – I was good at sport, and I never had problems making friends. I think some of the teachers liked me. I was disruptive because I was so desperate to get out of the classroom, but I think some of them knew I meant well.

My first school was Beaconhurst in Bridge of Allan, which was a private school. I remember staying behind to do my homework. It was basic stuff, but I really struggled with it, and when I couldn't do it no one seemed to think it was a big deal. It's all new and strange to everyone at that age. By the age of seven, though, I was starting to wonder if maybe there was something different about me. I was communicating fine, making friends in the playground, but I noticed that I wasn't picking up things as well as the others. But when you're so young, it doesn't really register – you don't think about why you're not reading or writing, because you're so absorbed in just being a kid.

Everyone's in the same boat, but one by one people start to climb out and to find their feet. I never did. I was still splashing around in the water, and every day I felt as if I was drowning. That was when I started to develop stomach pains, off and on to begin with, but they were to grow worse and plagued me until the day I walked away from school.

I was unhappy at Beaconhurst, but things got better when I moved to Riverside Primary, a state school in Stirling, at the age of nine. It was a bigger school and seemed to me to be a happier place. Teachers took more of an interest in me. They kept sending me out of the classroom, but I think they liked me. That was where I met Jenny Mailer. She worked in admin at the school, and whenever I was sent out I would go along and talk to her. 'What have you done this time, Kenny?' she would say, and then she would chat to me, tell me I needed to concentrate.

A couple of other teachers were really kind to me and even came to see me when I was off school for about six weeks towards the end of my time there. My stomach pains were kicking in with a vengeance, and the stress started to rise to a new level. I'd had two years at Riverside and the first year and a half were the happiest of my schooldays. But the last few months were haunted by the realisation that high school was approaching. I knew it would be different there. I knew it would be harsh.

My first day at Wallace High was a bad one, set up by an incident in those last few months at Riverside. I had already had my first taste of being bullied and labelled stupid. 'Oh, here comes Thicko!' and 'You're the guy that can't read' – all that. Then I broke the nose of the school bully, which made things even worse. I never looked for fights, and that was the only time I ever punched anyone, but if someone was going to fight me, I was going to fight back. In the playground at Riverside this guy had been winding me up something rotten, just chanting 'thick, thick, thick' and I clocked him one. Sure enough, after that I became known as the school bully – the school bully, and thick with it.

On my very first day at Wallace High, the cousins of the guy whose nose I'd broken came looking for me after school and chased me down the road. I ran up to a random house and hammered on the door, shouting, 'Nana! Nana! Let me in!' Understandably, the old lady inside didn't open the door, so these guys gave me a good kicking. Within the first week, the headmaster had issued me with a warning. He knew I was disruptive, he said, and he was ready to expel me. And so it was that the tone of my high-school years had been set.

One teacher, however, was crucial for me back then – a guy called Norrie Bairner. The teacher strikes in Scotland in the mid-

1980s nearly killed sport in schools, but Norrie would get in at 7.30 a.m. to give us an hour of training and touch rugby in the gym. He and others like him were called scabs by the striking teachers, but Norrie had always done this for free anyway, and he kept my enthusiasm for sport going, as he did for loads of other kids. Although it was my cousins, Hamish and John, who introduced me to rugby, Norrie Bairner's commitment to helping us kids play sport would help me in my life in more ways than I could have imagined.

The school has been pulled down since I left, and a new one built. The place I remember was a big lump of concrete with dirty windows, dark corridors and nothing at all to inspire a kid. It was a big school with around a thousand kids from all walks of life, everything that Stirling had to offer. I remember the gates and the big car park in front of it, always with lots of cars. We played the coin game against the front of the school, where you had to throw a coin as close to the wall as you could without touching it. The winner took all the coins home with him.

Whether or not I had coins in my pocket, going home was always emotional. I used to walk from the bus stop to the farm. The minute I walked away from the bus I could wind down and most of the time that meant tears. There was a hedge in front of our house that I used to jump over so I could save myself the extra twenty yards and get home quicker. Sometimes I would get home too fast and still be crying, and I would rush upstairs to straighten myself out.

On one particularly bad occasion, I stood in front of the bathroom mirror in a rage and punched myself over and over again.

It was at the height of those worst times, between the ages of eleven and fourteen, when every day was an ordeal. There seemed no let-up. It wasn't as if I had the odd good day in between the bad ones. They were all terrible. The frustration was unbearable. Why wasn't this stuff going in my head? I punched myself until my face was inflamed. It's common for a schoolboy to invent accidents to explain to his mother the black eye that someone had given him at school, but that evening I had to invent one to explain the black eye I had given myself. It would not be the first time that rugby provided me with a way out.

But before anyone starts to feel too sorry for me, the headmaster was right – I was a troublemaker. Being a troublemaker and struggling in the classroom have a chicken-and-egg relationship, but in short I found troublemaking the best way to get out of class. A teacher would say, 'We're in the science lab now, please don't turn on the Bunsen burners.' Well, how could I resist? Most of the work I can remember doing was copying out lines. I don't remember doing any homework at all, but three words I do know how to spell are 'I', 'must' and 'not', because I wrote them so many times. I must not talk in class; I must not be disruptive; I must sit still.

It wasn't long before I was put in a remedial class. I remember lots of empty chairs. There were just the six of us. The others came from rough parts of Stirling. There was a guy who was basically a traveller, although he would have hated me saying it. These days he would be described as a bit bling. 'I don't know why I'm in this class,' he used to say. 'Yeah,' I would agree. 'I don't know why I'm in it either. It's a joke!' One of the girls, I now think, had ADHD. Another guy went on to be a painter. We were an odd bunch. I stood out because I was the only one who would come to school in uniform. And I would always come in. The others thought nothing of skipping school. I was fine with getting myself sent out, but getting myself expelled was never an option.

My best mates at the time were Jason Yarrow, who would go on to play squash for Scotland, and Gavin Carlin, who probably would have played rugby for Scotland if he hadn't wrecked his knee as a teenager. They knew I had problems, but, again, it was never discussed. I would just turn left to go to my classroom and they would turn right for theirs.

For woodwork and science, however, we were all in the class together, and it was in a science class, at about the age of thirteen, that the last hopes for my school career were snuffed out. There were no empty chairs in that classroom, so there was a bit of an audience. I said to the teacher that if she could read me the questions, I really felt I could answer them. It was meant to be a way of showing her I was vulnerable, but it came across as if I was some upstart telling her how to teach. She hauled me up in front of the class and read the questions to me. I got something like eight out of ten of them right and I was euphoric. 'You see! I told you! I told you I could do it!'

She hit the roof and sent me out. Nothing new in that, but this time it was different and I remember it as if it was yesterday. This punishment was for being full of myself, when in fact I had just felt so overjoyed that I might not be so stupid after all. It crushed me. If that teacher came in now, I wouldn't even recognise her, but that was a turning point. After that, I thought,

'Right, I've just got to get to the end of this. Get through school, enjoy my rugby, and that's it.' I didn't care anyway. For a long time it had been assumed by my family, as well as by me, that I was going to end up on the farm, whatever happened, so the fact that I wasn't getting anywhere in the classroom was looking more and more irrelevant. I wasted the three years that followed at high school. I simply waited for my time to run out.

# 2

# Growing Pains

By my mid-teens, I was starting to make waves as a rugby player. Hamish and John were always off playing rugby, and, when I was old enough, it had seemed natural to go along with them to Stirling County rugby club. Hamish would pick me up and leave me to run around with the minis in the early years. He was a great player – the best in our family – a big man with massive shoulders and an even bigger heart. He left Stirling to join West of Scotland, a club in Glasgow, who at the time were in the top flight when Stirling were in the one below. It caused a bit of a stir. He was a prop forward. They used to complain that he spent too much time running round with the ball in his hands, but these days he would have been capped just like that.

We had a good mini-rugby team at Stirling County. We just loved playing, and that was enough motivation to do well in the competitions that we entered. We used to reach the final on a regular basis, as much as anything because it meant we could play more games than if we got knocked out. We used to go to tournaments every weekend in Edinburgh, Glasgow, even the Borders. We never cared about the weather – I remember some kids turning blue in the cold. I wasn't the best player in the side, but I was always in the team because I was quick and strong and worked hard. I made friends with a lad called Mark McKenzie, who I would go on to play with at various levels. I played prop, and Gareth Flockhart, another who would become a good friend, was the other prop. Between us, at hooker, was a girl called Alison McGrandles. A guy we used to call Ginger was the other hooker, and he was mad that he couldn't get in the side ahead of Alison. He was a great guy, but the banter was killing him and he gave up rugby in the end. Maybe he took some comfort from the fact that Alison went on to win seventy-odd caps for Scotland Women.

We were a good bunch of kids, but I don't remember a lot else about those early days, other than that I never passed the ball, and by the time I was a teenager this was becoming a problem. In my rugby career, I have played in every position – didn't last too long at fly-half, it's true, but I've played every-where. For a while it seemed likely I would end up at openside, but I was always adamant I wanted to be a back. By the time I was thirteen I had convinced them I should play at outside centre. This is where people started to resent my refusal to pass.

Sandy Bryce, a well-known referee, was our coach. He said to the team one day, 'Right, no one pass Kenny the ball today.' The team followed his orders to the letter and by the end of the game I was seething with anger. Sandy sat me down and said, 'That's how everyone else feels when you get the ball.' So I had lessons to learn, but by then I was in love with the game.

Sandy was also a farmer, and I used to help him level the pitches every summer.

'Och, I'd love to play on this pitch one day,' I mentioned to him when we were working on the first-team pitch.

'You'll play on it,' he said. 'You'll do more than that – you'll play for Scotland.'

'No, no. I just want to play for Stirling County,' I replied.

That wasn't strictly true – I'd had ambitions to play for Scotland for a while by then. When I was twelve, my mum bought me a Scotland jersey, when Scotland won the Grand Slam in 1984, but I wouldn't wear it. I wanted to earn one the hard way. I wanted the one my hero Andy Irvine had worn.

By the time I was fourteen, it looked as if I might have a chance to win the junior version. Gavin Carlin and I had made it from Wallace High School to the North and Midlands Schoolboy team. This was the route into the Scotland Under-15 team, which took on Wales every year. I'd played really well all season, now at full-back, and I went along to the trial. Everyone was saying, 'Och, you'll get in. Nae problem.'

As the time for the announcement approached, I was off school with a bad throat – it was at the lowest part of my worst times at school. I was seeing specialists about all the ailments I was going down with, but none of them knew what was causing them, and neither did I. One of the doctors eventually asked if I was having problems at school, and suddenly the connection was made. My body was full of tension because of the stress. Looking back, it may even have been a kind of depression.

Now this worry about making the Under-15s was adding to the mix. I kept ringing Gavin, asking, 'Have you heard yet? Have you heard?'

Then one day, he rang me. 'I've got the letter!' he said, and his voice trailed off as he realised I hadn't. My heart sank. I remember going through to my mother, crying my eyes out.

'That's it! I can't play rugby any more! I'm not good enough!' I wailed. It looked then as if that jersey she'd bought me was going to stay in its cellophane forever. But mum was to become a constant source of support to me in my rugby career, and it started then. 'This will make you stronger,' she said. 'In a few years you'll think of it as the best thing that ever happened to you.'

At the same time though, the rejection ripped the heart out of me. I felt embarrassed by it, because rugby was always my trump card. Useless in the classroom, maybe, but rugby? I was meant to be good at that. Why didn't they want me? People said it was because I wasn't from the right school. There was a public school bias, they reckoned, and they may have been right. Gavin was so good, it didn't matter what school he went to. He was my best mate, so I was really chuffed about him making it, but when I went back to school, everyone was patting him on the back and

I was dying inside. I cried for days, but it was the best thing that could have happened to me.

Hamish took me aside and said, 'You've always told me you want to play for Scotland. So what's changed? This is nothing. The Under-15s mean nothing.' He was right about that. None of that year's side went on to play for Scotland. Not one of them even made the Under-18s. In Gavin's case it was because of that knee injury. Who knows how far he could have gone, but for that? For the most part, though, rugby at that age is not a reliable indicator of who is going to make it – not that it felt like that at the time.

———

Hamish was becoming more and more important to me. He was married now, and for a while I felt a bit uncomfortable going round to see him and his wife Jean, who has always been known as Bash. I thought that maybe they didn't want a kid hanging round any more. In the end, he broached the subject, saying that they hadn't seen so much of me lately. I told him my concerns, and he was shocked. 'Don't be stupid! We love ya! Get yourself over here!'

So many of my best memories on the farm involve Hamish. When I was a young lad he would let me sit with him in the cab of the tractor, but he told me I had to hit the deck any time I saw a policeman, because it was illegal to have a child with you. Whenever we went out on the road, I spent most of the time cowering behind the driver's seat, not that any of our local policemen would have really cared. They weren't exactly patrolling the lanes.

My routine was to run or cycle over the fields to meet up with Hamish, John, Ally and Kelso as soon as I got back from school. I remember hot days with the roof off the tractor, and running around chasing sheep. All good, wholesome stuff.

Hamish and John were taking on the family business. My father had been an institution in the farming community, and they were the next generation. They had bold new ideas about breeding cattle. They were into embryo transplants and the like. That wasn't my father's scene at all – for him, you bred a calf and waited for it to grow up. Hamish and John were far more entrepreneurial – they wanted ten calves, not one. They would take an award-winning cow, extract its eggs and end up with virtually a production line of calves.

My father, however, had been known to import semen. That was how we ended up with the cow to end all cows, Powis Innocent 29th. Not exactly a catchy name, but what a cow! She won the Scottish Winter Fair in the mid-eighties, and we drove her down to the Royal Show in Warwickshire the following summer. Hamish and another cousin of ours, Jas, took me with them in the lorry. I was thirteen and it was the best twelve hours of my life. They fed me lemonade shandy – Top Deck – all the way down and I thought I was such a lad. Soon I was feeling a bit giggly, then I was bloated and finally I threw up. Bubbles can do that to a wee lad. Trouble was, after all that time in the back of a lorry, it was our prize cow that was really wasted. When we opened the doors at the end of the journey she basically fell out.

People were coming over asking, 'Where's this great cow of the Logans?' And the poor thing was fucked – battered, bruised and shaky on her feet. She wouldn't perk up and stayed in a comatose state all week. My father had driven down separately with my mother, and he knew something had to be done. We weren't going to win with her in that kind of shape, so Dad said, 'Right, there's only one thing for it,' and he fed her half a bottle of whisky, straight down her throat in one, just before show time. That did the trick. Suddenly the cow was on fire and she won the show.

She was a special cow and ended up buried in our garden. We had her head stuffed, and I still intend to put it on display, when we've got the house for it.

———————

If you went by what they reckoned at school, the prospect of me owning any kind of house was verging on nil. Written off by my teachers, and by the selectors of the Scotland Under-15 team, I was starting to develop a determination to prove people wrong. Not in the classroom, where I, too, had given up on ever achieving anything, but on the rugby field and on the farm.

I spent a lot of my youth walking round the farm, looking for things I could do or make. I used to love doing that – maybe I could turn this into a go-kart, maybe I could hang that up and make something out of it. When I was fifteen, I made a fair bit of money by selling wood. I came across a massive tree trunk one day, and asked my dad what he intended to do with it.

'Ditch it. It's too big to cut up,' he replied.

'Can I have it?' I asked.

So I took a chainsaw and slabbed the whole thing, then spent an entire Sunday breaking it up into small pieces with an axe. I got a hundred bags and started filling them. My dad asked me what I was going to do with them and I told him I was going to sell them.

'Don't be daft. Nobody's going to buy wood,' he said.

''Course they are!' I replied. 'Those old folk down the bottom always need wood for their fire.'

I got my mate to bring his tractor round and we loaded up the trailer and went from door to door. I sold the lot in one day. A hundred quid. So I started doing that regularly and made a bit of money.

I was desperate to work on the farm full time, and that finally happened when I walked away from school that day. I was shitting myself as the exams approached, like anyone else I suppose, but for me it was nothing to do with whether I would pass or not – I knew I was never going to do that. My school life had been one long exercise in dodging the fact that I couldn't read or write, and here was the grand finale, the reason all of us had ever started going to school in the first place. For everyone else it was a question of measuring how much they had progressed in the past ten years or so; for me, those exams could only ever serve to expose the fact that, in all that time, I hadn't got past first base.

I don't even remember what they called the exams we used to take back then as sixteen-year-olds in Scotland – I think it was

Standard Grades. I do remember that my first exam was English. I sat down in this huge room and wrote my name at the top of the paper. But that was as far as I got. The paper might as well have been written in French. I looked out of the window, and then around at row after row of my schoolmates, bent over and working away furiously, and I just thought, 'Why am I here?' I looked at the mess of my scribbled name on the paper. 'What is the point of this? This is it. It's finished.'

I got up and walked to the door. The supervisor intercepted me and asked what I was doing.

'I can't read,' I said. 'I can't even write my address. There's nothing for me here.' And I left school for the last time.

Straightaway I was given a job on the farm at £50 a week. Now I was taking on the big, bad world and I couldn't read or write. My mum was filling in forms for me, and within six months she had set up extra classes. It was only then that dyslexia was first mentioned.

At school, a history teacher, Deirdre Wilson, had become involved in the remedial classes – I think she found it interesting and liked to help people. Maybe she saw some potential in me, because she said she wanted to help. She and my mother organised for me to go round to her house once or twice a week after I'd left school, and I did it for about a year. It was Deirdre who was the first to diagnose me with dyslexia. It was a great relief to know what the problem had been – even that there had been a problem at all – but it was frustrating, knowing that all I could do was keep trying.

It was all about picturing words in your head and keeping

them in there. We played memory games at her house – there was the clock and the TV, and the table, which was by the sofa, which had five cushions on it. I did more homework with her than I'd ever done at school.

The first book I read was with her. It was *Lassie*, written for nine-year-olds. I went through it word by word, and after a page I was exhausted. I just couldn't take any of it in. Deirdre was fantastic, and I'll always be very grateful for the effort she put in, but the work we were doing together wasn't making any real improvements. I soon realised that the endless struggle to get round, or just to cover up, my illiteracy was going to continue indefinitely.

———————————

Those early years of my life, both the agony of school and the happiness of the farm with my family and my cousins, came to an end suddenly in November 1990, when I was eighteen.

It happened during the Scottish Winter Fair, which was held in a couple of huge arenas, acres wide, in Ingliston, out by Edinburgh Airport. The fair was a festival for the farming community, with shearing competitions and all sorts. Hundreds of cows were on display, each one in its own pen with pictures and records of where it had been, its pedigree, and how much milk it produced. Our cows looked immaculate – we used to wash them every day, oil them up, clip them, polish their hooves, puff up their tails. It was like Cruft's but for cows. Farmers from all over the world took part. We were there every year. My father had actually won it a couple of times.

You did your business in the bar every night. There was a big drinking culture – after we had done our day's work, we used to head straight to the bar in the arena for a few beers.

It was a Wednesday, and I'd had a normal day at the fair with Hamish, mucking the cows out, followed by a couple of pints in the evening. Hamish left for home at about 10.30 p.m. with his brother John, a guy called Andy and Gareth Flockhart, my mate from the rugby club. Hamish had left the bar, but for some reason he came back in to find me. I was standing at the corner, and Hamish waded through the throng towards me.

'See you tomorrow, pal,' he said. 'Have a good night! Don't forget, you're a star!'

'Yeah, whatever!' I jeered at him, and off he went, back through the hordes and out of the door.

Hamish joined the others in Gareth's car, and was keen to head towards Edinburgh – to Corstorphine – to get some chips, while the others wanted to get back to Stirling. While they were debating, Gareth missed the slip road, so they carried on towards Edinburgh city centre.

In Corstorphine, Gareth parked the car on the other side of the road from the chippy, while the others got out. He wanted to turn the car round, but it was quite busy, so he decided to wait for them to return first, something he would go on to blame himself for, in that irrational way you do.

John and Andy were the first to get back into the car, and they waited for Hamish, who had told them to go on ahead. He never came. Soon they became aware of a commotion near the chippy.

When they went to investigate, they found Hamish lying on the side of the road, unconscious.

I don't know what had happened to him – no one does. There was a bus driver who said his wing mirror had hit Hamish's head. There was some ice about that Hamish may have slipped on. And there was a kerb – the only thing we do know – that he snapped his spinal chord on as he landed.

He was taken to hospital, but to begin with only his immediate family were notified – his wife, his brothers and parents. I had gone to bed, unaware of what had happened, and went straight back to the fair when I got up. My father was told next morning, and so was Jas Logan. Soon they were saying to themselves, 'Who's going to tell Kenny?' They knew how close I was to Hamish.

Jas was given the task. He led me out into the tented walkway between the two arenas and through a flap into a little area where there were no people.

'He's all right, though, isn't he?' I said.

'No, he's bad.'

'So, what, he's broken his legs?'

Jas told me he was in a coma, and I fell apart.

They wouldn't let me go to see him just yet, so I was wandering round the fair in a state of desperation as the news gradually got round. No one was talking to me. Everyone knew Hamish, and most people knew that he was my buddy. I was with him all the time during my teenage years. My father was getting old by then, so a lot of those rites of passage a father and son might go through at that age I went through with

Hamish. He was the guy who would stand up for me. If my brothers were being nasty to me, it would be Hamish who pulled them up for it.

I was shaking my head, saying, 'There's no way he could die,' but everybody at the showground was leaving me alone. I swear they were actually walking away from me. It didn't seem real. None of it did.

Hamish's family called me to the hospital to see him that afternoon, and there he was, this great slab of a man, the life and soul of any party, supremely confident – he was simply the man. Except now he was just lying there, hooked up to God knows what. He had a tiny scratch on his pinkie. That's all he had, a tiny wee scratch, and I thought it was going to be fine, that he would wake up any minute. I went through to a little room where Uncle Archie, Auntie Margaret, John, Ally, Kelso and Bash were sitting, all of them in tears. I sat down with them and they told me the doctors were going to turn off his life support machine. And that was it – he was gone.

That night I went to the rugby club for training, thinking he would have wanted me to – after all, he'd taken me there for the first time, all those years earlier. I remember seeing about fifty folk, slightly distorted through the window, gathered together in a kind of square inside. They were all shocked by the news. Hamish had left not just his family, but a whole community. Four thousand people attended his funeral. He had brought fire and passion and enthusiasm into everyone's life. People just wanted to be around him, and if you were in his company, you had a good time. He left an impression on everyone he met. It wasn't just his family who were bereaved.

At the rugby club that night, no one really knew where to look. On the field, Brian Ireland, our openside, asked me if I was going to see him in his coffin. I said I didn't know. He didn't think I should. He said I should remember him the way he was. I hope I would always have done that anyway, but I'm glad I took Brian's advice.

The weeks that followed were horrific. It felt like a part of me had gone with him. Tears are all I remember. And then I started seeing him on the farm. I'd look round quickly and see this figure, and I would be running towards it before I realised.

I was haunted by those last moments with him in the bar. Why had he come back to find me? He was meant to be seeing me the next day anyway, but he made a point of saying that last goodbye to me. 'Don't forget, you're a star.' His words still echo in my head.

It reminded me of something he'd said to me a couple of weeks before he died. He'd said, 'If anything happens to me, make sure Bash and the kids are all right.' I told him to shut up. 'I might get hit by a bus,' he replied, but then he made light of it with a kind of bellow that was his trademark, a sort of cross between General Melchett's bray and Elvis Presley's croon. Was it a premonition? I've wondered ever since, did he somehow know he was going to die?

Two years later, my father died, which was hard, but we knew he was dying and he was well into his seventies. Hamish was thirty-five with a young family. I went round to see Bash and the kids. Dawn and Callum were two-and-a-half and four, which is roughly the age my kids are now. We told them that their daddy had gone to heaven. 'Oh, right,' they said and off they pottered, and as they grew up, all they heard were stories of what a great man their father was. They're doing really well now, but it must have been so hard. They are amazing young people and a credit to their mum.

Bash still lives in the farmhouse she and Hamish built together. Only now is she starting to consider the idea of a new relationship. For fifteen years or so she didn't see anybody. 'How can I replace the man?' she used to say. 'He was my hero.'

My way of dealing with it was to visit his grave every time I played rugby. From 1990 until I left for Wasps, six years later, I paid my respects before every match, whether it was local or overseas. Sometimes I would sit down and talk to him about the game that was coming up, other times I might be late, so I would rush into the graveyard, give a Hamish bellow, then rush back out again. He was buried in Logie Kirk, the local church where Gabby and I were married.

The family had already ordered a plot for his father in the graveyard, but Hamish ended up taking it. There was a little chip in his headstone, where I put my first Scotland badge. The badge was still there when we were married ten years later. He had introduced me to rugby, he had been my mentor on the farm – rugby and the farm, the two things that had got me through the ordeal of my school years. And for a long time I felt as if I didn't want to take to the field, any field, without him.

# 3

# Stirling Work

We were a good bunch of youngsters at Stirling County. The success we'd had at minis level and beyond had continued with the Under-18s. We reached the Scottish Cup final at Murrayfield when I was sixteen. I was on the bench for that one, and we lost to Melrose, but I was in the starting line-up for the final the following year, against Melrose again, and this time we won.

On the back of our success at Stirling County, I started to win recognition from the regional selectors. Within two years of my rejection by Scotland Under-15, I was selected for the Scottish Youth Under-18 team, which took on Scottish Schools Under-18 every year. In those days, the Youth team were considered the riff-raff, the ones who had dropped out of school, and we were playing the high-fliers, the ones everyone had high hopes for. The game was played at Murrayfield, and we were sent off to the away changing room and given white shirts to wear, Scotland's change strip. In every way we were made to feel like the ones making up the numbers. Which just made it all the more satisfying when we beat them.

They didn't like it – the schools team, I mean, although it wouldn't surprise me if the powers that be hadn't liked it either – because they were private-school boys who played rugby all the time. For us, though, it was a real scalp, and I felt I was back on the bike, having fallen off at Under-15 level. My love for rugby and Scotland was raging again. I remember wearing that white Scotland jersey with the 15 on its back everywhere I went, with no sense of shame – I was just too excited. Now I had a Scotland jersey I had earned, and wearing this one was not a problem at all.

Meanwhile, we'd turned into a handy wee team. Weirdly, our finest hour was probably our last game of the season, beating the touring Japanese at Murrayfield. I don't know what became of any of the lads in that Japan team, but they were brilliant. They'd been on tour for about three months round the world and beaten everyone – New Zealand, Australia, England, everyone. We were unbeaten as well, so this was talked up as the finale of their tour. I think they had rescheduled their trip home to take in a game against us.

We'd fancied our chances when we saw them for the first time, because they were tiny. Then we took to the field and, oh my God, they were physical. It was like being hit by a bomb. I went on a run down the wing and had one guy to beat. He was a wee feller, so I thought, 'Right, I'll bump him out the road.' Next thing I knew I was in a heap about ten yards the other side of the touch-line with a dead arm. I looked at the guy in amazement, thinking, 'How did you do that?' It must have been the martial arts.

I had settled at full-back now, and my stock in trade was catching high balls and going off on long runs – never passing the ball to anyone was still a problem, but I was fast and strong, so I was often able to get away with it. I did all my training on the farm. My working day involved hard physical graft anyway, which gave me an advantage over others in the fitness stakes. There were a few guys back then who took rugby seriously enough to go to the gym after hours to work on their conditioning, but it was amateur, so on the whole guys were still just turning up for evening training a couple of times a week at the club and then for the game on Saturday. The work I was doing on the farm was giving me an edge.

Sheep played an important part in my regime. When we were herding them, I used to run with the dogs. Sheep are brilliant at beating people. They've got a lethal step on them, and they move very much like Jason Robinson. Shaun Edwards later told me at Wasps that the secret to tackling Robinson was not to hesitate. He could bamboozle you with those shimmies, but he wasn't actually moving off the spot, so if you just carried on with your hit, you would get him. Same with sheep. If I'd only met Shaun when I was nineteen, I could have been a better shepherd.

The sheep often used to beat me, but I took plenty of them down as well. They were a joy to tackle, because they're such big, furry things, but if you collide with a sheep's head, it's like getting hit by a stone. And they're not afraid of using their heads. Or their horns – I once got cracked in the ribs by one of them. In general, my dad was more bothered about the damage we might do to them. Hamish and John used to cheer me on. They'd get me psyched up – 'Come on!' they would yell at me, and if I missed one, it was, 'Well, that's just not good enough.' You had to fling yourself at them and take them down by grabbing the fur – that was the key.

We used to chase cows as well. Cows were different. You wouldn't tackle a cow. But if you were fast enough to get in their eye line while they were on the run, they would change direction. So some of them might bolt for a hole in the hedge and I would go sprinting after them to try to head them off. The calves, in particular, needed herding. They were like maniacs running around. Bullocks (castrated bulls) and heifers (cows that hadn't had any calves yet) could be pretty crazy, too, if they wanted to be, jumping over fences and running through them. We would often get phone calls in the middle of the night to say they'd escaped, and we'd have to chase after them down the road to get them back. Then, when a heifer became a first-calfer (a cow that has had one calf), she would lose a bit of craziness and become more like a mum. And once they'd become third-calfers or fourth-calfers, they were docile, just walking round the place – they'd seen it all.

And then there were the bulls. You didn't get into the pens

with the bulls on your own. You weren't allowed to – they could quite easily kill you. I remember my father being tossed into the air by one of them. He managed to crawl under a feeder while someone else distracted the bull. They say if you're incapacitated by one, you should always lie on your front. Lie with your face up and the bull will crush you with his head; lie with your face down and he's not so sure. But it's a bit like that other theory that the best way to deal with a bull is to charge at it – no one's ever had the balls to find out if it's true.

Herding bulls involved tractors and/or pitchforks. Another option, of course, was just letting them do their own thing if they really wanted to. We let them walk around a field that we called the whale park. It was called that because they once found the remains of a prehistoric whale there. It was below sea level and in the past had been underwater, but now it was a boggy field with a deep ditch round it. When it came to the breeding season, we would leave a bull in the whale park with twenty heifers and say, 'Go and enjoy!' Quite often, we would find a heifer stuck in the ditch. If she wasn't letting the bull have his way, he would get angry and push her in there. Getting them out was hard, and sometimes heifers died in there. They would panic and thrash about, trying to heave them-selves out, but the ditch was like quicksand to them and they might either drown or die of sheer exhaustion.

Breeding was a huge part of our business. You could try to do it the old-fashioned way, but artificial insemination was becoming more common. The bull would be taken off to a place where they presented him with a fake cow in order to harvest his semen. You can buy semen from all over the world. We used to have semen salesmen turning up trying to sell us the stuff. It could cost two or three hundred quid a squirt for the pedigree stuff, others would be maybe eight quid, or they might offer you one batch of semen for so much and throw in another lot for free.

I accidentally harvested a bull's semen myself one time. He was a small bull and his balls had only just dropped. I was mucking out his pen when suddenly he came at me from behind and threw his front legs over my shoulder. He may have been small but he still weighed a couple of hundred kilos. Despite staggering under the impact, I managed to grab his nose ring, which is one way of bringing them under control, and got the frisky feller off me. Later my dad saw me and asked what I'd been doing.

'Mucking out the bull pens,' I said.

'What's that on your back?'

I took off my jacket and it was covered in white stuff.

'One of the bulls jumped on me, Dad.'

'Well, he's obviously hammered into the back of you.'

It was true. I had to accept the fact that I'd been spunked on by a bull.

Chasing animals wasn't the only job that got you fit – mucking out the calf pens did, too. It was horrible, and everyone did their best to avoid it by finding urgent jobs somewhere else when it had to be done. I always seemed to get lumbered with it, though. We were still doing it by hand back then and it was hard work. If you hadn't mucked out a pen for about a year, say, there was a lot of dung to deal with – a ten-foot by ten-foot pen a couple of feet deep. And it was rock hard. Breaking into it was like trying to rip up concrete. Except it was shit. And once you'd broken through the hard stuff at the top, it became softer and smellier the further down you went. You ended up stinking.

It was great for fitness, though. We used to race each other, shovelling shit into wheelbarrows, carting it away and rushing back for the next load. At the end of a day like that, it felt like a job well done, and you had the muscles to prove it. If only it had been so good for the back.

Other training devices included shifting hay bails and lifting weights. We used to have what we called 56-ers lying round the farm – 56 kilogram weights that we used for measuring wheat and barley. I used to do a squat with one in each hand in the old days, and by the time I was playing rugby seriously, I would do a set of ten every time I went past the weights. I didn't know about the dangers of free weights, and I paid for it later with the back problems that blighted the second half of my playing career. It would flare up on *Strictly Come Dancing* as well. After a couple of years of professional rugby, the physios put me on a regime designed to get me through to the end of my career. It involved never doing another squat, partly because my legs were already strong from all those 56-ers in my youth, but mainly because my back had been so damaged by them.

---

So I was back in the Scotland system and now people were starting to notice me at Stirling County as well. I had finally made my first-team debut in a cup game against Ayr on a dark and frosty Friday night in early 1990. That season, Stirling had been promoted to the top flight for the first time in their history, and the guys in the first team were local heroes to us. I was in awe of them and remember sitting in the changing room looking round and thinking, 'I can't believe I'm playing with these guys.' Each Saturday the youth teams would finish their games and come across to watch the first team, so I had been watching them every weekend for years. Now I was playing with men. I might have played for Scotland at youth level, but this was the first time I had ever played with the big boys. It was a big moment for me. This was the field I used to help Sandy Bryce to tend while dreaming of taking to it as a Stirling County player. At last my time had come.

The game went well – we won. I remember doing the simple things right – taking high balls and making my tackles. More than anything, I was keen just to prove myself. That's probably the most important thing in the make-up of any first-class sportsman, that passionate desire to keep showing yourself worthy. You may not always manage it, but without the desire you don't have a chance. I don't think it ever left me, that childlike nervous energy. Maybe it was particularly strong in me because of the problems I'd had at school and that I still had in adult life. I'd never been accepted in the classroom and, even now that I'd left it, I lived in constant fear that my inability to read or write would be exposed. That meant I relied all the more on my rugby to improve my self-worth – if I couldn't prove myself on the rugby field, I really had nothing. That was how I used to feel.

So coming off the pitch and having people say to me, 'You're not a bad wee player, are ye?' made me feel a million dollars. I sat in the changing room in a daze afterwards. 'They think I'm all right,' I kept saying to myself.

That was as far as praise would ever go at Stirling. It wasn't the kind of club to talk you up. The only person who ever said to me, 'You're going to be a star,' was Hamish, which was hugely important to me in its special way, but the Stirling mentality was important, too. You had to earn everything. They had a very similar ethos to the one I would encounter at Wasps. No one was a super-star and if anyone thought they were, they wouldn't last five minutes. In a lot of ways, Stirling County and Wasps were very similar – two clubs who overachieved and were never popular, but whose players were fiercely tight-knit.

The other thing that I remember from my Stirling County debut that night was that I took a kick at goal. Little did I know how goal-kicking would go on to dominate my career, so much so that a lot of people probably remember me for that more than anything else. And I doubt they all remember me fondly for it.

Kicking at goal really is a mug's game, especially if, like me, you take to it in a casual manner and don't specialise in it until it's too late. You can play terribly but kick five from five and you get all the headlines. Then you can have a blinder but miss a couple of kicks and you get slated. I wouldn't go so far as to say I was a fool to take it up, because I loved it, especially at Wasps, but my goal-kicking brought on the darkest hours of my career.

So it was appropriate that I should take my first proper goal-kick on that dark night in Stirling. In fact, the whole episode summed up my attitude to kicking. Jimmy Stewart, our regular kicker, went off injured. We scored a try in the corner at the end of the game and when it came to taking the conversion, our captain asked out loud who fancied it. No one said anything, so being the new boy and eager to please – I was always eager to please, right the way through my career – I found myself sticking up my hand. Why not? I'd taken a few shots before in training, and it would be no bad thing to have another string to my bow. And, you never know, I might actually get it.

They lobbed me the ball. There was no tee, so I made a dent in the turf near the touchline with my boot, plonked the ball in it, took a couple of steps back and thought, 'Right, just whack the bloody thing.' As a routine, give or take the odd adjustment, it was about as technical as my kicking would ever get – right the way up to kicking for Scotland.

I struck the ball well and it sailed towards the posts. Or maybe that should be the post, because it hit the left-hand upright. I should probably have taken that as an omen, but, no, the boys reckoned it was a good effort, and the satisfaction from this extra pat on the back became a part of everything else I took away from that first game for Stirling as an eager seventeen-year-old. How could I now separate goal-kicking from the general excitement I felt at the start of my senior rugby career? I couldn't. And so it happened from then on every time the question was asked, 'Who's going to take the kick?' muggins here would put up his hand. 'Duh, I'll do it.' It's how I ended up with every kicking job I ever had. It's how I ended up doing it occasionally for Stirling County. It's how I ended up with the job for Wasps. It's how I ended up kicking for Scotland. In short, no one else was stupid enough.

———

In the Stirling County team that night was a guy called Robbie Mailer. He was the son of Jenny Mailer, who had been a great comfort to me at Riverside primary school. When I went to Wallace High, I had come across Robbie and his sister, Nicola. Robbie was four years older than I was, and he fancied himself big time. He used to wear tight jeans, red-and-blue Kickers and these luminous jackets. In his own eyes, he was the school hero and the setter of trends. In the eyes of the rest of us, he was nothing more than Nicola's brother.

Nicola was a couple of years older than I was, so at school we never really got to know each other too well. She was a good-looking girl, and so were her friends. I went out with a few of them, gradually working my way towards her, and not long after I'd made my debut for Stirling, I started going out with her. She was at university in Dundee, and I would go up to see her when I could, usually after a day's work on the farm. When I couldn't, I would go out on the town in Stirling with Robbie, who was fast becoming my best mate. It got to the stage when I was seeing more of him than I was of her. As it turned out, he would go on to be my best man, but Nicola wasn't to be my bride.

_____

As if enough landmarks in my life hadn't already taken place at Stirling, my first game against England was played there as well. After the Under-18 set-up in Scotland, where we had been split up into those who went to school and those who didn't by administrators who might as well have been living in the nineteenth century, we all came together at Under-19 level. Suddenly, we had quite a serious team. Tom Smith and Gregor Townsend were in the squad, although the star back then was another local lad from Stirling County, fly-half Mark McKenzie, one of the best goal-kickers I ever played with. He was the younger brother of Kevin, who would go on to play hooker for Scotland.

Scotland's Under-19 game against England in 1991 ended up being played at Stirling County. I couldn't believe my luck. Representing my country at my home ground was one thing, but for it to happen against England . . . There was a big crowd – two or three thousand thronging round the pitch and packed into the stand – and all my family and friends came along.

England arrived and the anticipation became almost unbearable. We didn't know anything about them, and they didn't know anything about us. As youth players, this was going to be the biggest challenge any of us had yet faced. Would we be up to it? I remember that familiar nervousness as we sized them up when they got off the coach. One of them was a tall lad who was to pack down at No. 8. It turned out his name was Lawrence Dallaglio. At that point I'd never heard of him. That was going to change over the next few years.

It was a hot, sunny day in spring, a couple of miles from the farm I'd grown up on, at the club where I'd learned the game. Everyone I'd ever known was on the touchline and a few more besides, and there was a game against England in the offing. Anything seemed possible.

And it still felt that way after the game. It was a hard match – that big guy bursting off the base of the England scrum was obviously a good player – but we all played well, and in the best Hollywood tradition the winning try was scored by me, the local school drop-out made good, in front of his home crowd in the glorious sunshine. Perfect.

It was a good try, but it has got better with every passing year. These days it features a massive hand-off on the hapless Dallaglio and a scorching run past my opposite number, Jon Sleightholme, their right wing. Whether it actually featured all that at the time I'm only half sure. The one thing I do remember clearly, though, is touching down in the far left-hand corner. Stirling Castle was in front and the Wallace Monument was behind, and just on the other side of the hill was home.

Not so much in the Hollywood tradition was the fact that it was to be the first and only time I would taste victory over England. I would never be on the winning side against them again, not that I knew that at the time. As far as I was concerned, my record stood at played one, won one. As I said, anything seemed possible.

We hit the town that night with the England boys, and I remember getting on well with Dallaglio and Jon Sleightholme. We had a fair bit in common – we were extroverts and liked to have a good time. Lawrence was a big, larger-than-life character – a party man, basically – and it was the start of a long friendship.

That was typical of rugby back then. We had played hard, and in our case we had won against the odds. Then we came together afterwards to socialise and let our hair down. Rugby at the highest level is in danger of losing that. We are the last generation of players in first-class rugby who grew up in that amateur environment. Nowadays, players never know that lifestyle, and you do need to let your hair down. Aside from anything else, playing big games in front of big crowds is a high that you need to come down from, and socialising is a way of doing that. You talk to some professional footballers, who have to perform like that maybe twice a week, and they take pills to get to sleep after a big game. Well, I'd rather have a couple of beers than a sleeping pill.

That was how you developed relationships with players from other teams. You'd have a few drinks together, then you'd go away and not see them again for maybe even a couple of years, but the next time you'd pick up where you'd left off. The game was already changing in the early nineties, but amateurism had a few more years to run, and socialising with the opposition still played a big part.

———

At the end of August 1991, we were given our first taste of life with the big boys. I still qualified at Under-19, just about, and we went with the Scotland senior team to Bucharest. They were going for a Test against Romania as part of their preparations for the World Cup that autumn. We went along to play our Romanian equivalents.

It was an eye-opener from start to finish. The airport in Bucharest was deserted and we waited about an hour before we realised the baggage handlers were on strike. The Scottish Rugby Union (SRU) had to sort it out and by the time we got our bags back they were each a few items lighter than they had been when we'd checked them in. The streets of the city were lined with beggars and prostitutes – the poverty was quite a shock to me. It was my first real trip away from home.

We took on Romania on Friday, and there were further shocks. These guys were huge and bearded – there's no way they were nineteen. To be fair, I think it was actually meant to be their Under-21 side, but I swear some of them had grey hair. One of the props looked older than my dad. We protested, but the Romanians just shrugged. They said it was down to all the duck they ate. The duck?

Well, we lost. They gave us a good pummelling. Gregor Townsend and I played well, though, which was the start of both of us being noticed by the senior management. However, the most memorable moments of that tour were brought about by the antics of the senior players. The Under-19s came off the pitch that afternoon and that evening we were pummelled for a second time by a bunch of older men. Quite a lot of Scotland's top players were not playing in the Test match the next day but were along for the ride – Gavin Hastings, John Jeffrey and those guys. After our game we went into the bar and they were all downing vodka like crazy men. I remember John Jeffrey smacking me about a bit and putting me in my place. Duncan Paterson was the manager, and he stayed at the bar all night buying more and more drink. They were all going mental.

It was the same story after the senior team's Test match on the Saturday afternoon. Again, Romania won, which was a huge shock – their men were no less physical than their 'boys' had been against us, winning 18–12. Afterwards, we all came together for a big dinner in a massive communist-style hall – huge white walls, big curtains and all that. There were about two hundred people there, but the senior players were on a mission. Finlay Calder led a posse of all those who had played in the Test match earlier in the day, approaching David Sole, the captain, at the top table to drink wine with him. Sole had to down about twenty glasses.

Meanwhile, the rest of them were getting out of control. They were wearing these brand new grey 1991 World Cup blazers in preparation for the tournament that autumn. Finlay Calder and John Jeffrey started to rip the sleeves off each other's blazers, and soon they were all doing it – Craig Chalmers, the Hastings boys, Derek Turnbull, Derek White. We youngsters watched in amazement as things deteriorated. They were behaving like animals. But we soon got into it. This was brilliant – our heroes on the rampage.

'Come and do us!' we cried. 'Here we are! Take our sleeves off!'

The breast pockets were next to go, then they started to rip each other's trousers along the seam of the leg. Meanwhile, some people were starting to get very angry. David Sole, twenty-odd glasses the worse for wear, was sitting there fuming at his team-mates' antics. He may have been incapacitated by then, but he was a very diplomatic man and he was not happy. Duncan Paterson was furious, and eventually he marched the main ringleaders out – Chalmers, Calder and Jeffrey to the fore – their blazers now sleeveless with the pockets hanging off and their trousers flapping in the wind.

The next day when we gathered at the airport, we were a mess. I remember Damian Cronin trying to wear Iain Milne's trousers with what I swear had a waist of about sixty inches, which might fit Del Boy nowadays but back then looked a bit ridiculous on him. People were wandering round in their sleeveless blazers with severe reprimands ringing in their ears, but the punishment didn't stop there.

In order to save a bit of money, the SRU had booked us on a local Romanian airline. We took off from Bucharest but landed again about an hour later, still in Romania, so that we could refuel for the trip home, because it was cheaper that way.

We all got off the plane and hung around in this airbase. There was a café there where the sweets on sale had mould on them. After about three hours of hanging around we were getting restless, and all the more so when we noticed the plane's captain outside with his hat on sideways. He had a hammer and was banging away at the front wheel of the plane. Everyone gathered round the window to watch him. This didn't look right. What was he doing? The captain came in to tell us that they had a bit of an issue with the front wheel. It wasn't very safe and they weren't sure it was going to work.

After another hour the captain returned and said they reckoned they'd fixed it, and on we all piled, like lambs to the slaughter. Not that we had a lot of choice. It didn't look as if there were going to be many other planes flying to Edinburgh in the next decade.

Our concerns grew even stronger when the pilot asked everybody sitting at the front of the plane to move to the back in order to give the front wheel its best chance. All the big lads piled into the rear of the cabin. The plane began to trundle along the runway, and it trundled for quite a while. We were looking at each other, thinking, 'Shouldn't we be in the air by now?'

We cleared the fence at the end of the runway by a matter of feet. You could pretty much hear the plane creaking and groaning but at least we were in the air. Fingers crossed for the rest of the journey.

After a couple of hours, a terrible screeching sound came from one of the doors. The seal around it had gone. Literally. It had been sucked out into the stratosphere. The noise was deafening. This time we really did start to lose our cool. 'We're going down, boys! We're all going to die!' And we were only half joking. The pilot dropped the plane to a lower altitude, and the flight attendant tried to stuff towels in the gaps round the edge of the door and to secure them there with tape.

Then came the moment we'd all been dreading and longing for at the same time – the landing. As the plane came in, it was rattling and shaking so much that it was difficult to tell at what point we had actually touched down, but when we started bouncing up and down as well as rattling and shaking, we knew we had hit the ground.

When everyone was confident we weren't going to die – although I didn't really feel sure of that until we were a few hundred yards away from the plane – you'd have thought Scotland had won the World Cup a couple of months early with all the whooping and hollering. I've never been so relieved to get off a plane in my life.

There were a couple of journalists with us and the headlines the next day were of how Scotland's World Cup chances had nearly gone up in smoke in more ways than one.

But, hey, the SRU had saved themselves a few hundred quid.

# 4

# Up and Under

Not long after Hamish died, my father discovered that he had cancer of the pancreas. He and Mum decided not to tell any of us about it to begin with. My mum was also told that he had between three and six months to live. She told no one that, not even Dad. It probably helped him to make the most of his final months, and to prolong them. I don't think it occurred to him that he would do anything other than carry on working as usual and get better. Fair play to him, he did the first part of that, and although he would never get better, he lived for nearly two more years. None of us knew anything about it for the first year, but by spring 1992 the cancer was starting to take its toll and it became clear to us that he was gravely ill.

I was now hell bent on getting a full Scotland cap. I was nineteen and a Stirling County regular with a load of caps at various age-group levels to my name. I wanted my father to see me play for Scotland. Hamish had always said that I would do it and that, when I did, he would be there. That was no longer possible, and when Mum told us Dad was ill, I realised I might not have long to win that first cap before he died. Dad was far too reserved a man to have told me I was going to represent my country or that he would be there when I did, but that didn't mean it wasn't important to either of us.

Even so, I didn't seriously think I would make it for a wee while yet. It turned out I was a lot closer than I realised. The game that swung it for me was a match on the back pitches at Murrayfield between Scotland Students and Scotland Under-21s in the spring of 1992. I was playing for the Under-21s, and we were the warm-up game for the Students World Cup. The Students had some serious players – Ian Jardine, Rowen Shepherd – and a lot of them were over twenty-one.

In a few months' time, Scotland's seniors were off to tour Australia, and all the selectors were there. One of the referees came up to me just before we went out and said, 'If you play well today, you'll go on that Australia tour.' I thought he was joking – I'd never even considered it happening so soon. Gregor Townsend was playing for the Students and we had a guy called Derek Bain, a brilliant fly-half. They were the stars at the time. If anyone was going, it would be those guys, I thought.

That game was probably the best I'd ever played at that stage in my career. Everything went perfectly – I was running from my own half, scything through people, taking high balls, setting up tries. I think I might have scored one as well. At half-time that ref was looking at me knowingly, and by the end people were patting me on the back. The selectors were scribbling notes, talking to each other. I remember sitting stunned in the big changing room at Murrayfield afterwards, our side having won 28–23. It was dawning on me that I might be in the reckoning for a Scotland cap.

I was in a pub called The Birds and Bees soon after that with Nicola, when I got a message from my mum to come home urgently. Fearing the worst, I rang from the pub, but it was nothing to do with Dad. Mum told me that Bill Hogg, the secretary of the SRU, had rung. Could I phone him? I was back home in a flash.

'Hello, this is Kenneth Logan,' I said to him. I was still Kenneth back then for official matters. It was Bill McLaren who started calling me first Ken, then Kenny Logan, which is how it stuck.

'Are you available to tour Australia?'

In the amateur days, they had to check availability. Of course, everyone made themselves available, especially uncapped nineteen-year-olds, but they still had to check. Strictly speaking, I should have asked my dad if I could take the time off work, but I couldn't contain myself.

'Yes, I'm available. When is it?'

'This summer.'

'Am I going?'

'We don't know yet. We'll tell you in a week's time.'

A few days later, I was in the fields when my tractor phone (the farmer's equivalent of a car phone) went off. It was Graham Law, who was then the rugby correspondent for the *Scotsman*.

'Congratulations,' he said. 'You've been picked for the tour to Australia. How do you feel?'

I felt as if I'd achieved something massive, despite those years of being dismissed by teachers at school; as if I was, instead, proving Hamish right. For years he had said that I would play for Scotland. Now I was a big step closer to that goal. The misery of rejection by the Under-15s seemed a long time ago.

It was to be a new start for Scotland with the retirement of Finlay Calder and John Jeffrey after the 1991 World Cup, when Scotland lost in the semi-finals to England. I remember watching that game like any other fan, and here I was, about to go on tour with these people. David Sole was soon to retire, but he was captain again for this tour. Some of the great names, and some of my heroes, were there – the Hastings brothers, Tony Stanger, Craig Chalmers and Iwan Tukalo.

I was one of nine uncapped players, and three of us were youngsters taken from that Students/Under-21 game – Derek Bain, Gregor Townsend and me. Derek was possibly even more talented than Gregor, but he would never play professional rugby, which was a shame. He didn't have the all-consuming hunger for it. Gregor and I loved rugby – Derek wasn't that bothered. He was the kind of guy who could pick up a golf club and be a scratch handicapper. He loved life outside rugby. He went on that Australia tour and just stayed out there. Gregor, meanwhile, was the youngest of all of us – just eighteen, about to turn nineteen when we were picked. He had always been a golden boy, and this was the start of a great career.

I was about to turn twenty, and my call-up had not been so predicted. Even at Stirling County there were mixed emotions when I got the call. Assuming I got a game on the eight-match tour, this would make me the first player from the club ever to play for Scotland, and everyone, myself included, had assumed that honour would go to Ian Jardine. 'Jardy' was about seven years older than I was and had been the star of the club for a few years, as they moved up through the ranks to the top division. A few of the committee men at Stirling County didn't do much to hide from me their feeling that it was ridiculous for Scotland to take a kid like me on tour. At least that's how it felt to me. I think there was quite a bit of ill-feeling from some of the people at Stirling – towards the SRU, not towards me, but I felt a bit of it. Jardy was brilliant about it, and there's no doubt he should have been on that tour. He would get his cap in time, and in time I would get my pats on the back from Stirling, but the reception of the news to begin with was luke-warm.

Emotions were mixed at home, too. There was no doubting the euphoria over the official letter confirming my selection, which came towards the end of March, a week or so before my twentieth birthday, but as the tour approached my father was becoming frail. He wasn't yet bedridden, but the illness was taking hold. Mum later told me she thought he might die while I was away. That thought never occurred to me. My brothers and I had never been told that his illness was terminal, although we all knew it probably would be. Maybe I was being selfish by not considering the possibility more seriously. Pulling out of the tour never really entered my head, nor did the idea that Dad might die while I was away. And, in the end, thank God, he didn't.

Excitement turned to fear as the weeks ticked down to departure. This was going to be my first major tour away from home. I'd been on trips before, for a game here or there, but this was going to be six weeks away with people I barely knew. It turned out I wasn't going to be alone, though. Nicola said to me one day, 'Great news! I'm coming out to Australia!'

I wish I could say I was delighted. I put on a brave face, I put on a happy face, but all I was thinking was, 'How am I going to tell the team about this?' Here I was, a twenty-year-old, on my first tour with Scotland, and my girlfriend was coming out. I didn't know the form for these tours, but I was pretty sure it didn't involve girlfriends.

At a squad gathering, Gavin Hastings, a thirty-year-old legend of Scottish rugby, mentioned that his wife, Diane, was coming out, and I saw my chance.

'Oh, that's great!' I said, in front of everyone. 'My girlfriend's coming as well!'

You could actually hear the tumbleweed.

So many things for a young lad to worry about. But the biggest source of fear was my old foe, reading and writing. Playing rugby with Gavin Hastings and Iwan Tukalo seemed like nothing compared to the danger of them discovering I was illiterate, or thinking I was stupid.

The first hurdle I had to overcome on arrival in Australia was immigration. We had to fill in visa forms, and I didn't know what to do. So I grabbed Doddie Weir's form.

'Give us a look at yours, Doddie. Just to make sure I fill it in properly,' I said.

I copied it out word for word, which meant I filled in Doddie's name and address, not mine. I realised this as we approached immigration in Australia and I started to sweat.

'You've got the wrong form,' said the immigration officer. 'This is Doddie Weir's.'

I tried to make light of it. Luckily, he was a sympathetic guy – he may even have noticed I was struggling. He gave me a new form and I copied out my name and address from my passport. He volunteered to fill in the rest for me, because all the other details were the same as on everyone else's forms. So I cleared immigration in more ways than one, but I was constantly having to anticipate situations where I might get found out and to take steps to avoid them. I spent hours on that tour, during downtime, staring at a book, pretending to read it, trying to pick out words.

It meant I had to listen a lot. We'd be given schedules, which I could sort of make out, but I was always asking what time this meeting was and what we were calling such and such a move.

'You ask a lot of questions,' people would say. Well, the truth was it was because I couldn't read.

They gave us play books for our moves, with diagrams, which were all I could go on. I would often run the wrong line on the pitch. Sometimes I had just remembered it wrongly, but other times Gregor would point out that the diagram showed one thing, whereas if you read the text it said something else.

It was nerve-racking being on that tour, constantly nerve-racking, but exhilarating as well. I already knew Gregor and Derek Bain, because I had played rugby with them through the age groups, but I got to know people like Doddie Weir and Craig Chalmers. I didn't get to know David Sole so well, because he tended to keep himself to himself. It was his last tour, and I wish I'd had the chance to play more with him.

I was full of chat, which was a defence mechanism as much as anything. In time, I would learn to talk less, but I must have irritated a lot of people with my constant mouthing off. We each had nicknames that were written on our tour caps – another amateur touch that was still going strong – and mine was AMAC, which stood for All Mouth And Chin.

I don't remember being put in my place particularly. If anyone did, it was by humiliating me through drink. There were a lot of big nights out, and they picked on us youngsters in the kangaroo court sessions, where drinking forfeits were handed out as punishment for crimes on tour. Gregor struggled in particular. It was like taking a four-year-old out for a drink – he was throwing up, giggling and falling over after a couple of pints. I, on the other hand, used to take myself off to the toilets to be sick so I could get all the alcohol out of me. It was totally different.

Despite all the bluff of our off-field antics, it was what happened on the field that mattered. On 28 May I played the first game, in the sweltering heat of Darwin, for the midweek side against a Northern Territory Invitation XV, and I did well, even though we suffered an embarrassing defeat, 17–16. So I was on the bench for the first weekend game, against Queensland at Ballymore in Brisbane.

As the youngest guy it was my job to buy the wine gums, which were the standard food for the reserves – this was before the days of tactical substitutions, so reserves were never likely to get on. We were stuffing our faces, when one of the boys told me how Kenny Milne had once had to spew up behind the posts after he'd gone on for someone, having eaten too many. I laughed and had another one. I couldn't imagine myself getting on the field. But then Gavin Hastings cut his head open at the start of the second half, and in those days if you went off bleeding, you stayed off. Richie Dixon, the coach, gave me the nod.

'You're on at full-back.'

Whoa! I spat out the wine gum and felt the rest of the packet's worth welling up in my stomach. This was it. The Scotland first team. My big chance. On I ran. Almost immediately, Tim Horan launched a high ball. I took it cleanly and called a mark. Then I took a quick tap and swung my boot at the ball. It soared away sixty yards, almost to their 22. 'Fuck,' I thought, as the adrenaline rushed through me, and I caught my breath. I remember David Sole looking at me as he trundled off to the line-out. He didn't say anything, obviously, but he had at least looked at me.

We were leading 12–9 at the time, two tries to one, but Queensland had the Australia locks, John Eales and Rod McCall, just back from winning the World Cup, and they were cleaning us out at the line-outs. In the last minute, the score was 15–15, and I'd been playing well. Suddenly Paul Carozza, the Australia wing, went round his man and had one man to beat – and that was me. He was rapid, but I showed him the outside, which he took – I hadn't thought about it, this was just what I always did – and I smashed him into touch. Game saved.

It had felt so natural, because I'd done it so many times before, but I lay there realising that I had just done it for Scotland against one of the fastest wingers in the world. Scott Hastings grabbed me by the scruff of the neck and hauled me to my feet.

'What a tackle!' he screamed at me. And David Sole looked at me again.

I finally felt I'd arrived, and my tour went on an upward curve. We drew again the following Wednesday, 24–24, against the Emerging Wallabies in Hobart. In that game, we were getting smashed, when David Sole came on in the second half and practically turned it round single-handedly. The man was a phenomenon. I had been on the wrong end of another one of his looks at a training session before the tour. We were doing a sprint drill and he was in my group. I knew he was a prop, so I didn't try as hard as I should have done. A prop he may have been, but he was quick and he won. He didn't like the fact that he'd beaten me, because he knew I should have beaten him. The look he shot me that time, as we walked back for the next sprint, left me in no doubt about what he was saying – 'You always give one hundred per cent here. Don't think you can rock up as a twenty-year-old and beat me at half-throttle.'

I learnt a lot from him, the man who had led Scotland on their slow march on to the field at Murrayfield for the Grand Slam win against England only two years earlier. You just wanted to please him, and that was what made his captaincy so powerful.

The tour wasn't going well for us as a team. Gavin Hastings, who had injured his ankle as well as his head in that Queensland game and was suffering from a bad back, kept failing fitness tests, and before the first Test we had managed just one win – against New South Wales Country Origin XV, 26–10. The good thing for me about Gavin's injury was that I kept getting picked. In the end, I played in every game on the eight-match tour bar one, the first Test, when I was on the bench. In many ways, that was the most emotional game for me, as it dawned on me that I might get that cap soon and that Hamish wouldn't be there for it.

I had been in an emotional state quite often, as I struggled to cope with the excitement of what was happening to me on the field and the sadness I felt at being away from home. However, I was about to get a big surprise from Scotland.

We were on the team bus, on the way back from training to our hotel in Manly just after the team for the first Test had been announced. I looked out of the window as we drove over the Sydney Harbour Bridge and I remember looking at a huge ship in the harbour and thinking how proud Hamish would have been. I thought of my father, too, and wished they both could have been there. Nicola had arrived by then, but I hadn't seen much of her. She was with a friend and they were off all day, while I was training with the squad.

When we got back to the hotel, my room-mate, Alan Watt, a huge 6ft 5in prop, and I went up to our room. Watty opened the door and out leapt my cousin Ally and his best mate John Henderson, 'Hendy', an old friend of mine, singing, 'Meet the gang, 'cos the boys are here, the boys to entertain you!'

They'd come over to surprise me, and for a minute there was

bedlam, while Watty scratched his head. They were dressed in Scotland training gear and had managed to convince the hotel that they should be allowed into our room. It was not the first or last bit of bluffing they pulled off.

Just after my selection for the tour had been announced, they'd started secretly planning this trip. Unfortunately, I had accidentally heard about it when I walked in on their conversation at the farm, and the pair of them proceeded to put on an incredible act, pretending to have fallen out, so as to put me off the scent. They had spectacular arguments in front of me, and friends of ours back home were in shock at how badly their friendship had fallen apart. It had worked a treat. I'd assumed the trip was off. Everyone assumed their friendship was over – except them.

They became tour heroes. There was coverage of their trip in the local press at home, they were interviewed by the local press in Australia, they were interviewed by ITV. All the guys on the tour got to know them and welcomed them as unofficial Scotland players. Gavin Hastings invited them to join the team when we went out in the evening. The ten days they were there were magical for me.

Gav was finally fit for the first Test, but we went down 27–12, despite leading at half-time. Australia may have been the new world champions, and we may have been a team in transition, but one win from six at that point meant this was not turning out to be a tour to remember – unless it happened to be your first.

We got our second win the following Wednesday against Queensland Country Origin, and I played again. I knew there had to be a chance of being picked for the second Test that weekend, but I didn't do much more than play it safe. I felt I'd made enough statements earlier on in the tour. As we came off, I asked Iwan Tukalo how he thought I'd done. He had been a hero of mine for years, and as a youngster in the Scotland youth teams I had approached him for advice. He had been great – he'd even had me round to his house a couple of times, giving me help and showing me exercises to improve my step. On this tour, though, I was starting to emerge as a threat to him, and our relationship began to change, just the opposite of what would happen with Gareth Rees at Wasps when I started to push him out of the side. Reesy kept helping me and working with me in training, but Iwan didn't seem to want to know. After this Queensland Country game all he said to me was that he didn't think I had played that well, and I was gutted for a while. Until, that is, they announced the team the next day for the second Test in Brisbane. We were sitting in the team room. Richie Dixon announced Gavin Hastings as full-back. Then he said, 'Right wing, Kenny Logan,' and I couldn't help myself. 'Yes! Yes! Yes!' I shouted in the silent room. It was painful. That was how Tony Stanger discovered he'd been dropped, and he was sitting right next to me. His head fell, and I suddenly realised what it meant for him. I shut up pretty quickly and apologised to him, but I didn't listen to a word of the rest of the announcement.

At the end of it, I could finally relax and enjoy the realisation that I'd been picked for Scotland, the first player from Stirling County ever to win a full cap. Everyone was giving me a hug. I was jubilant. But there was one guy who didn't say a word to me. You've guessed it. David Sole.

We all got on the team bus and headed off for training. There were school kids and press there and more chaos as I revelled in my selection. We did our warm-ups, but still no word from Sole – not even one of his looks. 'This isn't right,' I thought. 'He's the captain.'

Then just as we were about to start the team run, he came over to me and, in the middle of the pitch, spent two minutes with me.

'Well done,' he said. 'You've deserved this. You've worked hard.'

There was no one around us and it meant more to me then. He'd waited for all the shit to die down and for everyone to go. That was how he worked. He was a quiet guy, nothing flashy, but when he spoke, you listened.

I had trouble sleeping the night before the game, but I don't think it really hit me that I was making my debut until I got home afterwards and was bombarded with pats on the back. When you're on tour, you're on your own. Among your team-mates, especially if you're new, you feel pressure to play it cool. After the initial excitement over my selection had escaped out of me, I spent the rest of the week trying to look as if I was taking it in my stride and that this was all part of the plan.

The idea of playing for my country, however, was nothing compared with the worry I felt over singing a song on the bus, which was the tradition for all first caps, on the way to training the day before the match. I didn't really know any songs. I would have sung 'Running Bear', because I sort of knew the beginning of it, but that was Gavin's favourite, so I was never going to be allowed to choose that one. That meant I was going to have to sing from a songsheet, and that meant having to read it. I wasn't bothered about the singing part, although I'm not much of a singer. If you can read, you can sing, as far as I'm concerned, and I couldn't read.

It was a short drive to the training ground, and as I got up to try to get away with 'Running Bear' the bus braked suddenly, and I fell forward. The driver told me to sit down, and the moment passed. To my amazement, it was barely mentioned again. Someone did ask out loud after the Test if everyone had sung their song, and I shouted, 'Yes,' and kept my head down. So I never had to sing that first song. It was more of a relief to get through that than it was to get through the game for my first cap.

It was a beautiful day in Brisbane for the second Test. I went for a coffee with Ally, Hendy and Nicola in the morning. They were the only people I could share my excitement with. Then I remember the police escort through the city and sitting in the changing room, looking round in wonder at my team-mates, just as I had before my Stirling County debut just over two years earlier – there'd been no police escort for that one. We ran out on to the pitch at Ballymore and the atmosphere was amazing.

The game itself didn't go well for us. Big Gav had pulled out with a back spasm just hours before the start. He'd played about a game and a half all tour. He had basically been on a Camp Australia trip. These days he'd have been flown home immediately, but he was such a legend that he got to stay with us. He spent most of the tour going off on boat trips, and, boy, did he get some stick for it from the rest of us. So, having psyched myself up to play on the wing, I was now pitched in at full-back, and Tony Stanger was reinstated.

I didn't play badly, but it was probably my poorest game of the tour. Michael Lynagh had me running around like a rabbit, chasing his kicks, some of them long, some short, and the Australians were pouring through us from the off. Probably the best tackle I put in was on David Campese, and it was off the ball. I'd tackled him legitimately to begin with, but he slipped away a nice offload. As he got up he tapped me on the side of the head and made some smart-arse comment about me being a novice. I was still on the ground, but as he trotted off I tapped his ankle and he fell flat on his face. 'Do you want a hand up, old man?'

But the scoreboard told no lies. We were beaten 37–13, five tries to two. And David Sole had gone over at the death for a consolation try. That was the last game in the world before the try became worth five points. So the next time you're asked in a pub quiz who the last man was to score a four-point try, you'll know the answer. That honour was the least Soley deserved in his last game for Scotland. He came in to the changing room at the end and hung up his boots on his peg.

'Why you doing that?' asked Dave McIvor, our blindside flanker.

'Won't be needing those any more,' said Sole.

'What size are you?'

'Ten.'

70

'I'll have 'em,' said McIvor, and he took them down and put them in his bag.

Looking back, it was the best tour I ever went on. Regardless of the results, I was out there playing with my heroes and playing well. It was still amateur and we had a great crack off the field. It was also an emotional time for me. Neither Hamish nor my dad could be there, but Ally and Hendy were, so I was able to share my first cap with some of my family.

Most of all, though, I had finally won that first cap, the first player from Stirling County to get one. Now I wanted more.

# 5

# Three Little Words

If there was ever a time in my life when I thought, 'I've made it,' it was then. I suppose it's quite common among young sportsmen who are suddenly thrust into the limelight from nowhere. There I was, a farmer's boy on five grand a year, returning to the small community of Stirling as some kind of conquering hero. Suddenly I was being offered a grand just to open a shop. Tommy Fergusson, the local coal merchant, who was also a friend of mine, gave me a car with my name plastered all over it. I'd arrived!

Mum and Bash, Hamish's wife, had put together a big banner

saying 'Welcome home, Kenny' and draped it across the front of the farmhouse, along with all kinds of decoration. It was open house all day. Friends and family came and went. Gareth Flockhart and a few of the rugby boys cooked up a big barbecue in the evening. People driving past tooted their horns.

I look back now and cringe at myself, lapping up all the praise, and believing it, but I was young, and I like to think it's the only time in my life when I got a bit carried away with myself. I will say that it was a relief for once not feeling that I was inadequate or that I had to prove myself. But it goes to show why second-season syndrome is such a problem in so many young sporting careers. I hadn't exactly become a world-beater − I'd made my debut for a team that went on to lose by thirty points on the other side of the world − but even to burst on to the scene in the modest way I did and to become the subject of the hype that followed was bound to turn your head just a bit. That's when a sportsman is in danger of losing the edge that comes from continually trying to prove yourself.

That said, I went mental in the gym that summer, working on my speed and power. I did too much. What I needed was a break. Sure enough, my performance levels dropped the following season, and it wasn't long before I was back to doubting myself and fighting so hard to get over those insecurities. It is better for a sportsman to be that way, I suppose, but it doesn't always make for a happy person.

Certainly my form for Stirling County suffered on my return. I said I wanted to play full-back, which didn't go down well, and I played pretty badly, which went down even worse. It was wrong for the team to have me at full-back, because it meant our best goal-kicker, Callum MacDonald, had to move to the wing. I needed pulling down a peg or two. But regardless of what was happening with my rugby, I was forced to grow up by bigger life events.

There's a picture of my return from Australia that summer with the welcome banner and lots of smiling faces. My father is in it, looking very old and weak. That's probably the last photo ever taken of him. Within a few weeks he was confined to his bed, and that was where he spent his final months.

I know he was proud of me, although he never quite said it. There had been a tear in his eye when the squad was announced. It turns out he didn't think he would be alive when I returned, but Mum reckons my playing for Scotland gave him a new lease of life. He was such a prominent figure in our community – a Justice of the Peace – and in his final days as a man about town he had a whole new set of handshakes to deal with, congratulating him on my success. As his condition deteriorated, Stirling County let Mum drive him to the edge of the pitch so that he could watch me play from the car. She parked at one end and the crowd would form round them.

Otherwise he spent his final days in his bed. He was laid up high on two mattresses, so that he could look out over his farm and watch the cows and the tractors coming and going.

I used to go up to see him at the end of the day. He'd always said that you never stop learning in life. He was still saying it when he was well into his seventies, but one day during one of my visits to his bedside, he said to me, 'I think I'm struggling to learn now.' A couple of days later it dawned on me what he was trying to say. He was dying.

My dad never really told me he loved me. I knew he did, but saying it wasn't his way. He may have been reserved, but he was also soft-hearted. He felt things deeply, even if he didn't like to show it. He wasn't the kind of person to go round repeating things, because, once he'd said something, he was so genuine it wouldn't occur to him that it would ever need saying again.

By the end, he could barely speak at all. One Thursday evening in November, after I'd finished work on the farm and changed into my rugby kit, ready for training, I went in to see him, sat down and talked him through what had happened that day on the farm. He seemed a bit far away, as if he wasn't listening. Then, as I got up to go, he tried to say something. It took him a wee while and I could barely hear it, but there was no doubting what he said. It was, 'I love you,' and I left the room in tears, because I knew then that was it.

I went off to training that night, realising I wouldn't see him again. I kept looking down the end of the pitch, expecting to see someone coming round the corner with the news. I remember running, with the castle at my back towards the Wallace Monument end, and passing to Gus Turner. As I stopped to turn round, I saw my brother Andrew walking up the pitch towards us. I knew what it meant.

I went home with Andrew, but I didn't want to go back into Dad's room again. I just sat outside in the corridor and talked to him through the wall. It was sad, but I was also happy that it was over. Even without his illness, I had accepted the fact that he was so much older than the fathers of other people my age. So I was well used to the idea he was going to die quite early in my life. Maybe I was even tortured by it. As a teenager I used to sneak into his room at night to check that he was still breathing.

Because I loved him. Not in the mad, knockabout way I'd loved Hamish and I loved my cousins, but in that reverential, slow-burning kind of way that you love the man you respect more than anyone else in the world. There was a big age difference between us, and I had always been his little lad, the only one of his three boys who had shared his love for the animals on his farm. So I think there was a bond there.

His death was easier to handle than Hamish's had been two years earlier, but it threw up more issues for us to resolve. The biggest was what we were going to do with the farm. One of my memories of that time is sitting in the undertaker's car after my dad's funeral, driving up the winding road towards the Sword Hotel, next to the Wallace Monument, where the wake was to be held. I was facing backwards, opposite my brothers and my mother, and it wasn't a happy conversation. Dad had just been buried, and I looked out to my right, over the expanse of the farm. Who was going to run it, now that he had gone? What were we going to do?

Andrew, my middle brother, didn't want to do it. He kept himself to himself and was much quieter than the rest of us, more like my dad, maybe, than anyone. He used to go off on his own windsurfing or down to the boxing club. For years he'd worked in the post office, and then he went away with the army. Dad was leaving James and me twenty-five per cent of the farm each and my mother fifty per cent, but Andrew was left a house in the grounds. He had never shown any interest in the farm, but that was about to change. He threw himself into it all of a sudden, almost as if it was his way of grieving Dad's passing. Suddenly, you couldn't keep him away from the place. He became interested in the cows, just as Dad had been. James was into working the land, and I was equally into both. But Andrew, again like Dad, was hopeless with the machinery. He used to crash the tractors into walls. If Andrew was driving a tractor, you more or less had to follow him round with a cement mixer and bricks, so you could put the farm back together again. Running a farm wasn't really an option for him. He was his own man. It just wasn't in his personality.

James was running his contract business cutting hedges, which was a part of the farm's operations that my father had given him because he had shown little interest in the rest of it. I think he'd had a run-in with Dad, and I remember Dad saying, 'That's it. He can have the contracting business and fend for himself.'

I really wanted James to stay with the farm. I felt that I needed his help. He is probably the most practical person I've ever known. He can strip a tractor down, build a house; he can work wood and steel; he can weld. He's the perfect farm manager, which is annoying, because that is exactly what he is now on someone's else's farm. Back then, though, he had a different vision for himself.

He and I had a fiery relationship, which went back to our

childhood. I was seven years younger and I spent a large part of my life tormenting him. He used to chase me for hours – it's how I got my pace, because he was quick. I think I must have been a nightmare. He would be about to throw my bike at me, so I would stand in front of his car. 'Come on then!' I was constantly taunting him. We would have a ruck, each get a punch in, and then I would run off again. He never caught me once.

Things are very different between us now. He asked me to be godfather to Claire, his daughter, which was an honour that brought tears to my eyes, and our relationship is better than ever, but it didn't improve, really, until we went our separate ways over the farm.

When we were sitting in the funeral car, driving up the hill to the wake that day, we each had an equal stake in it, but his focus was on his hedge-cutting business. He would help out on the farm whenever he could, but he wasn't going to look after it.

'I've got a business to run,' he said.

It was upsetting me. I wanted us to run the farm together. I wanted him to say, 'Let's make this work.' I'm a passionate person, and when things are flying around that's when you need to stand up and be counted. I felt I was the only one standing up on this one.

'Well, I'll do it then,' I shouted. 'I'll do it! I'll do it!'

It was a turning point in my life. Maybe *the* turning point. It was time to leave my childhood behind. I was twenty years old, unable to read or write, an amateur rugby player who'd just played for his country, a son who had just lost his father, and now I was in charge of a farm. I had to make decisions that affected people.

It felt too much at times. On more than one occasion I stopped the tractor in a distant field on the farm and wept. How could I deal with this responsibility when I could barely write my own name?

Putting a brave face on it was the only option – dry my eyes, pull myself together and head back up to the farm. I'd already learnt in rugby that showing signs of weakness, even if weakness was there, would be the first thing to undermine you. And there were plenty of people – family, neighbours, friends – to help me, even if my illiteracy was never mentioned. To this day, I don't know if any of them were aware of it. They may not even be aware of it now.

When it came to farming matters, Tommy Brewster, a neighbouring farmer, was a vital sounding board and became a kind of father figure. My cousins were there for me, too, John in particular. He was my other father substitute – to this day people think he actually is my father, which is not to say he looks old and decrepit. I was very close to all of Hamish's brothers – John, Ally and Kelso. I'd grown up with them on the farm, but John was the eldest and the most sensible, and if you ever had a question you needed answering, he was the man. When I go back to see Mum in Stirling, the first people I visit are Ally, Kelso, John and their families.

Muff Scobie, another cousin, the son of my dad's sister, Senga, was great, too. He was another rugby player, a prop like Hamish. He played for the Midlands and was forwards coach at Stirling County during my last couple of seasons there. He was very close to Hamish and was a hard man who never showed any emotion, but he carried the coffin at Hamish's funeral and I remember looking round and seeing the tears streaming down his face. That moment made a deep impression on me, and it was the same at my father's funeral, two years later in the same church, when Muff put his arm round me at the gates. I spent a lot of time with Muff in the years following my father's death, as I tried to cope with the farm. He sent over his bookkeeper, who was crucial to us for ten years, to help out with the accounts.

Then there was Mum, of course. She'd taken on a lot of pressure when they told her Dad had only months to live. It was a burden she'd lived with on her own and it was hard on her. She'd insisted on keeping Dad at the farm for those two years he'd lived, right until the end, and as a result he died a far happier man than if he'd had to spend his final weeks in a hospital. Mum has always been very strong, a good go-to person when there's a family crisis, and she remained strong for me in those years after Dad died.

Without any of them, I would have found life even tougher than I did. Because when it came to dealing with the rest of the world, outrageous bluff was my only real technique.

———

I was receiving quite a few invitations to make appearances around the town, but the one that really hit home came from Wallace High School. They wanted me to come back and talk to the kids. Jenny Mailer, Robbie and Nicola's mum, had set it up. It was very emotional for me, probably the hardest speech I've ever made.

Of course, as the day approached, I desperately tried to get out of it. I'd said yes in an off-hand sort of way, and I'd forgotten about it. I didn't have a diary – everything was in my head. When it dawned on me that I was going to have to do it, I panicked. I really didn't want to go back and see some of those people. The only thing for it was to invent all kinds of other engagements, but Jenny just said, 'That's fine, we'll do it another day.' It was a nightmare. There was no way out of it. I couldn't be busy every day for the rest of my life. So I broke it to her that I didn't want to do it, simple as that, and that I couldn't speak in front of so many people. But, just as she had in my junior schooldays when she'd consoled me every time I'd been sent out of class, she chivvied me up and said it would all be fine. The school was so proud of me and they were all rooting for me. That was a bitter-sweet revelation. If only they'd had so much time for me when I'd actually been a pupil there.

Before the speech, loads of teachers came up to me and shook my hand, telling me how they always knew I would be a success. One woman in particular reminisced about what a talent I was, and I remember she'd been one of the most sneering to me at school. It was embarrassing. 'Fuck off' was all I kept thinking. The only people I was pleased to see were Jenny, obviously, and Norrie Bairner, the man who had crossed the picket line during the strikes so that we could still play sport.

Norrie had to intervene when I really thought I was going to lamp the headmaster. Before the speech, I presented him with my Scotland jersey, the one I'd worn on my debut in Australia.

'Oh, that will make a fantastic prize for the raffle,' he said.

I couldn't believe it. I actually squared up to him.

'No way!' I said. 'That is a playing jersey. It's the first and only one I have. I've worked bloody hard for that shirt, and it's not going in some 10p-a-ticket raffle. It goes up on the wall or I'm taking it home.'

Norrie stepped in to have a word, and the headmaster was happy to put the shirt up, but it made me despair how some of these teachers could so miss the point. My hackles were up.

I remember sitting up on the stage in the huge hall with the headmaster and the local minister and a whole load of other head-masters from nearby schools. I thought it was going to be just a hundred pupils or so, but about five hundred people had turned up – teachers, pupils and their parents.

The headmaster introduced me. 'This is Kenneth Logan, former pupil, Scotland player, we're all so very proud of him, blah, blah, blah.' When it was my turn to get up, for a moment I froze. I was so nervous. My hands were wet and when I got to my feet my legs were shaky. It was the first speech I'd ever had to make. I looked out and started to recognise faces in the audience, each one a memory from those terrible days at school – all these faces swirling around in my head.

I had a piece of paper in my hand with headings that my mother had written down to try to help me: Australia, rugby, school, emu. That last one referred to a story that I'd planned to tell them about the Australia tour, and I just launched into it and didn't look at the piece of paper again.

When I'd been selected for the tour, I'd been given a load of stash, and I was so excited about it. One of the things we were given, along with the Scotland blazer that I was proudly wearing as I spoke, was a pair of Ray-Bans. I was chuffed with these sunglasses – they were Wayfarers, so cool. At the start of the tour we went to a game reserve in Darwin, and I was standing by an emu pen, alongside David Sole, Gavin Hastings and Tony Stanger. I was wearing my Wayfarers, and I thought, 'I'm all right.'

Then somebody clipped my head and my sunglasses fell into the pen, maybe about ten feet down. This emu started flicking them around the place. Everyone was laughing but I didn't find it funny. Those sunglasses meant a lot to me and I had to get them back. So when the emu lost interest and walked away, I jumped down into the enclosure and grabbed them. The emu turned round. For a moment, it looked at me and I looked at it. Then it started to run towards me. I leapt up on to a ledge and out of the pen, swinging my feet out just in time as it went for me. I straightened myself up, put my sunglasses back on and said, 'Lions anyone?'

It was a good story to get things going, but it was meant to make a serious point. Even tiny things can and should mean a lot to you. We must never be embarrassed or afraid to go all out for them.

The crowd laughed at the story, but my eyes kept going back to the teachers who had made my life such a misery and who were now sitting at the sides of the audience. The sight of them made me speak straight from the heart. I didn't mention dyslexia, but I described how so many of my former teachers had come up to me that day and shaken my hand, patted me on the back, told me how they always knew I'd do well, yet when I'd actually been at the school they'd never given me the time of day.

'I find it really frustrating,' I said, 'that their attitude has changed so much, just because I've played for Scotland and achieved something in their eyes. But any achievement is amazing. Passing your exams is amazing. Learning to read is amazing.' Little did they know how much I meant that.

I went to sit down at the end of it, and the kids got to their feet and clapped and cheered. The headmaster stood up to speak, but they just kept going over him. I found it hugely inspiring. I couldn't have done it again. It was a one-off. Some of the headmasters from other schools asked if I would come and speak to their kids, but I said, no, that speech was for one school only.

Wallace High, though, never asked me back.

––––––––

I may have suddenly become the pride and joy of my local community, but I could only make the bench for Scotland's first game of the 1993 Five Nations. Derek Stark was given his first cap instead of me against Ireland at Murrayfield. I didn't have a problem with it. Starky was very quick and he'd been playing well – but, deep down, I knew I was better than he was. I may not have been selected but I was still in the squad, and I was just happy to be involved and to watch and learn. Second-season-itis had me in its grips, and I was not the man in form. You just have to get through that second season, any which way.

I was having real problems with my concentration and with learning moves, thinking too much about everything. Throughout my career I was always at my best when I didn't think. I liked taking high balls under pressure, not when I had no one around me. I liked kicking goals that I wasn't expected to get; it was the ones straight in front that gave me problems. So I was trying to work all of this out in my head. Sometimes I would try to manufacture more pressure to make it look as if I had no chance of getting to a high ball, then getting to it all the same. But that meant I was thinking too much about not thinking too much, and so it was easy to get stuck in a rut.

I did get on for twenty minutes at the end of our last game – at Twickenham against England – and I played well. We were already losing – Stuart Barnes ran rings round us – but my highlight was when Peter Winterbottom ran at me, and I just launched myself at him and hit him backwards, spilling the ball. It was my second cap, and I got that adrenaline surge again – I can do this, I realised, this is as hard as it gets, and I can do it.

Well, it wasn't quite as hard as it gets. For me, that's playing against the All Blacks, which the Lions did that summer. I was never in the reckoning for that, but there was an uncapped Scotland tour to the South Pacific that I did go on. My mouth was in overdrive and they banned me from talking for forty-eight hours, which was fine. Trouble was they gave me a placard to hang round my neck, and I was supposed to communicate by writing on it. So even this joke had me panicking. My way round it was just to write 'fuck off' on the board, which for some reason I'd always been able to spell.

The other things that stood out about that tour were the frogs in Fiji and the transvestites in Samoa. They call the transvestites 'fa'afafines', and they are accepted as part of the culture. Some of them were stunning. Later on that summer, I happened to be watching *The Crying Game* with Robbie. We didn't know the ending, and I said to him, 'That girl looks just like the fa'afafines in Samoa,' and we all know what happened next.

And then there were the frogs. There are frogs everywhere in Fiji. When the rain started to pour down during our match, hundreds of frogs emerged from out of the bushes and invaded the pitch. We actually ended up playing the game on frogs. It was a surreal experience, matched only on that trip by the official outfits we had to wear – blazers, ties, long blue socks and shorts. The SRU's sense of humour knew no bounds.

The Lions were beaten by the All Blacks that summer, meanwhile, and the following November New Zealand came to Murrayfield and cut us to shreds 51–15. I was on the bench again, although I got on for my third cap as a blood replacement for Gavin Hastings early on. The score was 0–0 when I returned to the bench is all I can say.

Ian Jardine finally made his Scotland debut in that match, which made me and Stirling County very happy – the second man to be capped from the club, even if he should really have been the first. He was twenty-nine, and it was long overdue. He and I had played for Scotland A against New Zealand the weekend before. We gave them a good game, and Jardy played a blinder. He had to be in the side for the Test match. And I reckoned I had to be in line for the No. 11 shirt, but in order to accommodate Jardy, they shifted Scott Hastings out to the wing, so it was the bench for me again. I wasn't so happy this time.

Scott was no winger and, to be fair, he was quite embarrassed by the decision. He'd never even played there before. His opposite number, the twenty-year-old Jeff Wilson, scored a hat-trick on his debut, and Scott was all over the place. Dougie Morgan, our coach, copped a fair bit of criticism for it, which he survived, but this was the second of what turned out to be a nine-match run without a win.

The good news for me was that it meant I was in the team for the start of the 1994 Five Nations, and I became a regular. But it was a poor campaign. We got smashed 29–6 in the first game, down in Cardiff in the pouring rain. Gavin Hastings was coming under a lot of pressure as captain. People were saying he was getting too slow, too old and that the legend was no more. It was a tough time for him, but he inspired such loyalty in all of us and we were desperate to turn it round for him.

We came close against England at Murrayfield in the second game. Gregor slotted a drop goal at the end of normal time, and we were winning 14–12. Then, in injury time, the ref spotted a hand in the ruck with a blue cuff. Assuming it was a Scottish hand, even if it would have had to have belonged to a contortionist, he awarded a penalty at the death to England. There were huge protests. Initial suspicion fell on Jardy, who was on as a replacement. Afterwards on the news, they were even slowing down the film to try to identify the culprit. Jardy swore it wasn't him, and he was right. For some reason, England's shirts back then had blue cuffs on them like ours, and it later became clear that it had been Rob Andrew's hand on the ball.

Not that that changed anything. Jon Callard lined up the kick for England. I was standing behind the left post, and his kick was arcing wide. For a second or so, we were thinking we'd won. We went to celebrate, but, no, the ball somehow curled in just in time, and the final whistle went. We had lost 15–14. It was so dispiriting. We were on a losing run and to beat England would have been such a boost. Thinking for that second that we had won made it all the crueller.

Gav was so distraught he started crying when interviewed on live television. He was so honest and passionate about his country. He was a one in a million. We didn't actually know that he had cried until it was all over the news. Gav became a national hero after that.

I got on really well with him and his wife, Diane. He saw himself as a kind of mentor to me, although it was around then that his dad said to me, 'You want to tell my son to leave you alone and let you play your own game.'

It was true that Gav was a bit protective of me. Every time a high ball went up in those days I would hear this voice bellowing in my ear, 'GAV!' and I would roll my eyes. Not again. Any chance I could catch a ball? He used to call me the Young Pretender. He thought I was going to take over his mantle at full-back but by then I was enjoying playing on the wing.

'You know, I'm quite happy to take these balls myself now,' I said to him.

Our next match was in Dublin, and this time it was Gav

accusing me of crying. Even by Lansdowne Road standards it was a windy day. When we were playing into it we were fielding kicks right, left and centre. There was no chance of kicking them back, because the ball just stuck to your boot – if you wanted to find touch, you had to run it there. I took a blow in the face, and there was blood everywhere.

'I've broken my nose,' I said to James Robson, our doctor.

'No, you haven't,' he replied.

'Yes, I have. I can feel it.'

As I was talking, he grabbed my nose and wrenched it back into place.

'It's fine now.'

My tear ducts were smashed, so there were tears streaming down my face for the rest of the match. At one point Gav noticed this.

'What are you crying for?' he said.

It was a poor game, ending in a 6–6 draw, so we were still winless, and that's how it stayed for that Five Nations. France came over to Murrayfield two weeks later for the last game and beat us there for the first time in sixteen years. A miserable championship, then, with plenty of tears and a wooden spoon at the end, but at least I was now a *bona fide* Scotland player.

———

Around that time I took a decision that I still can't quite explain today. I got engaged to Nicola. Damian Cronin pulled no punches.

'What have you done that for, you idiot?' he said, when he heard. I was about to turn twenty-two and I had the vast majority of a promising rugby career ahead of me, let alone a life. He had a point.

I don't know why I did it. She was a lovely girl, and I was obviously keen on her. I had very close ties to her family. Robbie was my best mate, I'd known her mum since I was a kid at primary school, and her dad, Iain 'Old Man' Mailer as he was known, was a real club man at Stirling County, the guy who stood at the bar and told you all the good things you'd done on the field and let rip at you over the bad things. He was a good friend, too. So it was easy to get carried away with the happy-family side of it all. I felt under a bit of pressure to propose, although I don't know who from. It just seemed like the done thing, but it wasn't right for either of us. We joke about it even now. We were both too young, me especially. When we got engaged I almost wanted to brush it under the carpet. Six years later, when I got engaged to Gabby, I wanted to shout it from the rooftops.

Rugby was number one for me back then, which it always had been and always would be until Gabby became number one, something she did far more quickly than I ever thought anyone would. I was constantly away playing, or at training, or I was working on the farm, so I wasn't the ideal boyfriend, and maybe getting engaged to Nicola seemed like a solution to that.

So what did I do next? You guessed it, I went away with rugby. This time on the Scotland tour to Argentina that May. Things weren't going well between Nicola and me when we left, and I fell for someone while I was there – a gorgeous, raven-haired Argentine, about nineteen or twenty years old, who was a model for, bizarrely, Famous Grouse whisky. We fell in love but never kissed. I went along to a Famous Grouse promo with Shade Munro and met her there. We got on really well. After that I went to as many of the Famous Grouse promos as I could. It became a bit of a joke in the squad. 'Famous Grouse? Kenny'll do it!'

I just couldn't stop looking at her and her dark skin and brown eyes. She was a good Catholic girl who worked hard, because her parents didn't have much money, and I was a good boy, because I was engaged and didn't want to do anything stupid. On the last night she came out with us, and at the end of the evening I kissed her goodbye on the cheek. It didn't go down too well. Why was I kissing her when I was due to leave the following day and return home to my fiancée? The next day, though, she came round to the hotel just as we were leaving and gave me her phone number, told me I was an amazing guy and said she wished she lived in Scotland.

We played two Tests on the tour and lost them both, the first by one point, the second by two. The Hastings boys and Craig Chalmers were among a few senior players who didn't tour, so we were a young side. The first Test was special for three of us – Kevin McKenzie won his first cap, which meant it was the first time that Stirling County had provided Scotland with three players for a Test match, Jardy and I being the other two. Kevin, or 'Stumpy' as he was known, was a hooker and the elder brother of Mark, who was a goal-kicking fly-half – not much of a family resemblance, as we were to find out to our cost in the second Test. Stumpy was a feisty customer who was absolutely committed to his rugby and getting the best from himself. He was almost always the smallest guy in the team, but he worked like a madman in the gym, long before the game turned professional.

The management stuck with the same team for the second Test, even though we lost the first 16–15, and we were trailing 19–17 with time running out when I went on a run up the left touchline and got tackled. I slipped the ball inside, but my ankle was caught in the tackle and I fell to the ground, where I lay on the grass in agony, watching the play unfold. We had them on the rack, deep in their 22, and a try looked likely. The ball came back from a ruck, and Bryan Redpath passed it back to Stumpy, who was standing in the fly-half position in front of the posts. I knew what Stumpy was like – 'anything my fly-half of a little brother can do . . .' – and it was so obvious that he was going to go for the drop goal. I watched him line it up and screamed from the floor, as if I was in a war film, 'NOOOOOO!'

The ball didn't get off the ground. It didn't even reach the tryline. It spewed off towards the corner flag. Argentina picked it up, belted it downfield and the chance had gone. To be fair to Stumpy, he was the kind of guy who could have slotted it over in training. He was skilful and certainly ballsy enough to do it, but not at the end of a Test match with the result in the balance, not when Gregor was standing right next to him and not when the Argentine defence were in his face.

What was even more galling was that the player charging at him shouldn't have been on the pitch. The Argentine fly-half went down injured and while he was being treated a replacement came on. Then the fly-half recovered, but his replacement never left the field, and he was the one who put Stumpy off. Argentina played with sixteen men for a few minutes, and the referee didn't even notice. It was unbelievable.

I was carried off, cursing everything – a 2–0 series loss, an injured ankle, Argentina's cheating and my old mate Stumpy, the hooker who thought he was a fly-half. We called him Lescarboura after that, after the French drop-kicker *extraordinaire*, and it really wound him up.

I'd ripped my ligaments, so my ankle was put in a cast for the flight home, and I was instructed not to drink. So Jardy, Stumpy and I took three seats together in the plane and celebrated Stirling County's success by drinking Bailey's all the way home, and when we'd drunk the in-flight trolley dry we bought the duty free. By the time we got off the plane we were smashed.

That set the tone for the summer. Within days of getting home it was over between Nicola and me. She broke off our engagement. Robbie was furious with her and took my side. He obviously wanted his sister to marry his best mate. Her mum and dad were practically apologising. Old Man Mailer drove Robbie and me to the Highland Show that summer, dropped us off and we drank Rolling Rock all day and night.

After one night, Robbie talked me into ringing the Argentine girl. So I did, and she was going to come over. I told her I would get her a job and I looked into flights (one-way obviously). Her English was excellent, and she was all set, but her parents blocked it, saying that she hardly knew me. Which was a fair point.

It was the start of what we call the Rolling Rock summer. I had a broken engagement and an injured ankle to get over, and I did it with feeling. We had a great time. Every Friday night one of us would ring the other and simply say, 'Rolling Rock.' 'Rolling Rock,' the other would reply, and we were down the pub within minutes.

# 6

# End of an Era

I was young, free and single now, and the following season my rugby hit new highs. Scotland suffered a ninth game without a win in the autumn of 1994, against the touring Springboks. For stretches of the match we played well and there was a feeling that we might have turned a corner. I had a good game against Pieter Hendriks, and my confidence was starting to grow. If I could play well against this lot, I could play well against anybody, but it was doing my head in that I still hadn't been on the winning side in a Test match.

Dougie Morgan's job was on the line, and Gav was now suffering real pressure as captain. The next game was a friendly against

Canada on a freezing afternoon in January, a warm-up for the 1995 Five Nations. Ten changes were made to the team that lost to South Africa. This was meant to be a new dawn. It had to be.

That was the game when Damian Cronin shat himself. He hit someone so hard in a tackle that he suffered an involuntary expulsion of air – and he followed through. Those were the days when you weren't allowed to go off at half-time, but Damian told the referee he had no choice. 'Where's he going?' people were asking. I remember the medical staff coming down to see what was wrong, only to find him in the toilets wringing his pants out. Damian scored the only try of the game in the second half. Nobody laid a finger on him, and he was no speed merchant. It wasn't pretty (the game, I mean) but we won, at last, 22–6, and it marked an upturn in our fortunes.

An excellent Five Nations for us culminated in a Grand Slam decider against England at Twickenham. The highlight of our campaign, though, was a win in Paris – the first time we'd beaten the French on their home territory in twenty-six years. The main motivation was to stop the endless repeats of the black-and-white footage showing Jim Telfer's try in the corner in 1969. Every time we had an away match against France they dusted down the archive footage – 'The last time we won in Paris, Jim Telfer scored in the corner, blah, blah, blah.' Here we go again. We all said to him after the win, 'At least we'll never have to watch your try again, Jim.'

Whenever we played at the Parc des Princes, it was carnival time, with the brass bands and the cockerels, but this game will be remembered for Gregor Townsend's moment. The French scored a try to take the lead with about five minutes to go. In the dying moments, Gregor took the ball off Bryan Redpath, stepped inside and attracted about four defenders before slipping an outrageous pass out of the back of his hand to Gav, cutting the perfect line. Gav was in between the posts and, boy, did we celebrate.

We'd been told by Gav that whenever you win in France the tradition is to smash the plates at the after-match dinner. None of us knew any better – most of us hadn't been born the last time Scotland had had a victory in Paris. You did what your captain told you to do. So we smashed the first one, and someone cleared it up and brought out another, and we smashed that. In all, we destroyed about fifty of them.

It turned out not to be a tradition at all, but they kept bringing plates out, so we kept smashing them. I could see another Romania 1991 situation developing, and was rubbing my hands – senior Scotland internationals getting to behave like children. Brilliant! But Jim Telfer and Duncan Paterson soon told us to start behaving – within reason. The next morning we were still in our number ones and we were still drunk. We came home to a hero's welcome.

The match had been a triumph for Gregor, who was starting to fulfil the potential we'd all known about for so long. But more than for him, the Five Nations was turning into a triumph for Gav. He'd become Scotland's most capped player in the first game of the championship, a win over Ireland, and he was extending his points-scoring record with some superb displays with the boot. Having gone through such a dark period the year before, like the team itself, when people were calling for his head, he was now suddenly thriving as the captain of this young team, and we were all thriving under his leadership.

It was a special time for me. The following weekend I played for Stirling County, and we became Scottish champions for the first time – the first team outside Edinburgh or the Borders to win the title. Nineteen years earlier, when the leagues were first extended, the club had been placed in the bottom, the seventh division. It was an amazing fairytale, and so many characters from those years were there that day, including Ian Nelson and Kenny Crichton, who are no longer with us. The two of them were club stalwarts who had done so much to bring about our success. Ian had started up the mini- and midi-rugby sections. Nearly all of the championship-winning team had come up through them. He was there that day with a tear in his eye.

On the field, though, we had some real characters. The only thing missing from our win that day was Ian Jardine. His cheekbone got smashed against the French at the end of the game the week before. He was on fire that season. If there had been a Lions tour, he would have been on it. He was finally getting the recognition he was due after years of consistent excellence. When you were tackled by Jardy, it was like you'd been hit by a truck. The impact would shudder through your legs. He was quick, too. In other words, he was a less-skilful version of Brian O'Driscoll, but that season he had learnt to slip little passes away and he was causing havoc.

Elsewhere, we had Brian Ireland, 'Icy', an openside who was a nightmare to play against. He would have played for Scotland, had it not been the era of Finlay Calder and John Jeffrey. He should probably have been capped anyway, as should our skipper, lock Stewart Hamilton. Back then, national selection was all so political.

Big Hammy was about thirty-nine when we won the league. Renowned throughout club rugby, he was an icon at Stirling. He'd played in most of the divisions during our journey from bottom to top, although he'd gone away to play for Heriot's for a few years. One man who did play in all seven divisions – the first man in Scottish rugby to have done so – was John Henderson, the guy who came out with my cousin Ally to watch me get my first cap in Australia. We had a few injuries in the centre after we'd won the title, so Hendy was called into the first team for the Watsonians game, one of our last of the season, and played a blinder against Scott Hastings. It put him in the history books and put Scott in his pocket.

We beat Boroughmuir to win the title, although we hadn't expected it to happen that weekend. I fielded a high ball on our 22 and set off on a long run to their 22, which ended when I flipped the ball up to Gus Turner for the winning try. I was also kicking that match, because Mark McKenzie had gone off, and I slotted the conversion for a 13–9 win. About ten minutes after the final whistle, the news came through that Watsonians had lost, and we were confirmed as champions.

It was an amazing feeling to sit in the changing room that day, celebrating with my mates, some of whom I'd played with since I was a kid and some of whom I'd watched all those years. We closed the doors and sang our songs at the tops of our voices, the ones we always used to sing when we won. We were the outsiders in Scottish rugby, far away from the heartlands of Border rugby. Our songs were based on that, fostering a them-against-us mentality – 'No one likes us, we don't care.'

About four to five thousand people had crammed into the stand and round the touchline at Bridgehaugh that day. It doesn't sound much by today's standards, although our crowds were as big as the ones Edinburgh or Glasgow get now. The future looked so exciting. Rugby was about to turn professional, and there was talk of a European super league. As Scottish champions, we were put forward as one of the teams, but the SRU decided to go down the route of district rugby. I think that was a mistake. The game in Scotland has always been based around its clubs. That decision bypassed the soul of Scottish rugby, and it says something that the professional game in Scotland has withered to just two districts, neither of which is well supported.

The club game is withering, too. Stirling County get just a few hundred to a match now, because all the international players have left to play for districts that don't get enough support, or for clubs in other countries. In my view, at the start of the professional era, the SRU should have selected a handful of clubs in strategic locations and poured their resources into those. Probably four of them would be left by now as fully professional outfits, but they would be well supported and they would mean something to their local communities. But we went down the wrong road.

Certainly the community in Stirling was buzzing when we won that title, and so was I. My first senior trophy arrived one week and the next I was playing a blinder for my country as we beat Wales at Murrayfield to set up a second Grand Slam decider of the 90s against England. If asked to nominate my favourite try from my career, I would probably say it was the one against Wales that year. The only thing is, I didn't score it. I didn't score many tries for Scotland – thirteen in seventy appearances, although I did score another seven in two World Cup qualifiers against Spain and Portugal in 1998, but the SRU didn't award caps for those two games, so they don't count. Don't ask me why. Probably to avoid paying us win bonuses.

I don't know why I couldn't stop scoring tries for Stirling and then for Wasps but so rarely scored them for Scotland. Well, I do. I hardly ever got the ball. Most of my work for Scotland was defensive, chasing kicks or running them back. At Wasps we played far more rugby with ball in hand, and a lot of the rugby at Wasps was of international intensity.

When I went through that time of never passing the ball as a kid at Stirling, Sandy Bryce had told me that I would gain at least as much satisfaction from setting up tries as from scoring them, and he was right. Never was it truer than in 1995. I went on a sixty-metre run to set up the try that won Stirling County the title, and I did the same for Scotland against Wales the very next weekend. We were trailing by a point in the first half, when Doddie Weir gave me the ball on our 22, and I was off. Eventually, I had one man to beat, and maybe I should have gone for the line, but I had beaten four men already and I saw Eric Peters in support, so I took the tackle and gave him the try-scoring pass. The feeling was phenomenal. The roar from the crowd gave me goose pimples all over. Normally, the try-scorer is congratulated, but this time, I was the one getting all the pats on the back. Even Eric came to join in. It was later voted try of the championship. Dave Hilton scored a couple of minutes later, and that was the basis of a 26–13 win. Three wins out of three, and having been on a run of nine matches without a win, suddenly we were going for a Grand Slam.

At Twickenham for the last game of the championship, we were underdogs. England had a mighty pack of forwards, and Dean Richards, as he liked to do, kept his boot pressed down on our necks. That guy was a phenomenon. He could strangle a team practically on his own. Rob Andrew kicked his goals – seven penalties and a drop goal to two penalties from Gavin Hastings and two drop goals from Craig Chalmers – for a 24–12 loss. It was a massive anticlimax. The dullness of the game was one thing, but we had to deal with the fact that we'd had a shot at the Grand Slam and not taken it.

Despite that, it had been a good championship. People often forget how good a decade the nineties was for Scottish rugby. It started off with that famous Grand Slam that no one forgets, but we had another shot in 1995 and then again in 1996, and we ended the decade winning the last Five Nations, when again, we were one win shy of the Grand Slam – and for the third time, it was bloody England who denied us.

Scotland was a good amateur rugby nation. It was professionalism that killed us. By now there were serious rumblings on that front as the global game prepared for the 1995 World Cup. We Scots were not exactly at the cutting edge of it. Gav knew what was going on, and he was already acting as an unofficial agent for the rest of us. On the other hand, I was a farmer on five grand a year and had other things to worry about.

But there was boot money to be had. I remember Gav introducing me to some Japanese blokes when we were staying at Pennyhill Park before the England game in 1993. I was only on the bench, but they wanted to sign me up to wear Mizuno boots. They offered me £500 a Test match.

'What? Just to wear your boots?'

'Yes.'

'OK.'

The only problem was that Scotland had a deal with Nike to supply boots, but the players didn't see any of that. Mizuno were happy, as long as I wore their boots for Stirling, even if they paid me only for the Test matches that I was involved in. Those of us on boot deals with other companies blacked out the Nike logos when we took to the field for Scotland. The Nike boots were not as comfortable back then anyway – especially when they weren't lined with £500 – and by the time of the World Cup, Duncan Paterson, our manager, gave in to our complaints and said he didn't care what boots we wore as long as we won. The Nike deal was set to expire, anyway. So then we started polishing our logos. Craig Chalmers's Puma stripe was so white it was unbelievable. We used to practise lifting our boots in the air when we dived for the line so that the photographers would get the logos on the soles of our boots in their shots.

By 1995, Mizuno were paying me £750 a Test. By the end of a season, the boot money was pretty much matching my salary as a farmer. Still, it wasn't exactly mega-bucks, although they did give me a nice set of golf clubs as well.

---

Scottish rugby was still amateur in spirit and in name, even if a few sponsors did ask us to wear their gear, and it was with the excitement of old-fashioned tourists that we set off for the World Cup in South Africa that year.

Less old-fashioned was the idea that the SRU wanted us to bring our wives and girlfriends along, and they were happy to foot the bill, which was four grand each. I was seeing a girl called Nicky at the time, but it wasn't serious.

'Look, I'm single,' I said to the SRU. 'If I don't take anyone to South Africa, why don't you just give me two grand, and you can keep the rest?' They didn't go for it.

'Well, I'll take my girlfriend, then.'

'But you said you didn't have one.'

'I do now. I'm in love with her. Probably marry her.'

Nicky was delighted – a free holiday in South Africa for three weeks, thanks very much. Never did tell her I'd tried to take the money, though.

We were staying in Pretoria and the SRU put the girls up in Sun City, at the same hotel the Ireland squad were staying in.

The girls had a good time there – really good, if the Ireland boys are to be believed. But they're a bunch of wind-up merchants. Still, we never did play Ireland in that World Cup, which is probably just as well.

We hardly lived like monks, though. I was rooming with Craig Chalmers. Normally, an experienced player is paired with someone who is inexperienced, or it's old with young, or at the very least two players are put together who don't know each other very well. So Craig and I couldn't believe our luck when we were told we were sharing. I was the junior player, but by then I'd been a regular in the side for a couple of years, and I knew Craig well. We christened our room the Temple of Self Belief. Craig printed out stickers for our door that read: 'This is the Temple of Self Belief. No entry unless you believe in yourself.' All that sort of crap.

The minute we arrived, we were looking for a bit of action, and we got it. Craig, Doddie and I went out the first night. Security guards were detailed to accompany us everywhere, all tooled up with guns and what have you. We were told not to wear watches or jewellery. If thieves wanted to rob you, apparently, they just cut off your hand or finger because it was less hassle. Right.

So we took a security guard, Keith, out with us and ended up in a nightclub. The three of us were up on the stage making fools of ourselves, smashed out of our heads. I went off to the toilet at one point, and two guys came in after me. They started asking questions and being confrontational. I didn't think anything of it, but suddenly Keith burst into the toilet.

'Hey, Kenny, get out, eh!' he said.

I did as he said, and as I left I could hear him laying into these guys. They were thrown out, and he told me they were going to rob me and give me a going over. He'd seen them follow me in. It was classic, he said. Then he noticed one of his guns was missing and he rushed back into the toilet and found it under one of the urinals, where it had slid during the fight.

Needless to say, that was the end of our night. The next day in the team meeting we kept our heads down as the management told us they had heard reports of three Scotland players out on the town, and they warned us to be careful. They didn't go so far as to impose a curfew, but the implication was clear. The three of us went out again the next night, but this time we took Gav with us. If the captain was going out, it had to be OK.

We had a good night, but the upshot was that we all broke down with various problems. Craig was in bed for three days with tonsillitis; Gav had a bad back; I pulled my hamstring in training the next day; and Doddie had legs that were too long, or some complaint like that. The four of us realised we'd been stupid, burning the candle at both ends, and now we were in a race to be fit for our first game – against Ivory Coast in four days' time.

We made it, and the game was a mismatch. We won 89–0. Gav broke the record for scoring the most points in a Test match with 44. They said it would stand for ever. Nine days later it was broken – Simon Culhane scored 45 as New Zealand beat Japan 145–17, and that was without Jonah Lomu, who was already the star of the show, ripping through Ireland and Wales in their pool games.

The runners-up in our pool were going to have to take on

New Zealand, and we didn't want that to be us. The winners had to take on Ireland. After some of the stories coming out of Sun City, quite a few of the boys fancied that, I can tell you. To win the pool, we had to beat France in our final match, and the game held no fear after our win in Paris earlier in the Five Nations. We knew we could take them. We'd beaten Tonga in our second pool game, 41–5, and France weren't looking so convincing.

It was an epic. Again. This time, though, we were the ones who were scuppered by a last-gasp try. We'd led 13–3 at half-time, and even at the end of normal time we were 19–15 up. Deep into injury time, the French had one last shot at our line, and Emile Ntamack squeezed in at the corner with the last play of the game. It still makes me wince when I think of it – 22–19 to France, and we had a date with the All Blacks in the quarter-final.

We were so deflated in the changing room. It was the reverse of what we'd done to them in Paris. We'd had such a good season, and to lose in that way was hard to take. It was worse than when we'd lost the Grand Slam decider to England. We'd been in control of this one right to the very end.

We had eight days till the quarter-final on 11 June, so the management and Famous Grouse took us on a trip to the MalaMala Game Reserve to help us get over the upset of the defeat. We arrived late to a welcome party held under the stars, and went to sleep in our huts to the sounds of the animals on the reserve. Next morning, I opened the shutters and spied an elephant not too far away. Craig opened the front door to go for a piss, but he slammed it shut almost immediately and stood there, stunned.

'What is it?'

'There's a lion at the front door.'

'Don't be ridicu . . .' I started to say as I opened the door, but sure enough, there was this bloody great lion, just sitting there looking at us. They'd told us to look out for the animals, but this was not what we had in mind. We phoned reception – not sure Dr Livingstone ever got to do that – and they came and shooed it away.

Later, we were taken off into the reserve in some little jeeps. I was in one with Kevin McKenzie, Craig Joiner, John Manson and Jeremy Richardson. We had a spotter we called Stevie Wonder, because he couldn't see anything. 'Hey, Stevie! There's a lion over there!'

After a while, we were starting to get a wee bit bored – once you've seen one zebra you've seen them all. Craig Joiner and I were in the back. The beers were stacked behind our seat, and we started quietly cracking them open, while the three hard front-five forwards scanned the horizon for animals with Stevie. It wasn't long before we'd drunk nearly all of them, and Craig and I were dribbling. When we stopped the jeep for our evening picnic, the Stump and the Pump (Manson's nickname was 'Pumpkin', because of the size of his head) were furious that the girls in the back had been drinking all the beer. Craig and I could only giggle. The entire squad eventually pulled up in their jeeps, and we all had a massive picnic at dusk in the middle of the vast plain. It was the first proper drink we'd had together since the start of the tournament proper, and our spirits were reviving after the loss to France.

We still had to face the All Blacks, of course. I've played them five times in my career, and you never go into a game against them, or anyone else, thinking that you can't win, but you know it's going to be extra hard. The plan was simple – keep the ball away from Lomu, which is easier said than done. In the fifth minute he went round Craig Joiner and through both Hastings brothers to set up New Zealand's first try, and he did something similar for a try of his own before the first half was up.

It was a crazy match – like sevens at times – and we gave almost as good as we got. At half-time we were 17–9 down and still in it, but we made a couple of errors at the start of the second half and, whoosh, we were suddenly 31–9 down after they scored from both. We scored three tries of our own and could hold our heads high after a 48–30 defeat. It was the most points anyone had ever scored against the All Blacks.

We'd had a good season and were emotional that it had ended, all the more since that game was the last in the career of Gavin Hastings. He was chaired off the field by the hordes of travelling Scottish fans.

I was gutted when Big Gav retired. I loved playing with him. He'd been a hero of mine while I was growing up, and the privilege of playing in the same side as him hadn't disappointed. I just really liked him. Still do – he's a good friend. He wore his heart on his sleeve and he was loyal to his team and his friends. By the time he retired, he was playing the best rugby of his career, which was a massive feat in itself, considering the low he had gone through the year before. The critics were calling for his head at the time, but he turned it round, and when he finished those same critics were describing his departure as a huge loss to the game. He was an inspirational guy, a great leader. People like that make you want to play for them. Gav was never afraid to stand up to the SRU, and he was never afraid to put his neck on the line for his team-mates. I've known a few captains who tend to say what the coaches want to hear, but guys like Gav, Bryan Redpath, Gary Armstrong and David Sole were the opposite. That earns you the respect of your team-mates. Gav played his rugby from the heart, and when he finished it was the end of an era for Scottish rugby.

And that World Cup was the end of an era for rugby all over the world. Jonah Lomu steam-rollered England in the semi-final, but it was South Africa who stunned the world with their emotional victory in the final in Johannesburg. In rugby circles, 1995 will be remembered for Mandela and Pienaar and South Africa's World Cup, while behind the scenes another fundamental transformation was taking place. The lives of all of us who played rugby at the highest levels were about to change dramatically.

# 7

# Money Matters

In August of 1995, our sport was catapulted into a new era when the International Rugby Board (IRB) announced that the game was to become professional. The years that followed were the craziest any rugby player could ever know.

Was it a blessing or a curse that our careers coincided with the move to professionalism? Some might say a curse. The pressure and insecurity of your livelihood becoming dependent on something that had always been a joy was difficult to handle. Where before you might have been dropped if your form dipped, now you might lose your job, or at least suffer a pay-cut. Those early years were littered not just with players who couldn't handle the transition, but with entire clubs that were churned up by the revolution and spat out again in pieces. It was such an uncertain time.

When I was first approached about turning professional, just after we got back from the World Cup, the offer was for two-hundred grand, forty times what I was earning as a farmer. I couldn't believe it. That was to play in Kerry Packer's World Rugby Corporation, the rebel circus that finally forced the IRB to accept professionalism or die.

We are the only generation to have experienced the thrill of being an amateur one minute and a professional the next. These days a career in rugby is something that a youngster can aim for, safe in the knowledge that there is a fairly stable industry that will take him on if he can reach the right level. He will have a particular attitude towards it from the start. For us, the chance to make money out of rugby just appeared one day. It was all seat-of-the-pants stuff, making it up as we went along, and, God, it was exhilarating.

We were all poised to play for Packer. He had tapped up a figurehead in every international team, and Gavin Hastings was his man in the Scotland camp. When we got back from the World Cup, there was a squad debrief at Murrayfield that all of us attended, and after it Gav called a meeting. We were wary of having it in the changing room as there were always loads of people about. So it was 'Everyone out' and we met in the car park.

'Right, it's on,' Gav said. 'I've spoken to the South Africans, I've spoken to Packer. There's going to be a world league. The shit's going to hit the fan. The SRU can't do anything about it.

If this goes ahead, they're knackered. You've got to be prepared never to play for Scotland again.'

That was a big warning to those of us, like me, who were in the early stages of our career, but Packer had said there would still be an international game – and a Scotland team – even if it had to be a rebel opration. We all signed preliminary contracts with him and we weren't the only ones. All of Europe had signed up, the Australians, too. New Zealand were poised to do so. They just needed South Africa to sign, because they were world champions.

The rest of us were ready. In Scotland, we had all just gone with Gav on it. He'd never had any time for the SRU, and we were his boys. We did what he said. He told us it was going to change our lives. There were different tiers – I think it was fifty grand, eighty, a hundred, two hundred – something like that. I was twenty-three and I signed up on the two hundred grand tier. I was young and they must have thought I was going to do quite well. We met in lawyers' offices in Edinburgh, signed the final papers, shipped them off and waited. The English followed soon after us. Now it was over to New Zealand and South Africa. 'My God,' we all thought.

———————————

All sorts of things were going through my head at that stage. 'What am I going to do with all that money?' was an obvious one. 'Are we all going to be like Premiership footballers now?' was another. I was also thinking this can't be true. There's no way they're going to pay me that much. All the same, my tail was up. It was another time when anything seemed possible.

Before I knew it, I had myself a celebrity girlfriend. The television had been on at the rugby club in Stirling one day that summer, showing Kirsty Young in all her glory. 'She's fit,' I happened to say to a couple of the lads. At least, that's how I remember it. Maybe I'd made more of it, though, because we were out in Stirling a couple of weeks later, and one of the guys said, 'That bird you fancy is out tonight.'

Somebody knew Kirsty's brother, Iain, and had been given the tip-off that she was in a pub in Bannockburn, so we all headed over there. She was sitting at the back with her sister and a couple of friends. I was getting a lot of banter as we stood at the bar.

'Come on then, Logan. Get over there. Let's see how good y'are.'

'Relax, lads, relax.'

We sat at a booth in the front of the pub, and the boys were teasing me.

'C'mon, Kenny. You're big time; she's big time. It's perfect. You're made for each other!'

Eventually, after enough alcohol, I summoned the courage to go over there. We were all pissed – I'd been on it since the afternoon. I don't know what Kirsty was celebrating, but she'd had a couple as well. I don't think she knew who I was, but I soon told her. 'Hi, I'm Kenny. I play for Scotland.' It was pretty much as cringeworthy as that. We chatted away for a while, and then she came over to us and we chatted some more. There was a lot of tongue-in-cheek banter: 'Oh, so you're Kenny Logan, the rugby player.' 'Yes, Kirsty Young, star of the small screen.'

At the end of it, I asked for her number.

'I'm afraid I don't give my number out,' she said.

'Oh, well, that's all right, because I give out mine,' which is what I did, and we left it at that.

About four days later I was at home, and Gareth Flockhart was round. We'd just agreed to go out with a couple of his mates in Edinburgh and were getting ready to leave, when the phone rang.

'Hi, it's Kirsty,' said that ever-so-slightly husky voice.

'Fuck!' I thought. 'Just hang on a second, Kirsty.'

I put my hand over the phone and signalled madly at 'Jumbo', as Gareth was known.

'It's Kirsty Young!' I whispered at him. 'What do I do, what do I do?!'

He leapt up and held his hands out in a calming way. 'Just be cool!'

'Hi, Kirsty. Sorry about that. Y'all right?'

'Yeah. What you up to?'

'Oh, nothing much. Might go out.'

'Do you fancy coming through?'

Hand over the phone again. 'She wants me to go round! What do I do, what do I do?'

'It's cool. We'll go to Glasgow.'

'Yeah, Kirsty, that'd be cool. We're actually just leaving. About forty-five minutes, OK? Where do you live?' I signalled at Jumbo to write the address down.

When I put the phone down we both went mental, whooping and hollering.

'You're a magnet!' Jumbo kept saying. '*She* phoned *you*! Brilliant!'

Then he looked at my T-shirt. 'You're not wearing that, obviously.'

'Why not? It's cool.'

'You've got to wear a shirt. She's gonna want to unbutton it and see your body. Guaranteed. She canna unbutton your T-shirt.'

'Don't be so daft.'

'Trust me.'

Jumbo drove me round to her place in Glasgow that evening and then went off to see his girlfriend, who was a student there. Kirsty let me in. She had this gorgeous three-bedroomed flat. I walked in and she offered me a drink. It was all a bit surreal, but we were soon getting on well, and we talked into the small hours.

At 3 a.m. I decided it was time to go and I called Jumbo to come and pick me up. Then I turned to her. It was that awkward stage at the end of a first date. It had gone well, we'd had a few drinks. Oh, and she was a TV star. So I didn't really know what to do. I gave her a little kiss on the cheek, then one on the lips. She put her arms round me, and soon we were kissing properly. And, sure enough, five minutes later she was unbuttoning my shirt. I started laughing.

'What's the matter?' she said.

'Oh, nothing. I'm just ticklish.'

For the next few dates I made sure I followed Jumbo's advice to the letter. But I couldn't keep relying on his chauffeuring services, which was a shame, because every date Kirsty and I had for the first few weeks of our relationship was at her place. She wanted no one to know about us to start with, so everything had to be behind closed doors until we were sure we wanted it to continue.

She'd had problems with ex-boyfriends and was paranoid about any media attention.

I turned up for our second date in my sponsored car. It was a Mondeo Si, full body kit, the bollocks, and it had my name plastered all over it, as well as the name of my sponsor, Fergusson Coal. Kirsty took one look at it and said, 'You can't park that here.' So I had to park it about five hundred yards away and walk. I went through the same charade every time I went to see her. Her flat was round the corner from Hughenden, the ground where Glasgow played. I had mates in Glasgow who would say to me, 'I saw that bloody car of yours again. What's going on? Who you seeing?'

I played a straight bat to all questions, but I was happy with our arrangement. I was twenty-three years old, thinking I was about to earn more money than I'd ever dreamt of and I was seeing the golden girl of Scottish television. Why wouldn't I be happy with that? She was good-looking and we had a great laugh together. If we had to be secretive, so be it. We found plenty of ways to amuse ourselves at her place.

She had recently had a bad experience with her former fiancé, Mike Antoniou, a double-glazing salesman who, according to press reports, got involved in a brawl. Kirsty broke off the engagement but was still concerned about him coming round. Once, he had stormed into the studio while she was presenting her chat show, *Kirsty*, and got into a fight with her producer, demanding to see her while she was on air – not the kind of thing you want. When she broke off the engagement, he told his story to the tabloids. This was all a couple of months before I started seeing her. She didn't want him coming round and finding me with her, because he'd probably be off to the press again, but I thought, great, let's see what happens. He did come round one evening. He was hammering on the door, but Kirsty wouldn't let me go down, so we left him to it.

She'd also gone out with Dominik Diamond, the guy who presented *Gamesmaster* on Channel 4. He used to ring her up, not realising that she and I had started dating. He was all right, though. I actually met him years later in London. I was in The Fine Line, opposite the Chelsea and Westminster Hospital, with some of the Wasps boys. Dominik's wife had just given birth to their first child, a wee girl, across the road in the hospital. He was in there celebrating and he came over to introduce himself, so we had a few beers.

But Dominik wasn't really her cup of tea. She needed someone more down the line, and she and I complemented each other well at that stage. Those first twenty-odd dates round at hers were easy and natural.

After a couple of months, we started to get a bit more adventurous, and one night we came back to the farm from a nightclub at about three in the morning with Jumbo and one of Kirsty's friends. The sun was starting to come up, and it looked as if it was going to be a spectacular sunrise, so we decided to take my car and a bottle of champagne and go to sit in one of the fields where the grass was about a foot long. We didn't go in it, usually, to avoid ruining it. Jumbo drove – the poor guy seemed to spend most of his life driving. We got to the field and Jumbo did his impression of a rally-car driver, spraying the grass this way and that. Eventually, he did one last handbrake turn to clear a patch for us, and we put down a picnic. The sky was a lovely red by now, the Wallace Monument was just in front of us, the Ochil Hills to the right, we drank champagne and had the music going. It was perfect.

Then Kirsty said she needed the toilet, so I told her to take the car down to the bottom corner of the field, which is what she did. It was a bit of an animal, my car, and I don't know what got into her, but by the time she got to the bottom of the field she was going so fast she couldn't stop. She smashed through the fence and carried on into a field of barley beyond. She left a perfect strip of flattened barley in her wake.

The car was torn to shreds by the barbed wire, and the top of the windscreen had taken the impact of one of the posts, which might easily have killed her if it had struck a bit lower.

Jumbo drove the car round to my mate Robbie Mailer's house to hide the evidence, and I called my sponsor, Tommy Fergusson, and told him the car had been vandalised – vandalised by Kirsty Young I was tempted to say, but that just seemed a bit far-fetched. As it was, when he saw the car, he didn't believe the vandalism line at all, so he asked me what had really happened and I told him.

'Fuck! *The* Kirsty Young?'

'*The* Kirsty Young,' I replied. 'I'm seeing her.'

'Fuck!' he said again. 'Take my car. Any time. Kirsty Young. Fuck!'

Tommy sent my car round to be fixed at Ogilvie's, a dealership in Stirling who, as luck would have it, sponsored Kirsty's car (in a more refined style than mine). That evening when I got home, Mum was going mental.

'Someone's trashed the field!'

'What field?'

'They've stomped down the grass, smashed through the fence.'

My brother James was livid as well.

'It's a joke,' he stormed. 'They've been rallying in there, hand-braking it, tyre tracks everywhere, the grass is ruined.'

I played along with the general outrage. This was one occasion when I had no problem with Kirsty's policy of secrecy, and she had never been more desperate than she was over this for the media to be kept out of it. This was very definitely our secret – and Jumbo's and her friend's and Tommy Fergusson's.

It turned out to be somebody else's as well. I was round delivering something to one of our neighbouring farmers, Peter Stirling, the following week. Peter's farm overlooked the field.

'Good night at the weekend?' he said.

'Aye.'

'How's your car? It *is* your car, isn't it? The one with Kenny Logan plastered all over it.'

He'd been up feeding his sheep at four in the morning and seen everything. You'll never get anything past a farmer. It was a fair cop, but I asked him, begged him, in the good name of Kirsty Young, not to tell anyone. Peter was true to his word. We were off the hook.

Eventually, in September 1995, Kirsty and I came out about our relationship. It was at the European premiere of *Braveheart*, held in Stirling. Kirsty had tickets for herself and a guest, and she decided the time was right to come clean, so I went with her. It was a great night. At one point during the film the projector went down and the lights came up, so Mel Gibson, give him his due, immediately stood up and started entertaining everybody while we waited for the film to come back on. He was brilliant, but I was shocked at how small he is. I met him afterwards with Scott Hastings at the party in Stirling Castle. Scott was backing himself with his best banter, while I was trying to tell Mel that I'd been brought up right under the Wallace Monument – that I was the real thing, if only he realised. Scott kept ruining my moment by going on about how we played rugby for Scotland, and then he brought out a Scotland rugby badge and gave it to him. Mel looked totally underwhelmed.

'It's Scottish,' Scott explained. 'It's a thistle. It's the rugby team's logo.'

'This really isn't going anywhere, Scott,' I murmured, as we both smiled at Mel. It was at that point that Mel wandered off to find someone – anyone – else to speak to.

At least the next morning I had equal billing with him on the front pages of the Scottish newspapers. It seemed Kirsty and I were every bit as interesting to the Scottish media as the premiere of the film of the year. I had a mountain of missed calls from my mates, mostly asking, 'Are you going out wi' that bird?'

I was and, in ways I couldn't have realised back then, it was to change my life completely.

---

I'd got the girl now, but otherwise any thoughts of a footballer's lifestyle were being put on hold. The Packer deal had gone up in smoke when the IRB announced in August that the game – or the game as run by them – was going professional. We didn't know it at the time, but we had all been waiting for Pienaar, South Africa's captain, to decide. If he'd jumped, the game would be unrecognisable today. There would almost certainly not be a World Cup. There might be an international game, but it would have been an add-on to a massive world league. Pienaar signed with the South African Rugby Football Union, the Springboks followed, the All Blacks signed with their union, and without their endorsement, Packer's enterprise fell apart.

A one-year moratorium on professionalism was agreed across the world, and the mad rush was set in motion to be ready for the start of the new era in September 1996. Looking back, just the ambition to be prepared for it was a joke. No one was even vaguely ready in 1995, and it was never going to be any different in 1996. There wasn't the culture for it in the committee rooms, or the crowds in the stands.

The idea of professionalism in Scotland was even more of a joke than anywhere else. There was no structure for it in 1995. In England, the millionaires moved in on the club game almost immediately, but in Scotland the clubs attracted no interest from investors. The SRU were forced to take the initiative and begin the rounds of securing their players. Some were already at English clubs. Others would soon follow.

Sir John Hall had been one of the first to buy himself an English club, Newcastle, and he set about assembling a dream team, blowing wages through the roof and setting the bar high for anyone who wanted a squad to compete. It was a standard that the professional game, even in England, could not support, but that didn't stop everyone trying to rise to it. Gary Armstrong and Doddie Weir left Scotland to join Newcastle without a moment's thought, and the SRU knew they had to act quickly before more left.

Kenny Crichton was the man they sent round. He was a Stirling County man whom I'd known for years. He had played a big part in the club's rise up through the leagues to winning the title in 1995, but he changed a bit when he joined the SRU.

Kenny met me at Stirling County and offered me a three-year deal. It was for fifty grand a year, which included everything, image rights and so on. Even after the Packer deal, fifty grand seemed pretty good to this farmer's boy, but the reality of the situation was that I couldn't commit to three years and I told him so. The big focus of my life at that point had become the farm. My brothers and I had all been working on the farm since my father died three years earlier, and James finally wanted out. He'd decided he couldn't carry on because it was getting in the way of his hedge-cutting business too much, which meant I had to find a way of buying him out.

I didn't want James to go, but I had to admit that our working relationship was not good. He is a very talented guy. He used to compete in the modern pentathlon, and he is amazing with his hands. I felt back then that if we'd gone into partnership, we could have made things work with the assets we had, but he was headstrong, and I was always away with my rugby. We just weren't getting on.

I had to organise the farm into a position where it could pretty much run itself before I could even think of going full-time with the rugby. The SRU's deal as it stood was a non-starter. I couldn't commit to three years with everything on the farm so up in the air, and the fifty grand they were offering, while seeming a lot to me, was not exactly market-leading.

Regardless of the stupid money Packer had been talking, which we were still coming down from, we all knew from our contemporaries what sort of money was starting to be thrown about in England, and Kirsty was talking about moving to London. That idea would never have occurred to me, but in this climate, the possibility of going to England was starting to materialise as something to consider seriously.

The other point I had to think about seemed shocking to good honest rugby folk back then but is a basic consideration for anyone in a professional sport, and that was the question of my value. I don't know if anyone else in the Scotland set-up had been offered more than fifty grand – if they were, I never heard of it, although some of the potential big-earners had already gone to England. I did know who else had been offered fifty, though, and I reckoned I was worth more.

What I told Kenny Crichton was that I would take a one-year deal, and he replied that a three-year deal was on the table, take it or leave it. I left it. Then Jim Telfer rang me while I was at Kirsty's place. I was in the papers with her quite a bit, which wouldn't have gone down well with him.

'We don't need superstars in this game,' he told me. 'We need rugby players. You need to get yourself off the front pages and onto the back, and you need to sign this contract. If you don't, you might never play for Scotland again.'

'Is that a threat?' I asked him.

'Work it out for yourself.'

I said I'd take the risk.

I was being bullish. We all knew which way the game was going, and the strong-arm tactics of the SRU weren't impressing very many of us. It summed up where we were, when the man in charge of taking us into the new era was saying that we didn't need superstars in the game. Later he would complain that there weren't enough of them in Scottish rugby, and it's quite obvious to anyone these days that superstars are exactly what you need. I'm not saying I was or should have been treated as a superstar, but I couldn't see how me being on the front pages was harming Scottish rugby.

I told Kirtsy what he'd said.

'That's ridiculous. Of course you need superstars,' she said. 'How else can you get kids to play the game?'

Jim Telfer was one of the best coaches I ever played under – a complete nutter but a great coach. He was not a natural administrator, though, and I reckon the development of the professional game in Scotland was slowed down because of this. He had been charged with taking Scottish rugby into the new era, but he was came from another time, when men were men and players were there to be whipped to within an inch of their lives.

He did have some modern ideas, but I feel they were wrong

for Scotland at that point. It was Jim who pushed through the idea of regional rugby. He had a strong vision for it, and no one really had the nerve to question him. Scotland went in ballsy with four regions – Edinburgh, Glasgow, the Borders, and the North and Midlands, who were named the Caledonia Reds. They thought that people would identify with these constructs and that they would turn up in their thousands. They didn't, and when it didn't look as if it was working, two of the regions were dropped like stones after only two years.

You didn't need to be Nostradamus to realise that the future of professional rugby in Scotland was shaky. The SRU maintained that I had to sign a three-year deal, and they offered me a loan to help with buying my brother out of the farm, repayable through my salary. It was flattering, but it wasn't much help. The rates they were offering were the same as the bank was offering, and I would rather have been indebted to the bank.

If they'd offered me a one-year deal and given me time to sort out my life, it would have inspired loyalty. But that's not the way the SRU work. It has always been a case of 'Those are the rules, and if you don't like them, you know where you can go.' And they were surprised when so many of us took them up on that and went elsewhere in search of employment.

In the end, we agreed I would stay part-time. It gave me a chance to concentrate on the farm and settle matters with James.

My dad had talked before he died about selling the herd. We all raised our eyebrows at that, but it sowed a seed in my head, and I came to the decision to sell the cows. I felt bad about it, and I don't think I could have done it if Dad hadn't suggested it first – this was his famous herd that he'd built up over years – but the sale raised vital funds, which were supplemented by the sale of the farm's milk quotas. I was lucky, because I sold the herd and the quotas at their peak – the following year the quotas disappeared altogether and were worth nothing – and the sale generated enough money for me to buy out my brother. We'd had lawyers and arbitrators in to value the farm, and after much haggling and stress the matter was finally resolved in 1997. Mum then made over to me ninety per cent of her fifty-per-cent share, and so I became the proud owner of my father's farm.

# 8

# Black Magic

On the rugby field, fortunes were mixed. The 1995–96 season was Stirling County's first as Scottish champions, and we were proving competitive again, although Melrose went on to take the title, beating us into second place. It was a strange time, though. Most of the team had ambitions to play professionally, and we all knew what that meant. The team was going to break up sooner or later. In the end, Stirling lost around fifteen players to the professional game.

The Five Nations of 1996 was another good one for Scotland – for the second year running we had a shot at the Grand Slam in our last game against England, and for the second year running we lost it. For me, though, it was a Five Nations spent mainly on the bench. With Gregor at fly-half, the coaches decided they needed to find room for a reliable goal-kicker, and that man was Michael Dods.

I'd been playing pretty well for Stirling County, but not well enough to get past the need for a marksman. We beat France that year at Murrayfield, 19–14, and Dodsy scored all nineteen of our points, including two tries. I went through the classic bench-sitter's conundrum. You always wish your team-mates well and I was no different. I was jumping around with the best of them when we won, but you also know that you're not going to be getting a game any time soon, and you don't like it.

The only game time I had in that Five Nations was in the next match – in Cardiff against Wales. I remember sitting on the bench, being covered in Jim Telfer's slobber. When Jim shouted, it tended to be accompanied by a fair bit of spittle, and I was sat in front of him. He was doing a lot of shouting, as usual, and I could actually feel it hitting me. I looked at my waterproof and it was covered in slaver.

I spun round at one point. 'Will you stop it?' I shouted, but he didn't hear me above the crowd. Then just before half-time Craig Joiner went down. Craig had got the other wing berth ahead of me. He was a Melrose man, which meant Jim loved him. If Jim had had his way he would have picked the entire Melrose team for Scotland.

I stayed where I was, basically sulking, because I was sure he would put someone else on. Suddenly, Jim whacked me across the side of my head, and I spun round again.

'What you doing?' I shouted at him.

'Get on the pitch! Joiner's injured!'

Thank God for that, I thought. He wanted me to go on after all *and* I wouldn't have to get drenched in his spittle any more.

Deep into the second half the scores were tied at 9–9 and we were on our own 22. I said to Gregor, 'Give me an inside pass. Their 10's drifting, and the 7 ain't getting there.'

So on the next play, Gregor turned it inside to me and I was off, from our 22 to theirs. I took the tackle of the last man and flipped the ball up to Ian Jardine, who got taken by the cover. We won a scrum, Gregor went over from a pop pass to level the scores, and Dodsy converted.

Wales scored late on but missed with the conversion from wide out. We had won, and the Grand Slam was still on, with England due at Murrayfield in a fortnight. We all went berserk, and I was thinking, 'I've got to be in the team now!'

Jim pulled us in afterwards to congratulate us. 'Right lads, one more game to go. Keep your feet on the ground! And, Logan, you keep your head down there as well!'

We'll never know if I was going to be picked after that, because in training the following week I went up for a high ball and, as I came down, I caught my finger in Scott Murray's jersey – compound fracture, bone sticking out in two places. That was me out. So selection for the England game was made easier. What followed was a rare example of us maybe being a bit complacent and the English being the more determined. Dodsy kicked three goals, but Paul Grayson kicked six, and we went down 18–9 at home. Another Grand Slam had passed us by.

That summer my focus was the Scotland tour to New Zealand. I was both delighted and stunned when they announced the squad. Not only was I in it, but Michael Dods had been left out. Jim Telfer had decided that, even if he was a decent kicker, Dodsy wasn't an international winger. He hadn't played that well, it was true, and he wasn't the greatest kicker in the world, but he had scored three tries and forty-seven points in the Five Nations. I thought it was a joke, leaving him out, but I wasn't complaining. Here was a new chance to re-establish myself and to vindicate Jim's decision to select me.

Most of my time in those days was spent trying to win his respect. I was particularly keen not to let him down on that trip. By picking me and not taking Dodsy, he was coming as close as Jim ever came to admitting he was wrong and to acknowledging that I could play a bit. I had to repay that, even if I knew he would never, ever say in plain words that he rated me.

Ours was a classic love-hate relationship. I really didn't like him back then, and I don't suppose he liked me, but I was always desperate to impress him, and not just because he was the Scotland coach. By the end of my international career I was very fond of him and our relationship was excellent, but it took a long time for us to get to that point. He would never admit it, but I knew I had his respect in my last couple of years as a Scotland international. In the nineties, though, it was different. Still, I reckon on this tour we may have taken the first steps towards a mutual understanding.

Jim loved all things to do with New Zealand. He was obsessed with the way they played rugby. If you were from New Zealand, he immediately loved you. If you were from New Zealand *and* you played for Melrose, you would have quickly become the most capped Scotland player of all time. And if you went to New Zealand and played well, Jim would have respect for you. I did all right on that tour, and I think he saw me slightly differently after it. Likewise, I saw him as more of a human being than the harsh taskmaster with no weaknesses that he liked to pretend he was.

Mind you, I could have done with showing him a bit more respect in Hamilton. It was in between the two defeats we suffered before the first Test – one an embarrassment in Northland that we lost 15–10, the other a great game against Waikato, which we lost 39–35. That second match was won by one of their forwards when he scored from a short line-out, despite quite clearly running round our hooker and into touch on his way to the line. Strangely, that winning try was never replayed on New Zealand TV.

We were staying in some condos in Hamilton. One time I noticed Jim watching TV as I walked past his window. So I went to my room to get the remote control, went back and started changing the channels on his set through the window. He just couldn't work it out. He was up and down. He didn't realise there was a remote. Then I put it to standby, turned up the volume, turned down the volume. He was going mad. He even phoned reception to complain – it was priceless. Scott Hastings walked past and I showed him what I was doing. He wanted to have a go, so I gave him the remote, knocked on Jim's window, then legged it round the corner. Scott was caught red-handed. 'No, Jim, it wasn't me, I swear!' was all I could hear as I left him to face the music.

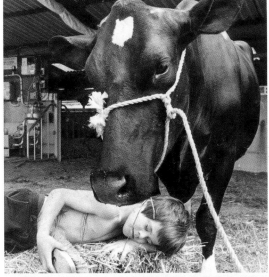

*Top left*: With my two big brothers.

*Above*: First day at Wallace High – I wasn't going to look so neat by the end of it.

*Left*: Snoozing next to Powis Innocent 29th. What a cow!

*Below*: So many of my best memories on the farm involve Hamish. Here, he's on the right receiving a prize with Manor Powis Duchess and me.

*Left*: Mini-rugby mates Alison McGrandles and Mark McKenzie showing me who's boss at Stirling County.

*Below*: Winners of the Under-18 Scottish Cup.

*Bottom*: Playing with the big boys. On the senior team 1991–92.

*Above*: With Hamish's wife, Bash, in the airport on the way to Australia with Scotland.

*Right*: All Mouth And Chin... plus some very cool Wayfarers and Derek Bain.

*Above*: Running out at Ballymore, 21 June 1992.

*Right*: 'Meet the gang, 'cos the boys are here!' The night of my first cap, with Ally and Hendy.

*Left*: I was so proud to represent my country while my father was still alive. This photo of Mum and Dad was taken a few months before he died.

*Above*: Love sick in Argentina.

*Left*: My drinking buddy on that 'Rolling Rock' summer: best mate Robbie Mailer.

*Below*: Carnival time in Paris, 1995. Gav was in between the posts and, boy, did we celebrate.

*Left*: Back to business with Stirling County. It was a special time for me.

*Above*: Scottish Champions for the first time. The future looked so exciting.

*Above left*: Scotland had to face the All Blacks in the 1995 World Cup. Still, we set the record of the most points scored against them.

*Above middle*: I was gutted when Big Gav retired. It was a privilege playing in the same side as him.

*Above right*: Playing against Wales in the 1996 Five Nations. It was my only game in the tournament, as we let another Grand Slam pass us by.

*Bottom right*: Trying to win Jim Telfer's respect in New Zealand in 1996, but it was like playing people from another planet.

*Top left*: Finally professional and breaking through with Wasps against Bath in 1997.

*Top right*: Premiership champions, 1997. Scoring the try that sealed it against Northampton.

*Middle*: We were in full party mode. The celebrations went on for two days.

*Bottom*: But partying (here with Shawsy) and a carbs overload, were a recipe for disaster for the new season.

*Above*: Scoring my fifth against Spain in 1998. I would have equalled the national record if the SRU had awarded caps.

*Above*: Celebrating victory over the Welsh in the 1999 Five Nations. I took over the kicking duties for the first time in international rugby. It felt good.

*Left*: Experiencing my first taste of the downside of kicking, losing against England 21–24.

*Bottom left*: But I kicked the final penalty in Paris and we beat the French to earn the title.

*Below*: Five Nations champions, 1999.

*Above*: There was nothing for it, but to win the Tetley's Bitter Cup with Wasps. Handing off Tom May of Newcastle in the 1999 final.

*Above*: But it was really the Alex King show.
*Below*: Celebrating with Nigel Melville and the boys.

Down in Invercargill the week before the first Test, we ground out a grim 31–21 win against Southland. The tour was not going well, and Jim's temperature was rising. He thought our attitude stank, and we were supposedly professional, or near as damn it, so he reckoned he had an extra reason to go for us. Jim's idea of professionalism was that you should train all day every day. In that sense, he was the worst possible person to guide us in that transitional period, in my opinion. Have him in there as a coach, yes, but he was manager now and all-round guru, and a man less suited to being the kind of visionary we needed back then you couldn't find. Ian McGeechan was what we needed, but he wouldn't return for a few more years yet.

'Why ye no' trainin'?' Jim would say to us.

'We're tired, Jim, we're taking a break.'

'Why ye tired? I'm no' tired. If yer getting paid fifty grand a year, ye should be trainin' every day.'

For Jim it was rugby twenty-four-seven. Everyone brought videos for the bus and Jim's were all on rugby – boxes of them. He thought if we had a five-hour bus ride, we should be watching rugby, rugby, rugby, but we wanted to watch something else. I was in charge of videos, and I put on *Basic Instinct* at one point.

'Ach, all yer interested in is birds wi' nae pants on!' Jim said, in disgust.

We fell about laughing.

After the game against Southland, he called us in for a meeting and unloaded on us. Everyone was getting it.

'Craig Joiner. How many caps have you got?'

'Sixteen, Jim.'

'Every one's a gift. Gary Armstrong, when was the last time you played well for Scotland?'

'Well, I thought I played all right against France. . .'

'You know the last time you played well for Scotland? 1990's the last time you played well for Scotland.'

We were all sinking into our chairs, waiting for our turn, and at the end of his tirade, he said, 'Anyone else got anything to say?'

Kevin McKenzie stood up. He was the fines master on the tour. 'Aye. I have.'

'What is it, Kevin?'

'I just want to read out the fines, Jim.'

We were all covering our eyes now. Don't do it, Stumpy, don't do it. The fines were light-hearted. This was really not the time to read them out. Jim was stunned, but Kevin was not to be deterred.

'Jim, I've noticed you've been walking about in your stockings with no slippers on. That'll be a £10 fine. Also, Jim, you've been using a clipboard that is not an SRU clipboard. That's another fine. And, Jim, yesterday I noticed you turned up too early for the team meeting, so all in all you owe us £35. And that's the end of the fines, Jim.'

Jim stared at us, speechless, and then stormed out.

I don't know why Stumpy did it, probably just to break the ice, but he went for Jim properly in the team meeting after the disastrous first Test in Dunedin, which we lost 62–31. We had been ripped apart. Jonah Lomu was in the team that day and scored a try, but it was Christian Cullen and Jeff Wilson who really took us to the cleaners. Cullen was incredible. He'd scored a hat-trick of tries against Western Samoa the week before on his debut as a twenty-year-old, and against us he scored four. His international record that night read two games, seven tries – not a bad start.

I had a poor game. I got an early hit in on Wilson, but after that it was grim. I missed Cullen on each of his first two tries, not that I was the only one. He ran through practically the entire team for his first and about half of it for his second. Then I missed Wilson badly for Cullen's fourth. It was like playing people from another planet. Every time you got the ball, four of them were on you; every time Wilson or Cullen got it, none of us were anywhere near them.

That New Zealand side were the best team I ever came across, and a lot of people consider them the best that ever played. Jim wasn't thinking that, though, and he launched into us again. He called us gutless and spineless bastards. That was when McKenzie, the smallest man in the team, stood up and hit back.

'Don't you ever call me or anyone else in this room spineless! I would fuckin' die for Scotland! You call me spineless again, Jim, I'll take you outside and show you who's spineless. And, I'll tell ye, it won't be me!'

And from that moment on Kevin McKenzie was Jim Telfer's best mate.

The following Tuesday, the midweek team beat Bay of Plenty in a high-scoring but close game, 35–31. Derek Stark scored a hat-trick and after my performance in the first Test I was terrified of losing my place. I couldn't sleep that night.

Jim kept faith with me, though, and I had a much better game in the second Test at Auckland. It was a horrible, wet day, but we played much better. All the same, it was one of those times when you think you're in a close game, but then you look up at the scoreboard and think, how did that happen? They beat us 36–12, and you'll just have to believe me when I say we did well against them. Jim came into the changing room afterwards and was happy – that's how well we did.

I remember Barry Stewart making his Test debut for us at tighthead prop, having just turned twenty-one a couple of weeks earlier. He was up against Craig Dowd, and it was the first time I'd really noticed what was going on in the scrum. I looked at Barry and thought, I'm sure he's not supposed to look like that. His nose was practically touching his arse. It was almost inhumane for this lad, however big he was, to be going up against Dowd. That All Blacks front row was the only one I ever looked at and thought, 'Wow.' Then I'd look up and see Jeff Wilson standing opposite me.

There was nowhere to turn against that lot. They went on to win the Tri Nations that year at a canter (43–6 against Australia two weeks after our second Test) and then take New Zealand's first series win in South Africa, earning themselves the nickname, the Incomparables. I had no problem with that name. If you ever got anywhere near them, they would just blow you away, as if they'd pressed a button. They'd let you get near them just to make it more interesting.

I played with some of them in 1999 for the Barbarians against Ireland. Ian Jones was captain and at one point, with the game still close, he said to us, 'Right, let's lift it for ten minutes.' I was thinking, 'I thought we *were* lifting it.' Then we lifted it, and I thought, 'Oh right, that's what you meant.' Ireland were blown away for that ten minutes. Then they came back, so the call went round again, let's lift it for another ten, and so on, until Ireland were beaten.

In 1996 the All Blacks were showing us all what it was to be professional. When we returned home that summer, it was time for us to show what we'd learnt.

———————

The bell rang for the official start of professionalism at the beginning of the 1996–97 season, but we were caught between the two stools. The break-up of the Stirling County team was about to begin, given an extra little nudge by what happened to James McLaren. That was a good example of how the desire to be seen as professional was making fools of people who were still amateur.

In our game against Melrose that autumn, Craig Chalmers was clinging on to Jim's foot at the bottom of a ruck, so Jim lifted it up to get free. Chick immediately started writhing around on the floor clutching his face. It was the best acting performance I've ever seen, and I still congratulate Chick on it to this day. He claimed he'd been kicked in the face. At the start of the new era, the SRU wanted to make a big statement on foul play, so they gave Jim a twenty-week ban for it, even though there wasn't a mark on Chick's face, and the solitary camera hadn't picked anything up.

McLaren appealed against the ban, and the SRU not only rejected it but upped it to twenty-six weeks instead. Brilliant. McLaren went to England, changed his name from James to Jim and played rugby league for six months. I'll say it again – brilliant.

The administrators were not the only amateurs in town, though. Most of us in Scotland still were, and I was no different. By then I had been courted, not only by Scotland, but by Sale and, quite strongly, by Newcastle. Sir John Hall entertained me at St James' Park for a Premiership match between Newcastle United and Southampton. Doddie Weir and Gary Armstrong were putting pressure on me to join them there. I had a good look round Kingston Park and talked to Rob Andrew.

What they were doing was exciting, but the problem of the farm kept coming up. Newcastle wanted me to go full-time, and although it was closer to the farm than any other English club, it was hard to see how it would work. They were offering me sixty grand a year, plus win bonuses, so it was significantly more than Scotland had offered, but I said no, because they wouldn't be flexible over the farm.

By the end of 1996, Kirsty had decided she was off to London. We were keen on each other, and she reckoned I should go down there with her. The idea terrified me. Yes, there was the fear any farmer's boy would suffer going to a big bad city, but most of all it was the thought of going down there when I couldn't read or write. I might have been a kick-arse farmer by that stage, lording it over hundreds of acres of land, but my dyslexia meant I was totally dependent on my mother and my bookkeeper. I didn't even have a credit card. I only ever used cash, because I didn't want to get involved in any writing, not even signing my name.

I'd become dependent on Kirsty, too. We were good for each other at that particular time of our lives. The Scottish press were all over us. They hung on Kirsty's every move. I was well known in rugby circles, but not in the grand scheme of things, so I was getting my first taste of the bright lights. The media were always interested in Kirsty's boyfriends, but they were probably disappointed with me in the end when it became clear I wasn't a nutter. Her mum and dad, on the other hand, loved me seeing her, because I was a sensible lad. They are lovely people, and I got on really well with them – still do.

I was flattered that someone like her would want to go out with me, but, equally, I was good for her after some of that previous aggro she'd suffered. She needed someone reliable. Her career was rapidly on the up, and a settled private life was not only a help but something she hadn't had before.

A turning point in her life, and also in mine, was when she contracted meningitis in 1996. She was up in Aberdeen doing some TV show, when she rang at about six in the morning, saying she wasn't feeling well and she'd had to call off this TV appearance. She didn't sound right at all – very vague and drowsy. I said I'd come up in the car, but she told me she'd rather get some sleep and that I should come up at lunchtime.

I phoned her mother and said if we left now we'd be up there by lunchtime anyway, so we drove up that morning. We got to Kirsty's hotel at around half ten, by which time she was throwing up and drifting in and out of consciousness. I went straight down to reception and they gave me a number for a doctor.

The doctor was off to see a patient and didn't want to come. I told him I thought this was serious. I was panicking, so I lobbied him passionately. It was obvious from her eyes that she was drifting away, and I argued with the doctor that he had to come immediately. He asked about her symptoms. One of the symptoms of meningitis is that you can't bend your neck forward and touch your chest with your chin. Kirsty had this and most of the others on his checklist. He agreed to come over right away.

Apparently it was a close call. The doctor said if we'd not come up when we did, she might have lapsed into a coma, and from there death was a serious possibility. As it was, she was rushed to hospital and had a lumbar puncture, the works. She stayed in hospital for a week. It was a frightening time, but she pulled through and made a full recovery. Kirsty says it changed her and made her more focused and ambitious. It affected me in a similar way. Hamish had always said to me to live life to the full, because you never know what's round the corner. Here was another reminder of that, as if his own death had not been enough of one. It was not long afterwards that Kirsty decided to go down to London, and I went with her.

As a couple, we were going strong, each of us feeding off the other's virtues. Not only was I a steadying influence emotionally, I also brought my farmer's boy practicality into her metropolitan lifestyle. On one occasion I had a near-death experience of my own, when Kirsty turned on the electricity supply that I had switched off while changing her light sockets. I got the full 240 volts.

She was good for me, too. I have always been drawn to intelligent women. I don't know whether it's because I never had it at school, but I need to be pushed and stimulated or I lose interest quickly. Kirsty was making a success of her life despite a bare minimum of qualifications from school. Those qualifications put her in a different league from the one I was in, without any at all, but her success added extra weight to the idea, which was still only developing in my mind, that it is possible to be clever without having been awarded bits of paper from your school or university, and certainly to make a success of your life without them.

I was finally forced to tell her about my dyslexia. She was driving me back to her flat when she suggested we went to the cinema that evening.

'Yeah, why not,' I said.

'Well, pick the paper up and see what's on.'

The usual panic kicked in as I leafed uselessly through the pages.

'I can't find it,' I said, slapping the paper shut.

'Yes, you can. It's in the middle of the page.'

Like a schoolboy again, I turned to the page as instructed and stared at it, wondering how to get out of the assignment I'd just been given, and if maybe this time, by some miracle, I would be able to read the words. It was no good, and I became increasingly agitated. I never minded so much disappointing my teachers, but I didn't want to risk my relationship with Kirsty. I shook my head.

'There's nothing on. Let's just get back home,' I said and threw the paper on the back seat.

She must have noticed something weird about my behaviour, because when we got back she asked me why I hadn't read the listings. I broke down in tears, thinking that this was the end of our relationship, and I told her I couldn't read or write. Her reaction surprised me. She didn't laugh, she didn't walk out, she didn't even think less of me.

'Why didn't you tell me about it?' she said. 'It's no big deal.'

And I believed her. It really didn't seem to bother her. She was interested in it, more than anything else. She didn't actively do anything about helping me get over it, as Gabby would do later, but her reaction was still a big step forward. Gabby doesn't hold back on these things. She understands me much better than Kirsty did, which is why just letting this go was not an option for her – she could see what dyslexia was doing to me, and she pushed and pushed until I did something about it. Kirsty, on the other hand, just didn't think it was an issue at all, for me or for her, and that actually helped. It began to dawn on me that this condition that had crippled me in so many more ways than just not being able to read or write was actually not that big a deal to everyone else. It didn't make me an outcast.

Despite that, the great service Kirsty did for me was to go down to London and suggest I go with her. In doing so, she was pushing me more than I'd ever been pushed before. I don't think I'd have ever gone if it hadn't been for her. If she'd stayed in Scotland, or if she'd never even been in my life, I would most probably have signed for the SRU and never left. However much we were to grow apart when we got there, I will always be grateful to Kirsty for making me go to London. If she hadn't, I might never have met Gabby. And I might never have played for Wasps.

# 9

# A Professional Outfit

The offers really started to roll in around Christmas 1996, as the London clubs were alerted to my interest, with Kirsty all set to move down. Harlequins and Saracens came in strongly, and then Wasps and London Scottish followed. But it was Wasps who appealed most.

There was an end in sight now to the saga over the farm. The running of it would be settled within a few months, but as yet I couldn't walk away from it and that remained a concern. Nigel Melville, Wasps' director of rugby, shrugged his shoulders when I told him. He said that for the rest of that season, at least, they were happy for me to fly down on Thursday for training, stay down for the match on the weekend, then fly back after it. They offered me a deal that covered the rest of the current season and the following two. It worked out at eighty grand a year, plus a ten grand relocation fee and win bonuses of £750 a match.

Wasps were winning a lot back then. They'd lost just twice in the league at that point and were top of the table. Their Heineken Cup campaign had been up and down, but one of the ups had been a 77–17 win in October over the champions, Toulouse, that had stunned European rugby. They were a young team on the up, and I wanted to be a part of it.

I went down to look around with Kirsty at the end of February 1997. She had dressed me for the occasion and I was happy to go along with it. I admit that I was just keen to please her back then, and as a result I found myself changing. A lot of my friends at the time weren't afraid to point it out. They were right. I was vulnerable and maybe I had become a bit reliant on her. For this particular trip she'd dressed me in a brown velvet shirt, black jeans and a pair of brown velvet shoes with a golden chain across each buckle. I looked a right chump. I wouldn't have signed me.

We turned up to watch Wasps play West Hartlepool at Sudbury, the old ground that had been their home for decades. It was just a field, really, in the middle of a housing estate near Wembley, with a rickety clubhouse. Wasps had begun playing most of their home games at Loftus Road, home of Queens Park Rangers in Shepherd's Bush, but for the smaller games they still played at

Sudbury. West Hartlepool counted as one of those. It was an easy win, and I spent most of the day shaking hands. I knew Damian Cronin and Andy Reed, who were playing for Scotland with me in the Five Nations. Lawrence Dallaglio I'd met several times over the years at Scotland–England games from the Under-19s upwards. Gareth Rees I also knew from the international circuit, and I was introduced to a load of young Englishmen – Alex King, Andy Gomarsall, Joe Worsley, Will Green. The club were pretty excited about them.

I came away knowing that this was where I wanted to be. Gavin Hastings, who was unofficially my agent at the time, wanted me to join London Scottish, where he had a connection. They were in the second division with serious ambitions about joining the party in the professional top flight, and were offering 120 grand a year, but I'd made up my mind. Wasps had phoned me directly and we had negotiated directly. I wanted to test myself in a new environment, to see how good I could be, or even how good I really was. Wasps were at the top of the English league, and I knew that this was the place to find out, with a host of ambitious youngsters on the way up. I liked everything about them.

Also, they were the only club that were happy for me to spend half the week in Scotland, which, regardless of the farm, was a good way to ease into things and to lessen the impact of homesickness. I knew I was going to suffer from that. I remember going to see the president at Stirling County and telling him I was leaving. I'd been at the club from the age of seven, nearly eighteen years, and I walked away from the place in floods of tears. I was crying my eyes out again when I said goodbye to my mum and drove away from the farm that first weekend – and I was due back the following Sunday. I never thought I would find another place like home or another club like Stirling County. But I did in Wasps. In fact, it was an even better place for me than Stirling had been.

The weekend after I'd visited Wasps for the West Hartlepool game, I was up at Murrayfield for the Five Nations Test against Ireland. Jim Telfer walked down the aisle of the coach to speak to me. He didn't look too happy.

'I hear you're going to Wasps.'

I nodded.

'Think you're going to be big time, do ye?'

'Don't know,' I shrugged, but I thought, 'I'll show you, you bastard.'

The SRU in general were fuming. There was only one guy there I respected back then – John Jeffrey. He really didn't fit in with them. He was a guy the SRU should have nurtured but they ended up pissing him off, just as they did all the recently retired players. I couldn't understand why former players slagged off the organisation so much. But I was beginning to. It seemed to me it was all about control with the SRU. All they were worried about was having their mantle taken away from them. They were not interested in growing the game or in new ideas. They'd bang on all day and night about how great things were in their day, but if you actually wanted to talk about the future with them, you could forget it. They are much better these days in that respect, but back then they were only interested in the past.

We beat Ireland well that day 38–10, our only win in the 1997 Five Nations, which was a bit of a comedown from the shot at a Grand Slam we'd earned ourselves in each of the previous two years. That left us with just the match against France in Paris two weeks later, and this time the French were chasing a Grand Slam. But before that, it was down to London for my Wasps debut.

———

The club wasn't quite fully professional then – a lot of the guys had day jobs – so training at Sudbury was still in the evening. I turned up on a dark Thursday night, wearing my Scotland tracksuit bottoms, just to let them know I could play a bit. Everyone was looking at me but keeping their distance to begin with, them from me, me from them. It's not easy, joining a club two-thirds of the way through the season. Normally, you meet for pre-season training when the slate is clean, but here I was, supposedly a big-name signing, intent on taking someone's place without having done anything.

Gloucester were in town that Sunday at Loftus Road, and I was so nervous. It was a new kind of pressure. This wasn't the nervousness of the new cap with nothing to lose. Here, great things were expected of me, the club's new signing with a wage to match, and yet this was going to be the highest standard of rugby I'd ever played, outside major internationals.

Sure enough, it was much more physical than anything I'd experienced with Stirling. This was the English league proper.

Wasps were top of the table, but everyone was waiting for this young side to collapse now the season was getting to the sharp end. Mind you, early March it may have been, but there were still nine matches out of a twenty-two match league programme to cram into the last couple of months.

Gloucester came at us from the start and took an early lead. They had us rattled. I remember my first touch. I cut through, and out of the corner of my eye I could see a Gloucester player coming after me. The trouble was I was so used to playing for Stirling, who played in red, white and black, similar to Gloucester's colours, that I passed the ball to this guy. He couldn't believe it, and he turned round and legged it towards our tryline. We all had to chase back to get him, and I got the first of many rollockings from Dallaglio.

'Logan, what the fuck are you doing? You don't pass to the opposition, you twat! Do they not teach you that in Scotland?'

'I'm working on it,' I said. 'I think I've got it now.'

One thing I was to learn at Wasps was that if you made a mistake, you got to know about it, and Lol was the first to tell you. That was the first of many times he gave me 'the look', the special Dallaglio glare. It put you in your place, all right, and I knew then there would be no comfort zone at this place.

I wasn't having a great game. We'd got the lead back by half-time, and in the second half we pulled away to a 36–10 win. My match ended a couple of minutes before time. I was at the bottom of a ruck, getting a bit of a shoeing, and someone caught me in the back of the head.

'Not so easy over here, is it?' said Phil Vickery, as I was led off. There was blood everywhere, and, by the time they'd put the stitches in, the game was over.

In all other respects, the game had been an eye-opener for me. I was impressed with what I'd seen, even if I felt hugely frustrated that I hadn't contributed much to the performance. It was obvious Dallaglio was a special guy, wading into the famous Gloucester pack. He threw a few punches and got yellow-carded for it early on. Alex King, the young fly-half who was already in the England squad, was a class act, and I was already looking forward to playing outside him some more.

Rob Henderson, the Ireland centre, had joined just a couple of months before I did and looked as though he was going to be a big laugh on and off the field. Gareth Rees, the Canadian, was solid as a rock at full-back, built like a prop forward but with the deadliest boot. He kicked twenty-one points that day.

I was killing myself for not getting in on the act with these boys. I hadn't exactly covered myself in glory on my debut. Kirsty had come to watch and a group of us went out that evening, but it was a quiet one. I was beating myself up and I didn't get much sleep that night. People used to think that I was casual about my performances and therefore that I didn't care – Jim Telfer certainly used to think that – but it was just that I didn't want people to see that I was bothered. Behind closed doors, I used to give myself a really hard time, even when I'd had a good game. It was an attitude that fitted in well with the culture at Wasps, where people were ruthlessly honest with themselves and each other, but that was no consolation. I sat on the plane to Scotland the next day feeling pretty subdued.

There was no time to dwell on it, because the Five Nations match in Paris was imminent. Results-wise, Scotland had suffered that championship, going down heavily to Wales 34–19 and England 41–13, but we'd played well in patches and we'd enjoyed that big win over Ireland the week before at Murrayfield. We'd beaten France two years running in the competition, which was unheard of, but there was no joy this time. Going for a Grand Slam in the Parc des Princes was motivation enough for this seriously good France team, even without them wanting to avenge our two wins. They got vengeance, all right. They were rampant, and we came off battered, 47–20 to the worse. I returned to Wasps determined to get back into the winning habit.

———————

My next game for Wasps was against Orrell at Sudbury – the last time Wasps were ever to play there. That was when things really took off, so much so that people often think it was my debut. I scored a couple of early tries – in the first seven minutes – and was starting to feel a bit more comfortable, even if Orrell were bottom of the table and on their way down. Wasps were also looking comfortable, certain to remain top of the table for another week. On the half-hour, Orrell kicked long and we chased back. Gareth Rees gathered the ball on our 22 on one side of the pitch, while I was running back on the other. Without any warning, he launched an American Football-style pass in my direction from fifty yards away. I'd never seen anything like it. It was Reesy's trademark innovation, and no one has ever mastered it as well as he did. I caught the ball, gathered myself and looked up to see one man in front of me. I beat him and ran off for my third try. Half an hour gone in only my second game, and I had my first hat-trick at the club. I knew then I was going to enjoy myself at this place.

I scored a fourth before half-time to bring up a 50–5 score at the break. In the second half we scored two more – for a 62–5 win – but the second of those was by me, netting me a five-try haul, a league record that stood for a few years. I should have had six. The touch-judge called me back for one, saying my foot had gone over the line. There was no way . . .

But five was enough to be getting on with, and any caginess between me and my new team-mates evaporated that night. I was the new boy and I'd just scored five tries. I was going to pay. Out came the tequila slammers. Everyone was given five. Dallaglio was in charge. 'A toast to Kenny, the new signing, and his five tries,' and it was bang, bang, bang, bang, bang.

I couldn't believe it. 'These boys are on a different level,' I was thinking. 'How can they drink so much?' Out came another five each, and I was staggered – staggered and staggering. I later found out that the others were doing water, but I was trying desperately to keep up with them and prove my worth. They destroyed me. We did the next five, and then Dallaglio said, 'Right, five more.' I was shaking my head, begging for some sort of sanity to be restored, but he was having none of it. Mind you, Lol probably *was* doing tequila. Downing shots of water wasn't his style at all.

I don't remember much about that night, but we bonded, and

the Wasps era of my life had well and truly started. We were young, single and on top of the league. The routine was simple – we drank hard and we played hard. Every Thursday night after training we partied and, as long as we won, we were at it again every weekend after the game. We used to congregate in our special spot by the bar in the Leopard Lounge on the Fulham Road every Thursday night.

It was heady stuff, although I always felt I needed to be reasonably discreet. Not only did I have a girlfriend, but she was high-profile back home. I was not as exhibitionist as some of the boys. When challenged about it, I would cite the Scottish press as the reason for not going the whole way with some of the antics. I got a lot of grief for it at the time. Top of our chosen sport we may have been, but they all thought the idea of press intrusion ridiculous. Lol was to learn the hard way a couple of years later, but I genuinely felt I had to be careful back then.

---

My relationship with Kirsty was starting to take the strain. However exciting my new lifestyle with Wasps, it was not great for relationship building. Kirsty was living in a flat in Earls Court, which served as my base. I would turn up on Thursday, go to training and return in the dead of night after an evening out with the boys. That kind of thing wasn't her scene at all. I was twenty-four, going on twenty-five. Kirsty was twenty-eight and couldn't wait to get to thirty.

The idea that she was old before her time was nothing new. On her thirtieth birthday, her sister gave her a cake that read: '30 at last!' It was an open joke among her family, and it was an almost-as-open joke among my friends. The Wasps boys reckoned I was on my best behaviour when Kirsty came out with us.

For all the drinking and partying, I was still nervous about London, and I did look to Kirsty for reassurance. I was regularly the little boy lost. On one occasion around then, I was called with about fifty others, to Birmingham for a gathering of players who were in contention for the Lions tour to South Africa that summer. We were given a presentation on how amazing it was all going to be. Then they gave us forms to fill out, and I felt the sweat gather on my brow and that familiar sick feeling in my stomach. I was back in the exam room. There was no way out of this one, though – no dramatic exit, no mother or girlfriend to help. How was I going to complete the form? We were being asked there and then to register our availability for the pinnacle of any rugby player's career. But I couldn't tell anyone about my secret, so all I could do was hide my blank form under the table. They probably thought I just hadn't turned up.

In dealing with my life in London, I had my new family at Wasps to see me through the bits involving rugby and partying, and for all other times I had Kirsty. She was relishing life in the city. Even in Scotland she was what we farmers used to call a townie, and she handled the move to London with no problem. She thrived on it.

Everyone had said that going to Channel 5 was a backward step – new channel, dodgy reception with more chance of people seeing snow on their screens than any recognisable images of her. But she was good at her job, and if you're good at something, whatever decision you make, right or wrong, you'll end up going the right way.

Channel 5 launched a week after my five tries at Orrell. They were exciting times for us both and, without realising it, we were becoming more engrossed in our own worlds. She was the face of Channel 5 News, famous for the way she perched on the edge of the table as she read the bulletins. She had always been a mature girl, and now reading all that news was making her a very serious girl, too. Her life was taking her to places very different from Loftus Road on a Sunday afternoon, or dancing on the stage at the Leopard Lounge with your shirt off on a Thursday night.

If the cracks in our relationship weren't yet visible, it was only because we each had our own circles to mix in and our own glories to revel in, so we could put off facing up to the way we were growing apart.

—————————

The Wednesday after the Orrell game in March, Wasps recorded a good win over London Irish at Loftus Road, 31–18. The mad rush to cram in all the remaining fixtures was on. In one way, we were lucky. The boys had been knocked out of Europe and the Pilkington Cup early on, so we could concentrate on the league. Leicester, who were second in the table, had made it to the European final, and the weekend after the Orrell game they reached the final of the Pilkington Cup by winning at Gloucester. That meant they were facing a backlog of games. It was to cost them.

Leicester and Bath were the standard-bearers of English rugby, and they were on our tails, with Bath in third place. What's more, we had to play both in the space of five days. In the first game, we took on Leicester at Welford Road on a filthy wet Wednesday night.

The place was packed – 17,000 crammed into the stadium under the floodlights – and I realised that this was what I'd come down for. Not that it was a laugh that night, far from it. In those days, the Welford Road pitch was a bit of a bog at the best of times, but it was really heavy that night – and so were Leicester, led by Martin Johnson.

Leicester also had Dean Richards, and it was back to the bad old days playing for Scotland against England. In senior rugby, I never beat England, and I never won at Welford Road. We actually did pretty well that night, but the ball always seemed to end up back in Deano's hands, and the cry would go up, 'Deano! Deano! Deano!' Leicester would just flock around him and start marching forwards. 'Deano! Deano!' As a winger, there was nothing you could do. I spent most of the match walking backwards, getting depressed. 'Deano! Deano! Deano!' It was relentless. Needless to say, no tries were scored that night. Two late penalties by Joel Stransky, the Springboks' drop-goal hero in the 1995 World Cup final, secured Leicester an 18–12 win.

Now we were just four points clear of Leicester at the top. They had two games in hand and a better points difference, and we had a match against the champions, Bath, that weekend. The hacks were sharpening their pencils, ready to plunge them in when the inevitable collapse kicked in. The script still had us, the young upstarts, bottling it in the final straight. Leicester were everybody's favourites.

Bath also had an outside chance, and they came to Loftus Road, needing to win. It was a fantastic game. Bath were leading 25–18 with five minutes to go. We were wobbling, but we had character, and right at the death Alex King squeezed into the corner for a great try, which Reesy converted from the touchline with the last kick of the game. That 25–25 draw all but knocked Bath out of the race, and meant that Leicester had to keep winning. However, the busy schedule was catching up with them, and instead they started losing. A run of three defeats away from home in nine days, including a 47–9 hiding at Bath, knocked the stuffing out of their challenge.

I know all this now mainly through looking it up. At the time, I wasn't following the title race at all. I was in my own little bubble, preoccupied with personal performance and not letting my new team-mates down. As a winger, you have to be selfish, like a striker in football. I knew if I did well, the team would benefit, so I didn't dare be distracted by other things, such as who was going to win the title. We may have faltered a little that week, picking up just one point against our two closest rivals, but all I knew was that I hadn't scored a try for two weeks.

That changed the following week on a sweltering afternoon at Saracens. The game went well – we won and I scored two tries – and it confirmed, if confirmation was needed, that I had made the right decision. Playing a standard club game against Francois Pienaar, Philippe Sella and Richard Hill was the kind of environment I wanted to be in. We were keeping ourselves in pole position and the rest were running out of games.

Two weeks later, after a good win over Sale, we were at Franklin's Gardens against Northampton, and even I knew that if we won we would be champions. The weather had turned again. It was a wet Saturday afternoon in the Midlands at the end of April, and the game wasn't pretty. Shane Roiser, my partner on the other wing, scored a brilliant try in the first half, but the game was tight until the end. As the clock ticked down, we were leading 19–15 and were under the cosh. Reesy put a grubber kick through, and Nick Beal fumbled it. Reesy was on to it in a flash, which shows how much was at stake, because the man was not nimble, and he fired a pass out to me. I had a clear run-in and took the ball round to the posts for the try that sealed it.

We were champions, and I started leaping up and down, waiting to be mobbed. No one came. It had been a breakaway try, so the others were all scattered at various points around the pitch, and I was left jumping up and down on my own. It was hugely embarrassing. And it was shown repeatedly on the national news.

Otherwise, it was an amazing day. Champagne was being sprayed in the changing room afterwards, and I tried to take stock. I had come down eight weeks ago, and here I was, already an English champion. We were in full party mode. The celebrations went on for two days.

It was a triumph of spirit and ambition for a team so young and unfancied, and set the tone for the club that was to dominate English rugby throughout much of the following decade. I knew almost immediately that I had joined a place with a special atmosphere. Many have left Wasps to go elsewhere, myself included, and found that other places just don't have the same spirit. In the eight seasons I spent there, I never came across one guy I didn't like, or one who was not totally and ruthlessly honest with himself and his team-mates. The quality of the person was all-important at Wasps. They were very good at bringing good people in. Sometimes, they brought in a guy because they liked him, and only then worked on making him a good player. They just had a feel for people and could sense when there was something about a guy that meant he had to be at the club.

I loved it from the start. I'd come from Stirling County, a small club who had come from nowhere to win the Scottish league on the back of spirit and talent. Wasps hadn't quite come from nowhere – they had won the title in 1990 – but they were another small club, whose spiritual home was a field in a housing estate, a pitch that would take about a couple of thousand spectators around its touchlines. The previous season they had been stripped of three key players in Rob Andrew, Dean Ryan and Steve Bates, who had been the first big signings in the professional era when Sir John Hall took them to Newcastle. To win the title the following season was a big statement for the young side they were building.

Amid all the partying we almost forgot that we had one more league game to play, away at Harlequins. Sure enough, the weather changed again, and the sun was blazing as we ran out to an ovation at the Stoop. There has been an age-old, bitter rivalry between Wasps and Harlequins, the two rugby clubs most often vying for the title of London's best. In honour of that, we took to the field in shirts that had 'Champions' emblazoned on them, and, if in the week leading up to the game we had not done much in the way of preparation, the importance of our arch rivals not making us look stupid in our champion kit made up for it.

The shirts did the trick – the shirts and the fact that Quins had been the only team to beat us at home in the league that year. The party carried on. We ran away to a 42–22 win, which included two more tries for me. That brought my tally to eleven in nine games and I ended the season as Wasps' top try-scorer in the league, despite having joined in March. The five tries against Orrell obviously helped, but playing in that side as a winger was a joy and such a refreshing change after so many games for Scotland where I'd done little more than chase high balls and make tackles. At Wasps that season we were almost always on the front foot, and the tries kept flowing. If only it could have gone on for ever.

# 10

# Feeling the Strain

After every party there is a hangover. I'd been in the reckoning for the 1997 Lions tour to South Africa that summer, but as our season was building to its conclusion the squad was announced – and I wasn't in it. We still had a title to win, so my disappointment was limited to hoping that an injury in the last couple of games of the season might open the door for me, but as the title celebrations gave way the reality dawned that I wasn't going.

There was a Scotland tour that summer, but I pulled out of it. The reason was that my back was playing up – bulging disk, L5-S1, the bane of my rugby career – but maybe also I felt down at not making the Lions. Staying behind was stupid, because Scotland were going to South Africa as well. I should have pumped myself up with painkillers and gone. If I'd been selected for the Lions I would have done it, so why not for the Scotland tour? In the end, the Lions needed a replacement for Ieuan Evans, and Tony Stanger was called up because he was there with Scotland. It could have been me. Tony was with Scotland in the first place as a replacement when I dropped out.

I'd been getting a lot of positive feedback from Lions selectors that season. I was scoring at will for Wasps, and even if Scotland had had a disappointing Five Nations, it had gone quite well for me. Ian Lawrie, a Scottish selector, was telling me it was between me and Nick Beal, the Northampton full-back, for a place on the tour.

Ian McGeechan was the head coach with the Lions. When I met him in the early days of my Scotland career, he'd said, 'If you ever want some help, give me a call any time. You've got talent, and I'd like to help you.' I never did. It just didn't register. Looking back, it was dull of me. Now I would be on the phone in a flash, but I was young and new to it all.

A lot of Northampton guys went on the tour in the end, and that's a lot down to Geech. They all did well. Everyone did brilliantly, which was what made it so hard not being there. The quality of player, the hard grounds, the superb coaching – I know I would have thrived as much as anyone if I'd gone. Instead, I chose not even to tour with Scotland and was left to sit at home with negative thoughts churning round my head. What if I'd filled out my Lions form? What if I'd phoned Geech and established a relationship? What if I'd gone to Northampton? What if I'd gone on tour with Scotland? These questions were driving me mad that summer. And my back was killing me.

Then Kirsty told me she wanted space, and we all know what that means. She'd already suggested I get a flat of my own, so I'd rented a place in Chelsea Harbour, which Wasps paid for. The boys called it the Logan Lounge – we had a lot of late-night parties there. That summer it felt like a dungeon. I was feeling lonely and sorry for myself. The Lions hadn't wanted me, and now Kirsty didn't want me. I'd come to depend on her too much. I still hadn't got a proper grasp of London, so I'd looked to her, which she must have found uncomfortable – although not as uncomfortable as I did. That summer I let myself wallow in negativity. I didn't have Kirsty any more, and most of my mates were off playing rugby somewhere else, so I had no one to score lots of tries with, and, even if I had, my back was buggered anyway. And pre-season training was around the corner. All in all, I was pretty heartbroken. I went back to Scotland and just wanted to stay there. The farm was now sorted and in the hands of a farm manager, so I knew those days in Scotland that summer would be my last for a while. The next time I headed back to London it would be for real.

Pre-season started in early July, but some of the guys were still away, and it felt flat. I was alone in the Logan Lounge, and doubting myself. The swing in mood from the end of the title-winning season to this point, barely a couple of months, was dramatic. I was having a nightmare in pre-season. The training schedule was horrendous. We were all full-time now, which meant there was no more running away back to Scotland for half the week, and my personal life was at a low, post-Kirsty. My two-year relationship with her was over, and my two-month honeymoon period with Wasps felt pretty much done and dusted, too.

We had won what was the last Courage League Division One title. Now we were all playing for the Allied Dunbar Premiership. The feeling was that here was a new start for the sport. Yes, last season may have been the first of professionalism, but this season we were going to be properly professional, honest. In short, the pissing around stopped here, and the fun stopped here, too.

At Wasps we were caught between two stools. The partying culture was never going to end there and then, but it overlapped horrendously with the blind leap we took into the full-time era. In 1997–98 the club game was professional at the most basic level. Fitness coaches today would cringe at what we were doing that pre-season. We had to run one hundred metres twenty-four times, and then we were straight into the gym to do some weights. It was barbaric, and the state of my back deteriorated even more.

I was overweight. We were all overweight. A dietician who had watched us train had told us that, if we wanted to train like that, we needed to stuff ourselves with carbohydrates. That was a green light. Alex King, my flatmate in the Logan Lounge, was back from England's tour of Argentina, which made me feel a bit less lonely, and he and I would go off to the patisserie after training. 'Gotta get our muffins in. Gotta get our sweets in. Bloody hell, look at the carbohydrates on these bad boys.' It was fine while we were beasting it on the training field, but as training tailed off we all ballooned.

So I was out of shape and down in the dumps. The only consolation was that Kirsty was struggling as much as I was. Her mother had told me as soon as we split up that she was all over the place. Kirsty was still ringing me, asking me what I was doing that night and so on. She was obviously confused.

On the last day in August we played our first game of the new season, a 38–21 win at Bristol. It wasn't a great performance, but I scored a try, and it seemed my form might be carrying on from the previous season. We all went out that evening. Kingy had bought himself a place and left the Logan Lounge, so I had a new flatmate, Laurence Scrase, another of my team-mates at Wasps. The next morning he and I were sitting round watching the news coming in from Paris. There'd been a car crash involving Diana. I rang Kirsty, who'd been anchoring the coverage at Channel 5. She confirmed that it was true and that they were saying Diana was dead. We were stunned. I kept ringing Kirsty throughout the morning for updates. I think everyone was just completely thrown by it. Kirsty must have been, too, because she suggested we meet that afternoon in the Fulham Road for a chat.

I went out for breakfast with Lawrence Dallaglio and told him I was seeing Kirsty later on. He shook his head.

'Don't get back with her, will you.'

'Why not?' I protested. 'I think she loves me. I think I love her . . .'

'Why would you want to? You're having a whale of a time. You're young and on top of your game. You get back with her, you'll lose your edge. You'll play shit.'

And, God, he was right.

The whole world felt a bit weird that day. I went straight from breakfast to meet Kirsty. We gave each other a big hug. It seemed like a relief to see each other. We dabbled with small talk for a while – we were both looking well, our families were all well. Then she said, 'I hear you're buying a house.'

It was true. Andy Gomarsall had been a regular on the camp bed at the Logan Lounge, commuting down from Cambridge the previous season for our various matches, training sessions and piss-ups. Now he wanted a place of his own in London. He and I had found a couple of mews houses in Chiswick – internal courtyard, gorgeous. He was moving into one with his girlfriend, Fran, now his wife, and I had a mortgage in place to buy the other. We were going to knock through a door between the two.

Out of the blue, Kirsty suddenly said, 'Why don't we buy one together?'

I did a double take, but she seemed serious, and it didn't take me long to agree. I loved her and I missed her. For all the drinking and partying with my new Wasps mates, I still felt vulnerable in the Big Smoke. I was a long way from home, there wasn't a green field in sight, Diana was dead, and being with Kirsty seemed easier than not being with her.

So within a few months we had moved into a new house. I said farewell to the Logan Lounge and hello to a more mature way of life. Mind you, our place was just off the Fulham Road, so I was still round the corner from the boys' favourite haunts. The best of both worlds, you could say.

Or a recipe for disaster.

———————————

Lawrence's words kept playing through my head. What if I lost my edge? What if I started playing shit? But the tries kept coming and the boys kept winning. I scored eight tries in the first five games of that season, and we won the first seven. After that opening game at Bristol, the season went straight into the Heineken Cup, and we played all six pool games in one block. We had Swansea, Glasgow and Ulster in our pool. Glasgow were my old district team, and I scored three tries in the two games against them. We cruised the pool with six wins out of six.

The squad had been bolstered with a couple of interesting signings. One was Simon Shaw from Bristol. He'd just been with the Lions in South Africa, and Alan Tait had told me great things about him from that tour. I would get on well with Shawsy, he reckoned, and he was right.

And there was another guy who turned up at the start of that season. None of us had heard of him. He arrived at the clubhouse in Sudbury at 6.30 a.m. wearing a T-shirt, shorts and flip-flops and was sitting on the doorstep waiting for us when we arrived for training. He was a short feller, but he must have weighed about 19 stone. 'Where are your bags?' we asked him. He held up a carrier bag. In it were a pair of pants and a pair of boots. They were all he had. He'd just flown over from New Zealand,

and he introduced himself as Trevor. Our kit manager, Malcolm Sinclair, took him off to get some training gear, and for the first few weeks his Wasps kit doubled as his everyday clothes.

His full name was Trevor Leota, a Samoan hooker, and the club was suddenly a more dangerous place to be. At his first training session, Kingy did a switch with me, and I was running through, when out of nowhere something hit me. It was Trevor, and it was like being hit by a rollercoaster. I was catapulted backwards, onto my back, and the ball that I'd had tucked safely under my arm just bounced pathetically on my head. I was out cold. Eventually, I could make out faces looking down on me.

It turned out it wasn't a one-off and we soon realised we had the most ferocious tackler in the world in our squad. In the years that followed, his mere presence frightened anyone in the opposition who had the ball. A player could have a four-man overlap, and he would see Trevor coming and panic.

When he got angry, you really didn't want to be anywhere near him. During training sessions it was funny watching professional rugby players putting up their hands to be on Trevor's team. He was soon banned from tackling in training, because he injured a couple of our players and it was just becoming too dangerous. He was a wonderful guy – ferociously loyal to his team-mates, and the hardest bastard you'll ever meet. You could hit him fifty times with an axe, and he'd just grin through the blood, 'Is that all you got, bro?'

We were feeling pretty good at Wasps around then – English champions, scoring freely with a squad as strong as ever. Same with me. I had my girlfriend back and the season was carrying on where it had left off. But something wasn't right. At Wasps, we were papering over the problems. We were all still overweight from the carbs overload in the summer. We were still out on the piss every Thursday night. My back was still giving me gip and Kingy was struggling with a knee complaint. Things were gathering to blow up in our faces.

In the second half of October they did just that. Saracens came to Loftus Road and turned us over. It may have been the middle of October and our eighth match of the season, but because of the Heineken Cup it was only our second match in the Premiership. It set the tone.

Kingy went off to have a clear-out of his knee and missed the next two games, and we lost them both. He came back for our home quarter-final in the Heineken Cup against Brive, the champions, and we lost that, too.

Wasps is one of the hardest places to be when you're losing. If you lose one game, the place is like a morgue. Lose two in a row and it's a crisis. Lose three and there are board meetings. That ruthless self-searching was the key to the success we went on to achieve, but it makes it bloody miserable when you're losing. I'd never experienced anything like it.

———————

The club season broke for a month after that, and I was glad to get away, back to Scotland for the autumn internationals. Didn't fancy all the bouncing off the walls that was sure to be going on at Wasps, with weeks to think about our collapse in form and no chance of doing anything about it.

But it was out of the frying pan into the fire. A pattern had been developing for a while with Scotland and the autumn internationals. We always seemed to get spanked in them. This was to be the worst autumn yet, and my relationship with Jim Telfer hit rock bottom.

Jim was always on my case – especially after I went down to London with a celebrity girlfriend. That kind of thing was never going to endear me to him, and it used to wind him up whenever the press spent time talking to me. 'What you talking to him for?' he used to say to them when I was mid-flow, surrounded by notepads. 'What's wrong with Tom Smith?'

Tom had been on the Lions tour that summer and returned a hero, but it hadn't made him any more talkative. He was one of a few forwards from the tour who were in pieces. It would take him about a year to recover.

Jim had been on the tour as well and was central to its success. One of the scrummaging sessions he put them through is part of rugby legend. The Scottish boys could have told the rest of the Lions about that. Jim had always flogged the forwards to within an inch of death. It used to be very funny to those of us in the backs.

'How many scrums did he make you do today, boys?'

'Fifty,' these broken men would say. 'Then we did another fifty on the machine.'

Jim used to run off suddenly and shout, 'Over here, boys! Now! As fast as you can!' And just as the boys were busting a gut he shouted, 'Now, sprint!' They would be on the point of collapsing, and Jim would get them to form another scrum. Sometimes, he would stand on them with his boots on and hit them with a stick. If a fight broke out, he would just watch it to see who came out on top.

Then there was his rucking net. We all had to do time under that. He had it designed specially and strung it from four posts at about waist height. We had to run underneath it to practise keeping our bodies low at contact. Then he would lower it and get us to do it again.

'Doddie Weir! Get yer heed doon!' Whack! Doddie was 6ft 7in. 'Ach, ye're as much use as a light hoose in the desert!' One time Mark McKenzie lifted his head up in a Scotland A session and sliced his nose open on the net.

Jim was colourful to say the least – wild and eccentric and brilliant at the same time. He was one of those people who could inspire loyalty by being horrible to you. The more he treated you like dirt, the more you wanted to please him.

I don't think I pleased him too much back then. A slap round the back of the head was his main way of communicating with me, and after I went to Wasps he and the other coaches thought nothing of dropping me. I had to be playing really well to get a look-in, which was good for me, I suppose, but there were some players in Scotland who turned up, wiped their arse and got in the team. If you had one good game, you were in. If I had eight good games at Wasps and one bad one, I was out.

'I see you're playing well, Logan.'

'Oh, thanks, Jim. Which games have you been down to see?'

'Och, I've been watching you on teletext.'

Great – but I'd made my bed, so that was fine.

Jim wasn't coach that season, because Richie Dixon was. I think Jim must have been technical director or something. Throughout my Scotland career, I'm not sure how often Jim actually was coach, but it always felt as if he was. He was there even when he wasn't. We used to see him sometimes when we were training at Murrayfield, standing at his office window, watching us through his binoculars.

Richie was a good coach. He'd coached me at Stirling County and was a good friend. He played a big role in our success, setting up the five-year plan that ended with us winning the title, but trouble was brewing for him now that he was Scotland coach.

We had Australia up first, then a weekend free, then South Africa. Kirsty wanted to go away to New York, and I was keen to have a mid-season break. We had one training session scheduled for the week after the Australia Test, so I asked Richie if I could take that week off, and he said fine, the session wasn't compulsory anyway. The boys at English clubs weren't being released anyway. I was just lucky that Wasps had given me the week off.

We put out a young team for that Australia game, with six uncapped players in the squad. It was Scott Murray's first cap, and James Craig was given a debut on the other wing from me. The first half was all right – we were leading for a lot of it and the score was 8–8 at the break. Then we collapsed. They scored four tries in the second half for a 37–8 win.

We were slated in the press, and Jim was furious. That night we were told there was a debrief at 9 a.m. In those days, debriefs could take three or four hours. You put the video on and sat through the whole game with the coach's finger on the pause and rewind buttons. When Jim got going, it could easily take more than four hours. Richie was the coach, though, so he started off, but it wasn't long before Jim had taken over, and we were in the middle of a marathon character assassination.

A few of us were looking at our watches and getting twitchy. It was now midday, and there was no sign of Jim letting up. The guys at English clubs had a plane to catch to get home, which was one thing, and I had one to catch so that I could go to New York with my TV star girlfriend, which was another.

Eric Peters put his hand up and said, 'Jim, the exiles need to catch a flight.'

'Fucking flight? No one's leaving this room until we've finished.'

I'd had enough. This session wasn't doing us any good. I stood up and said, 'Jim, I'm going to New York tonight.' There was a deathly silence. 'I've got to go.'

'Well, fucking go then,' he said. 'Fucking go.'

So I went. Yes, I had a plane to catch, but I was also proud to have stood up to him. Jim was treading on Richie's toes and he was laying waste to what little morale we might have had left.

Predictably, I was dropped to the bench for the South Africa game. I knew I'd played all right against Australia. I'd made eight or nine tackles and gone on a couple of runs. James Craig, on the other wing, had looked like a rabbit in headlights on his debut. He was injured for the South Africa game – Craig Joiner and Derek Stark were picked on the wings – but it would have been interesting if he'd been fit. Would he have stayed in the team? There was no doubt in my mind that I'd been dropped because

I'd gone to New York. In hindsight, my timing was not the best, it's true, and I probably shouldn't have gone, but the head coach had said I could, and I wasn't going to miss it just because Jim had overruled him and hijacked his video session to give us all a bollocking. Jim did that a lot, and it was a problem for anyone coaching Scotland when he was around. He had too much power. He was one of the best coaches the world had ever seen, but his authority ran out of control sometimes.

When the team for South Africa was announced, I asked the coaches if I could see my stats from the Australia game, but they said they hadn't been produced. I'd been dropped because I hadn't played that well, they said.

I trained hard that day. Then I saw Andy Nicol, who was captain at the time, and David Johnston, the backs coach, looking at the stats. I went up behind them, put my finger on my name and followed it across. My stats were good, as I'd thought. They moved the sheet away and tried to cover it up.

'You know why I've been dropped,' I said, and I walked off.

Turned out the bench wasn't a bad place to be for the South Africa game. If the defeat by Australia was bad, this was horrific – 68–10 was the final score, but that was nothing. The next weekend, Wasps went to Harlequins and lost 53–17. To Harlequins. Our bitterest rivals. It seemed there was nowhere to turn. I couldn't understand what was happening. None of us could. There were relegation play-offs for the bottom two in the Premiership that season, and we were now tenth, one spot away from the play-offs, ahead of London Irish on points difference. We stayed in tenth until nearly the end of the season. According to the record books, we ended up ninth that year. It felt like we were bottom.

There was no sign of any improvement with Scotland, either. Richie dropped me from the squad altogether for the start of the Five Nations in 1998. Then he and David Johnston resigned when the boys lost a warm-up game in Italy. The Italians were on the brink of being welcomed into the new Six Nations and they had also just beaten Ireland, but the defeat was too much for Richie to survive.

Jim Telfer took over the coaching with Ian McGeechan helping out round his Northampton commitments – the Lions' coaches in harmony again – and I reckoned I had no chance of seeing a Scotland jersey for a wee while. The press had been saying that Jim had rail-roaded Richie into dropping me, and I must admit I was astonished when the first thing Jim did when he took over was add me and Damian Cronin to the squad for the Five Nations. And he picked me in the starting line-up for the opener against Ireland.

At last, we won a game – 17–16 in Dublin. Only one point in it, but it was such a relief. It was the first winning side I'd been on for nearly four months.

It didn't last long, though. The following weekend I was back with Wasps and we lost 43–27 at Bath, then the week after that, back like a yo-yo with Scotland again, we went down to the French, and it was bad – 51–16 at Murrayfield. To be fair, the French were on fire that season and went on to win a second consecutive Grand Slam. They ran rings round us, and in those situations the winger is often the one who gets the bullet. There's nothing like a four-man overlap for making you look a fool, and every time a Frenchman ran at me he seemed to have at least four men outside him.

I was dropped for the rest of the tournament. In fact, I wouldn't play again for Scotland until November. I remember the following week being on the right end of a big scoreline for Wasps in the quarter-final of the Tetley's Bitter Cup at London Irish. I scored a try, my twelfth of the season but only my fourth since the end of September, five months earlier. My form was spluttering. I badly needed a break, and I got it six weeks later when I injured my shoulder. It put me out for the rest of the season and out of the Scotland tour to Fiji and Australia that summer (even Fiji managed to put fifty points past us on that tour), and I went back to Scotland to recuperate.

It had been a horrific season. Two years earlier, Scotland had had a second consecutive shot at a Grand Slam, and the year after that Wasps had been champions. Now both teams were at rock bottom. The wheel had turned so quickly, and a career as a professional sportsman suddenly didn't seem such a dream ticket. Wasps had had so many injuries and as champions everyone wanted to have a bit of us.

What applied to Wasps, applied to me. It was my second season in the Premiership, having blazed a trail in my first, and now people were on to me. I couldn't shake the back injury all season, my weight ballooned to fifteen-and-a-half stone and I'd lost pace. In the past, if things like that happened, a player always had a career and a life outside rugby to turn to. I'd had my farm to look after. Now that was no longer an option. Our hobby was our job, and if it wasn't going so well, there was no escape. Just like the team in general, I struggled with the new responsibilities of being a full-time professional and a champion.

We were young, we were suddenly being stripped of coaches and players by international rugby and we weren't ready to handle it. Things were so bad, we banned ourselves from going out on a Thursday night, but nothing seemed to work. We did at least make it to the Tetley's Bitter Cup final, but we were a few players short, and Saracens spanked us at Twickenham – not quite fifty points, but 48–18 still hurt.

My shoulder injury meant I missed that final, but up in Scotland that summer, nursing my broken body, I seriously wondered whether I would ever go back to Wasps. I wasn't sure I wanted to, and I was even less sure they wanted to keep me. With my niggling injuries and poor form, I was turning into an expensive luxury.

Sure enough, that summer I got a letter from Nigel Melville. In it he said that I was being put on the transfer-list.

# 11

# Glory Days

If my stalling rugby career wasn't bad enough, my relationship with Kirsty wasn't going well, either. Dallaglio had always said that I'd lose form if I got back with her. It struck a chord with me, because one of my policies up till then had been, if you're playing shit, bin the bird. It had worked in the past. It gets you out of your comfort zone. Gabby's been the only one where my rugby actually improved after I started seeing her.

Kirsty and I were back to the way we had been before the first break-up. These things never work the second time round. We bought the house together, but, really, she'd bought it. I was paying half the mortgage, but the mortgage was in her name. She was pushing thirty now, and I wasn't. Emotionally, we were going our separate ways even more than we had been before the first break-up. We hardly saw anything of each other because our jobs took us away at different times of the week.

She'd never been too comfortable with the mid-twenties rugby-player scene anyway, and the final straw came that summer. I'd been up in Scotland for a few weeks but was back for pre-season. I went out for a big night with the boys, and got very drunk, so I went home early with Robbie Mailer, who was staying with me.

Simon Shaw was meant to be staying with me as well, but we'd left him. So in the small hours of the morning he arrived at our place and tried to get in. Nothing was doing. Robbie and I were dead to the world. Neither of us was going to wake up to let him in. Kirsty may have woken up, but in those days she had to be up at 5 a.m. every morning to do her breakfast show on Talk Radio. Even if he had woken her up, she wouldn't have been in a mood to let him in.

Shawsy doesn't often get angry, but when he does there's enough of him, at 6ft 8in and pretty much 20 stone, to do some damage. He managed to rock a concrete bollard out of the pavement, and plonked it down outside our front door. Point made, he stormed off and walked the three miles to his house in Chiswick. Don't ask me why he didn't get a cab. It was a strange night.

So strange that I, apparently, got up in the middle of the night and pissed on Kirsty's clothes. That was a new low in my life. I have no memory of it – I was basically sleepwalking. Sleep-pissing,

I suppose you could call it. I'd never done it before (as far as I know), and I've never done it since. The shame I felt the next day when Kirsty told me about it made my crippling hangover feel like a tickle with a feather. I imagine her lying awake that night listening to a goliath hammering on the front door and her boyfriend in the corner urinating on her clothes. Probably not very long after that, she had to get up to go to work, opened the front door and tripped over a concrete bollard.

She wasn't pleased. She got back that afternoon, and I remember we went to see a financial advisor. I was still reeking of alcohol and apologising for my incontinence. We'd reached breaking point.

That weekend she went off to Babington House, a hotel and member's club that had just opened in Somerset. She phoned me on the Sunday to say she was staying another night. My suspicions were aroused. On the Monday, when she finally walked through the front door, I was at home.

'What's going on?' I asked her.

'Nothing.'

'Bullshit. Something's going on. Are you seeing somebody else?'

'Yes.'

'What?'

I hadn't expected that. I was stunned, and then angry. She calmed me down, saying that she hadn't so much as kissed him. Then I got my determined head on.

'We can work this out,' I said.

'No, I think that's it now. I really like this guy.'

The guy was Nick Jones, the owner of Babington House. She

must have genuinely liked him, because they're married now, with two kids. When she'd arrived, he'd carried her bags up to her room, and she'd thought he was the porter. Turned out he was a multi-millionaire porter.

That same day, she gathered some things together. As she left I said to her, 'If you go, that's it. Don't think you can come back. We're not doing this again.'

She nodded and was gone.

---

It had happened in a flash and I was left to nurse my wounds. But if one woman had walked out of my life, another had come into it – Margot Wells, wife of Allan, who had won gold for Great Britain (well, Scotland) in the 100 metres at the 1980 Olympics. Eric Peters had recommended her to me as a trainer, and I started commuting down to Guildford, where she was based. She transformed my fitness and my pace, and as they were the tools of my trade, she transformed my life.

I used to get up at 7.30 a.m. to get to Guildford by 8, train with her for an hour or so, then be back at Wasps by 10 a.m. By the start of the 1998–99 season I was lean and mean, and with Kirsty's departure sharpening me up mentally, I was on a mission. I'd been looking good in pre-season and I went to see Nigel in his office to offer him the chance of extending my contract, which had another six or seven months to run, for a further two years on the same terms.

'No, Kenny. You're on the transfer list.'

'Fine,' I said, turning to go, 'but it'll cost you more when you do extend it.'

The first game of the season was at Bath, and it was all over the newspapers that Kirsty and I had split up, although it was a few weeks after the event. We lost 36–27, but it was a great game and we could easily have won. I scored a really good try, and it felt as if something had changed.

Gareth Rees had been our goal-kicker for the past two seasons and was one of the best in the Premiership, but he got clobbered the next week in a match against Swansea, one of the Anglo-Welsh friendlies that were played that season with the English boycotting Europe. Alex King was also out, so I stepped up to take the kicks. Usual story – I just stuck up my hand when the question was asked. I kicked my goals that day, and got the gig for the next match, and then the next. Suddenly, people were saying, hang on, Kenny's really quite good at this. My style was the same as it always had been – plonk the ball down; whack it. As long as I had no time to think about it, I was happy. The boys were still running back across the halfway line as the ball was sailing between the posts. But it wasn't broke, so there was no need to fix it as far as I was concerned. Kingy came back; I carried on kicking. Reesy came back; I carried on kicking.

Reesy was a rock. He struggled to get back in the team that season, and a lesser man might have resented the fact that I had taken his kicking job, but he became my goal-kicking coach. He went out of his way to help me. Apart from anything else, he had become a really good friend.

I first met him playing for the Barbarians in 1994 in the Boxing

Day fixture at Leicester. After the game, Richard Cockerill got especially drunk. He was sitting at the table eating wine glasses. A little later, he fell over on a big carpet on the dance floor, and Reesy and I rolled him up in it. I remember looking across at Reesy as we did it, and thinking, 'This guy's a good laugh. I like him.' The Leicester boys were loving it. They went up to Cockers one by one and slapped him on the head, and there was nothing he could do about it.

I also used to meet Reesy on the international circuit. I remember in particular the opening ceremony for the 1995 World Cup in South Africa. The SRU had excelled themselves again in kitting us out in ludicrous gear. We looked like bus conductors – grey blazers, blue trousers, blue tie. On the breast pocket there was a thistle, the World Cup and a springbok. It looked more like a dog jumping over a teapot to get to a daisy. In the big marquee, with all the best players in the world packed into it, Reesy was the first to break the ice. He wasn't exactly looking a rock star in his Canadian outfit, complete with the maple leaf that everyone else knew as the exploding arsehole, but he was looking better than the awkward gathering of bus conductors that was the Scotland squad. 'Tickets!' he kept shouting at us across the room, and soon everyone was doing it. We were humiliated before a ball had been kicked.

However, kicking balls was now what I did for a living. I was whacking them over from all angles. Even from the halfway line I was landing about three in four. By Christmas I had racked up one hundred and seventy-one points in twelve games. I was loving it. Even if you didn't play that well you could kick five out of five and everyone thought you were a hero. Obviously, there was always the danger of the reverse being true – you play really well but miss a couple of kicks and everyone thinks you're a criminal – but at that stage I was back on track, and the idea of missing never even entered my head.

I was now living with Shawsy. Everything was amicable with Kirsty. Neither of us wanted a bitter split, and we came to a simple arrangement for the contributions I'd made so far to the mortgage. I bundled my clothes into a couple of bags and left everything else at the house – furniture, pictures. I just wanted away.

Little did I know that I was moving in with a woman in a 6ft 8in man's body. Shawsy was very house proud. He was an excellent cook and spent hours at the stove in his pinny, and, Christ, I had to be tidy. He had this beautiful house in Chiswick, open plan with floor-to-ceiling windows. His bedroom was a balcony-type affair overhead, and I was given a tiny little box room off the main living area, with a curtain across it for a door. If he'd really wanted to, which I reckon he might have when I started seeing Gabby, he could actually peer down into my room from his.

Shawsy was constantly rearranging the furniture. It was one of his favourite hangover cures – and we were hungover quite a lot during my stay. Thursday night piss-ups might have gone out of the window now that we had faced up to the realities of professionalism, but Saturdays and Sundays were still fair game. Many's the time I came back and thought I was in the wrong house. It was unrecognisable. He also liked to paint watercolours and thought nothing of going off to the wetlands in Barnes to paint the birds. For such a big man, he really was a big girl.

But not the girl for me. An altogether more attractive woman was about to walk into my life and change it for ever.

———————

It happened in the early hours of 24 January 1999. I was in the K Bar in Fulham with a few of the Wasps boys and in walked this blonde bombshell, who I recognised from the telly. She was with someone I knew, Tamsin from Sky Sports, so I sidled up to them and got myself an introduction.

I was dumbstruck. Dumbstruck and incredibly excited. I went through to the dance floor – I was that excited – to find Shawsy and Peter Scrivener, another of my best mates at Wasps.

'Scrivs, Scrivs, you'll never guess who's just walked into the bar.'

'Who?'

'Gaby Roslin.'

Scrivs went through to have a look. 'That's Gabby Yorath, you cock.'

Armed with this useful information, I moved in on a pincer formation with him, and we spent the rest of the night talking to Gabby and Tamsin, and when they kicked us out of the club, the four of us went to Vingt-Quatre, an all-night diner down the road, and had a full English breakfast. It was just a really good laugh. Everything felt very easy and natural.

I was back in the Scotland squad for the 1999 Five Nations, which was about to start, the last Five Nations before Italy joined to make it six. As we stood outside the café, waiting for a cab, I said to Gabby that she should come up to one of the Scotland games, and I put my arm round her. I'm pretty sure I've heard this in a movie, but it really was as if something went through me, like a pulse of electricity or something. She smiled at me, and I took my hand away immediately.

'What's the matter?' she said.

'Nothing, nothing,' I mumbled, but I was completely thrown. What had just happened?

In the taxi, my head was spinning. I didn't want to start seeing anyone. My life was going so well for once – I was scoring tries, kicking goals, back in the Scotland squad, young, free and single with no worries in my life. Why would I want to risk changing anything? Then there was the TV thing. I'd recently split up with one presenter – did I really want to get involved with another?

And yet. This girl was perfect. I had to give it a shot at least, didn't I? The taxi stopped outside Gabby's place and we both got out.

'What are you doing?' she asked warily.

'I thought you might make me a cup of tea.'

She looked at me sideways for a second. 'Come on then.'

I couldn't miss back then.

She'd just bought this house, and we both liked property, so she showed me round. We went upstairs into the main bedroom. It was empty, apart from a huge waterbed.

'That's been left by the previous owners.'

'Right.'

She jumped on to it. Well, that was an invitation if ever there was one. So I jumped on it, too, but when I hit the bed, she flew off it on to the floor. I rushed over to help her up. And then came the moment. There was a pause, and I kissed her. We went through all the usual is-this-a-good-idea stuff, so that was as far as it went that night. We slept fully clothed in her proper bed. Obviously, I didn't get a lot of sleep that night. Should I put my arm round her? Should I kiss her? Look, she's right there, lying next to me. All that kind of stuff kept me awake.

It was probably just as well because I was wearing a pair of Wimbledon boxer shorts my mum had bought me when she'd gone to watch the tennis. The next morning as I got out of the shower I managed to stand on the boxers and get them wet. I just stuffed them in my pocket and Gabby drove me back to Shawsy's.

Something had obviously happened between us, and on the way we talked about where we should go from there. We decided to take things easy. I was desperately trying to play it cool. I knew how my rugby and relationships did not always mix. I thought that I'd spent too much of my time with Kirsty trying to please her and not enough being true to myself. I couldn't let that happen again.

'If we do go out with each other,' I said to Gabby, 'don't try to change me. I am what I am. If you don't like it, forget it. Rugby is number one and I have to put it first.'

My piece said, I got out of the car and felt like the man. Later that day, she rang to ask if I'd left a pair of damp green and purple boxer shorts under the seat of her car on purpose. Didn't feel like the man after that, but at least we had our first date sorted.

The great thing about Gabby was that she understood about sport. A lot of girls would have taken offence at the idea of playing second fiddle to rugby, but she realised what I really meant. She'd been brought up in her dad's world of football, and she'd competed herself in the Commonwealth Games in rhythmic gymnastics. Putting sport first didn't mean you couldn't love anything or anyone as much as you did the sport, but it did mean there could be no compromises.

All the same, she became number one in my life quicker than I ever thought possible.

———————

My chances of winning her over were helped by the way things were going on the field. I was racking up the points and getting a lot of headlines.

'Is this normal?' she used to say.

I would shrug and say, 'Oh aye.'

I'd notched up more than two hundred points for Wasps that season by the time we met, and the 1999 Five Nations began a couple of weeks after that. Before Christmas I'd worked my way back into the Scotland team and scored seven tries in our two World Cup qualifiers – two against Portugal and five against Spain. Those were the games for which the SRU refused to award caps. Meanwhile, England beat Holland 110–0 in one of their two qualifiers and were all awarded caps. Mismatches they may have been, but they were World Cup qualifiers.

Duncan Hodge was the goal-kicker that autumn, and he kept

the job for our first game of the Five Nations at home to Wales. We were rank outsiders for the championship, 100–1 to win the Grand Slam. We started brilliantly though, John Leslie scoring a try after nine seconds – the fastest in history – but Wales worked their way back into the game, and led 13–8 at the break.

Six minutes into the second half, Hodgey was taken off with a broken leg, which forced a reshuffle that ended up the making of us. Alan Tait came on to partner John Leslie in the centre and Gregor Townsend moved to fly-half. It turned out to be a brilliant midfield. We were still trailing, 20–15, as we moved into the final quarter, but we blitzed them, scoring eighteen points in as many minutes to win the game 33–20. I took over the kicking duties for the first time in international rugby and kicked two conversions and two penalties. It felt good.

England were next up – at Twickenham – and the good thing was that people weren't laughing at our chances, but the game provided my first taste of the downside of kicking. We lost 24–21 despite deserving to win. England started well, but we were quicker and more inventive. Our new midfield were superb, and Taity scored two great tries. He was on fire. I converted all three of our tries, but missed three penalties. They weren't sitters, but they were straight from about forty-five metres out. I'd not played, or practised my kicking, since the Wales game two weeks earlier, because of a niggle in my knee. I struggled with the long ones, while the short ones felt easy. Usually I found it the other way round.

Afterwards, I was deflated. I remember sitting on the bus next to Taity, and he said, 'We might never get a chance like that again,' which was like a knife going through me. I knew if I'd kicked those penalties, we would have won. None of us was even thinking about a Grand Slam, but looking back now and seeing what a win that day could have meant, those misses are hard to take.

Taity was a good mate by then, although our relationship was based on antagonism. He antagonised me. When we played Ireland that year I went for goal with a penalty from about fifty-five yards out. Taity obviously didn't think I was going to get it. He eyeballed me aggressively.

'Just make sure this goes dead,' he said.

It had me seething, but I whacked it over. As I ran back I shouted at him, 'Don't ever fucking talk to me like that again.' I was furious with him.

It took me back to my schooldays and the feelings of inadequacy when schoolteachers gave me a hard time. For some reason, as a rugby player I thrived on that kind of confrontation, but as a goal-kicker I was a different person, more like the vulnerable schoolboy. I needed to be nurtured. I didn't need the extra pressure of people mouthing off at me. There's enough pressure on a goal-kicker as it is. That's why I was always good at getting the ones I wasn't expected to and vulnerable when I lined up the ones I was expected to score. At Wasps I had Reesy constantly putting his arm round me, encouraging me and telling me that I was kicking well. With Scotland, no one performed that role. Jim Telfer's approach was to pile on the pressure – 'Logan, you better kick well today.' I know now from having tackled my dyslexia that it was a case of overload – too many factors crowding in on my weak powers of concentration. Now I think I would stand up to Jim and tell him to concentrate on his own job and let me try to concentrate on mine, but I went into my shell.

Aside from that, spirits were excellent throughout that Five Nations. People were playing for each other. A lot of us played through injuries of some kind or another. Jim was brilliant as coach and had us buzzing. We were trailing 14–0 early on in that Twickenham game. Another year we would probably have folded, but we turned it round and should have won. We scored four more tries in the game against Ireland to win 30–13, and we were the darlings of the championship. England were still on course for a Grand Slam, but they weren't doing it with any style.

At Wasps, we were ticking along. Leicester were running away with the Premiership, but we were mounting another campaign in the Tetley's Bitter Cup, determined to go one better than we had the season before.

On the train down from Waterloo after one of our early cup wins that season, Alex King was talking to Nigel Melville. The mischievous pest saw me just behind him and asked out loud, 'So, Nigel, is Kenny still on the transfer list?'

'No,' said Nigel. 'But don't tell him.'

'Too late,' I said.

By the end of March I'd signed a new two-and-a-half-year deal, and I had a pay rise of forty grand a year.

I signed it after the Ireland game, while we were preparing for our cup semi-final against Gloucester, but that week I turned my ankle in training, which was the second injury of the season I had to play through. This one was bad. Margot put me on to one of the best physios around, Kevin Lidlow. He was a genius and somehow kept me going for the rest of the season, but I would need an operation on the ankle that summer.

It didn't seem to matter. Things were going my way. My relationship with Gabby was taking off. She wasn't so much like a girlfriend, she was becoming my best mate. Of course, she was gorgeous as well, but it was the way we just liked being around each other that stood out.

I would pick her up from the airport after she'd been on a work trip and say, 'I've got to go and see the physio.'

'OK. I'll come with you.'

She'd get into the car and off we would go. Kevin's clinic was two hours away in Thurrock. Neither of us noticed.

My ankle was strapped up for the Gloucester game, and I scored twenty points and won man of the match. We were in the final for the second year running.

Then it was the last weekend of the Five Nations, and in Paris we earned ourselves the title. The first forty minutes were incredible – one of the best halves of rugby I've ever been involved in. All eight tries were scored before half-time, and we scored five of them. Our running lines were dazzling. That midfield of Gregor, John and Taity reached new heights of brilliance. Glenn Metcalfe and I were having a field day running off them. Taity scored two more tries, and Gregor scored another, which meant he'd scored a try in all four games.

I'd nearly not made it on to the pitch, though. My ankle was heavily strapped and I'd had a cortisone injection. But I also had a ritual that I went through before every game, which was to jump up and touch the ceiling before we went out. Didn't matter how high the ceiling was – I had to touch it somewhere. The changing-room ceiling at the new Stade de France was high. I flung myself up at it and just clipped it, but when I came down on my ankle it felt as if it had exploded. I was in agony. Thank God for adrenaline. It was pumping through me, and I played through the pain.

I kicked well that game, five out of six, but the one I missed was a sitter. Taity had just scored our fourth try in the twenty-second minute, and as I lined up the kick I saw my face on the big screen behind the goal and winked at myself. My concentration, chronically bad at the best of times, was now completely thrown. I couldn't get the screen out of my head and not just because my face was on it. I hit the ball and looked up to see it cannon back off the post. I swore and as I ran back I saw on the big screen at the other end Taity effing and blinding.

'If we lose this game by two points . . .' he said to me when I got back into position. I laughed nervously. We were four tries to two up. Surely we couldn't lose.

Martin Leslie scored our fifth three minutes later – 33–12. That half felt ten minutes long. It flew by. The French scored a third try and a penalty to make it 33–22 at the break. In the second half the scoring dried up – it had to. I kicked a penalty to leave the final score at 36–22.

We were in the box seat. England were playing Wales at Wembley the next day, and if Wales could only win we would be champions. Nobody expected it, though. England were hot favourites to finish the last Five Nations with a Grand Slam.

After the predictable celebrations, I flew back to London the next day and went round to Shawsy's. He wasn't in the England team then, so we watched the game together. England were dominant, and it looked as if it was going to script. In truth, I never really thought it wouldn't. But Wales were hanging in there, and Lawrence, who was England's captain, made a crucial mistake when he decided not to go for the posts with a penalty four minutes from time. England were six points ahead and if they'd slotted the kick, they would have been home and dry, but they went for the line-out in the corner.

Shawsy and I were on tenterhooks. He wouldn't admit it, but I reckon he secretly wanted Wales to win. Whatever they say, you never really want your team to win when you've not been picked for it, and my excitement over Scotland's chances was rubbing off on him.

England's ploy of going for the corner didn't come off, and before we knew it Scott Gibbs was galloping through for the try at the end that brought Wales to within one point with the conversion to come. I leapt up. So did Shawsy. For a second we were jumping around the room. Then Shawsy realised what he was doing and stopped.

'Oh my God, I've got to live with you now,' he moaned, coming on all depressed.

'He's still got to kick the conversion,' I pointed out.

'Yeah, but it's Neil Jenkins, not you. He's never going to miss.'

Jenks didn't, God bless him, and my phone went mental. I spoke to Gabby, my team-mates, the press and Nigel Melville, who told me I could have the next couple of days off.

I went straight to Heathrow. Glenn Metcalfe was already there, because he was flying to New Zealand to get married. He'd watched the game on his own. I met him in the bar at terminal one, and English, Scottish and Welsh fans were patting us on the back. The English were brilliant. 'Well done,' they said. 'You should have beaten us anyway. It should have been the Grand Slam.'

The squad gathered in Edinburgh, and we celebrated again. On the Monday, at 5 p.m., they presented the trophy to us at Murrayfield in front of around 15,000 people, the first piece of silverware Scotland had won in the professional era. Ian McGeechan was poised to come in as coach after the World Cup that autumn, and he couldn't wait. The future looked so promising.

———————————

There was nothing for it, then, but to win the Tetley's Bitter Cup with Wasps. My ankle was starting to deteriorate badly now. They had found a piece of floating bone in it after the France game. I played three more matches for Wasps, but by the time the cup final against Newcastle came round, Reesy had talked Nigel into picking him and putting me on the bench. I don't begrudge him it now, even if I was fuming at the time. Reesy was up front with me about it and he had been totally selfless in helping me that season. He was right – my ankle was killing me – but I had scored seventeen points the week before in the win at Sale that clinched us a place in Europe, so it can't have been that bad, as far as I was concerned.

In the end I came on for Paul Sampson early in the second half and played pretty well, but it was the Alex King show. Kingy had been through tough times over the previous year or so. People forget that in 1997 he was the first fly-half Clive Woodward picked for England, but he had to withdraw with a knee injury. The next chance he'd had was on the Tour of Hell in 1998, when Woodward took a load of youngsters to the southern hemisphere and watched them get slaughtered.

Kingy came back from that with an injury and had struggled all season, but now he was hitting his form again. Playing opposite Jonny Wilkinson in that final, he was the King. My nickname at Stirling County had been King, and when I first arrived at Wasps Alex came up to me and said, 'There's only one King around here.' He never got a proper chance with England, but in my opinion he's the best fly-half English club rugby has ever produced. Show me another who has won as much. If your fly-half is winning lots of trophies, he's a good player. He was one of the best I ever played with.

And, boy, did he know it that night. We went to the Sports Café afterwards to celebrate and the final was being shown over and over on a big screen. At one stage near the end of the night, Kingy was hugging the screen. His try came up – it was a pretty special one, to be fair – and he was hugging himself.

I was watching from the bar with Dallaglio, Will Green, Scrivs and Shawsy. 'He's really lost it now.'

Little did we know, though, as we stood there happily celebrating Wasps' first ever cup triumph, that in no more than a week Lol would lose a whole lot more.

# 12

# The Big Man

In April 1999, Lawrence and I were at a testimonial dinner at the Hilton Hotel with the rest of the Wasps squad. At the end of it he said to me that he was going to meet some guys from Gillette, who wanted to discuss signing him up on a lucrative sponsorship deal. Did I want to come? I said, no, I reckoned I'd stay with the boys. Phew!

About a month later I got a phone call from his agent at the time, Ashley Woolfe. Had I seen Lol? No, why? He's all over the *News of the World*. Those guys from Gillette were not what they had seemed. It was all an elaborate set-up. They were undercover journalists, and Lol had jumped into their honey trap whole-heartedly.

He does everything wholeheartedly, that guy. He is the proudest Englishman I've ever known, and his belief in himself and his team is second to none. The flipside of it, though, is that he is continually pushing things – pushing himself, pushing you, and pushing the boundaries. It meant that as a team-mate, you were antagonised and inspired by him in equal measure. And it meant that when these people posing as corporate types offered him half a million to be the face of Gillette and plied him with alcohol, he got a bit carried away with himself.

I can honestly say that, in all the years I've known him, I've never seen Lol take drugs, or any other rugby player for that matter. Even if you wanted to dabble, you would have to find a way round the drug tests. I remember landing at Heathrow after Scotland training and getting a call from Gabby. There was a guy at the door wanting to test me. 'But I got tested yesterday,' I said. I was tested three times that week. They say it's random, but if you're playing well, you'll get tested. And after that Dallaglio scandal, the testers practically camped out at Wasps. In all, I would say I was tested about twenty times in my career.

We didn't see a lot of Lol after the story broke. He didn't exactly go into hiding, but he pushed away a lot of our attempts to help him. He was proud, and he was probably embarrassed. When we did go out for a couple of beers with him later that summer, there was tension about him. He became a different person, less open and even more focused. In many ways, it helped him become a better player. Having to resign the captaincy of England hurt him, though. He was one of the greatest captains England ever had. If it hadn't been for that sting, he would have lifted the World Cup in 2003. Martin Johnson was a great leader, but Lol was as good as he was. He was certainly more vocal.

If you made a mistake on the pitch, he let you know about it, with his head cocked forward in that way of his, the sneer on his face and those huge hands ready to maul you if they could. If you did something good, the body language was the same, but there was a grin on his face, and you felt a million dollars. His team-talks were legendary. I heard hundreds of them, and I can't remember any of them being the same.

One of the reasons we loved him and closed ranks around him back then was that we could take the piss out of him, not that he liked it much. He may have given hundreds of different team-talks, but he wasn't afraid to lift some of them straight out of a book or a newspaper. He was in mid-flow in the changing room once, and Shawsy turned to me and whispered, 'That was in the paper this morning.' Cue sniggering in the corner.

I wasn't afraid of annoying him, either. When I came back from the presentation ceremony after Scotland won the Five Nations, a couple of months before the drugs story, I obviously turned up in full Scotland kit.

'All right, boys? Good weekend? I tell you what, I might not be able to train today. I've been lifting trophies all weekend.'

This was a particularly touchy subject for Lol, since he was getting some criticism for his decision not to go for the posts towards the end of the Wales–England game. In training, I kept shouting to him, 'Kick to the corner! Kick to the corner!' But I kept my distance, because I knew he might kill me. Typical Lol – he ripped my Scotland hat off during one drill and tried to tear it to pieces.

'You fucking Scottish twat!'

'Er, can I have my hat back, please?'

Equally typically, when we walked off at the end of the session, he put a big arm round my shoulders, congratulated me and asked how the celebrations had gone.

We did have a little fight in training about a year later. Lol hadn't been playing because of injury but he was still attending England sessions, so when he turned up to training as we were warming up I gave him some banter.

'Don't worry, Lol, take your time,' I said. 'It's only us today. England training's next week.'

We started to move away for the next part of the warm-up, and out of nowhere he ran at me and smashed me onto my back. As we grappled on the floor, he rubbed mud in my face and made more comments about me being a Scottish twat. I was fuming and when he got up to run off, I tap tackled him and pushed his face into the mud, 'You English twat.' Then I sprinted off as if my life depended on it, which it probably did. The squad had stopped for some more stretching and I ran to the far side of them. My heart was beating at about two hundred miles an hour. He's gonna kill me. He's gonna kill me. Paul Volley saw him approaching and said, 'All right, Lol? Did you fall over or something?'

Lol nodded his head in defiance. 'Now I'm back,' he said, 'we'll probably start winning again.' And the boys whistled and jeered, 'Hey! The Lol's back!'

That was the spirit in the Wasps camp – you were constantly challenged by the antagonism, but even when you came to blows or slagged each other off there was a kind of warmth to it. That was embodied by Dallaglio as much as anyone, and the *News of the World* thing brought us tighter together around him. It also made us warier. The professional game brought new dangers.

We all felt a little nervous after the scandal. None of us was completely safe. Only a couple of weeks later, a chef and a barmaid at a bar where we used to drink were witnesses in a story published in the *Mail on Sunday*, pouncing on a piss-up we'd had there a few weeks earlier, after a game. They alleged that Lol was snorting cocaine. He successfully sued the paper and they apologised and paid his costs.

He couldn't sue the *News of the World*, because he had said everything he was reported as saying, even if he'd been duped into saying it by a cynical piece of deception. The mark of the man, though, was the way he came back from it. He held his head high and took the punches. Then he went on to win everything a player could win.

Lawrence is from a special family. They'd suffered so much when his elder sister, Francesca, died in the *Marchioness* disaster in 1989, so I suppose a run-in with a couple of undercover reporters was nothing after that. He is a perfect mix of his parents. His dad is a cool, elegant Italian with the gift of the gab, and his mum, who sadly died of cancer at the end of 2008, gave him the passion and the drive.

She was an amazing woman, one of the characters who made Wasps. When I turned up at the club for the first time, I didn't know who she was, but she seemed to have something to say to everyone. Her first words to me were, 'My son says you're a good player.' I was grateful – it was a nice welcome. It was also a standard being set. If you ever fell below that standard, you knew about it as much from Eileen as you did from her son.

One of our most outrageous wins was at Kingsholm in 1998. It was pretty unfair. We were losing 12–6 and the referee awarded a penalty to Gloucester. 'Kick to touch and the game's over,' he said. So they kicked to touch. And then he said, 'After the line-out.' The crowd were going mental at him. Kingsholm was the best club ground in rugby. You talk about the atmosphere at France games, but I loved playing at Gloucester. The hatred was exceptional.

Sure enough, we nicked the line-out, Kingy made a great break and flipped it to Will Green, who went in between the posts. There was pandemonium. Lol was standing full square in front of the Shed with his hands cupping his ears as they hurled abuse at him. I lined up the kick to win it and even the blokes in the corporate boxes behind the goal were jumping around like wild animals. The boos were deafening.

By the time I slotted the conversion, the crowd was already spilling on to the pitch and we all legged it for the tunnel. Kingy was interviewed on TV and was being jostled and jabbed in the ribs by the fans. Lol was giving and taking more abuse, while a few of the boys tried to shield him, which is when Eileen waded in and unloaded on those Gloucester fans. 'I was born in the East End,' she said afterwards. 'I can take care of myself.'

The gap at Wasps when Lawrence retired was massive. But so was the one his mother left.

———————

The timing of the *News of the World* sting was cruel because it happened just months before the start of the 1999 World Cup, the first one of the professional era. Lol was cleared of any drugs charges but fined for bringing the game into disrepute. At least, though, he was free to play, even if he was no longer captain.

In Scotland, our build-up was overshadowed by a strike over pay. It wasn't the first we'd had – the SRU were continually trying to find ways to save money – but this one was particularly heart-felt, because we were Five Nations champions. How had the SRU rewarded us? By cutting our pay.

It was the exiles, those players based outside Scotland, who called the strike, because we were not contracted to the SRU. Our match fees were being cut from £2,500 to less than a grand. There were improved win bonuses, but even if we'd won the Grand Slam, we would have been paid less than we were for the previous championship. And we knew how much the other British teams were on. In Wales, for example, on top of the match fees, you were paid fifty quid for each cap you'd won. For someone with fifty-odd caps, say, that meant nearly three grand a match before he'd even started.

Tom Smith stepped forward to help lead the negotiations. He

was still a quiet man, but he was now one of the most respected players in our squad. And one of the most feared. He is a sleep-walker – always a disturbing phenomenon, especially when you share a room with one. We stayed in our usual team hotel just outside Edinburgh for that World Cup, and I shared with Tom for the first time.

The first thing I did in any hotel was to take the mattress off the bed – because of my back, I preferred to sleep on the floor. In the middle of the night, I woke up with a start. Tom was leaning over me, his face inches from mine.

'All right, Tom?' I said nervously.

'Yeah,' he whispered.

'What do you want?'

He just rubbed his face with both hands.

'I tell you what, Tom. I might just nip outside for a glass of water or something.'

Suddenly, he ran over to the window and nestled his face in the curtains. That should have been my moment to escape, but I was fascinated. Then he ran back over to me and resumed his original position, squatting by my mattress with his nose practi-cally touching mine.

Enough was enough. I was out of there. I slid carefully off the mattress and legged it to reception.

'I've got to get another room,' I said to the girl on the desk.

'I'm sorry, Kenny, we haven't got any other rooms.'

'But I'm sharing with a psycho.'

'Oh, you're in with Tom, are you?'

'How did you know?'

'We always have this problem. Don't worry, we do have a room set aside for this.'

So Tom's waters ran deep, and people respected what he had to say, even the SRU. We boycotted training for a day in August, and eventually secured the same deal as we'd had before – not exactly a triumph, but we knew the SRU were deeply in debt. They had to cut costs, but you don't cut back on the one thing that can bring in the money, namely the players. Actually, they could have done that a bit. Some of the home-based players were on fortunes, because their agents had dreamt up big sums that they claimed their clients were being offered by foreign clubs. The SRU should have just invited those players to accept those offers. Instead, they tried to outdo them.

There was, and still is, this obsession with getting players back to Scotland. I can't understand it. Why not let them play elsewhere? Encourage them even. They'll be playing a higher standard of rugby week in, week out, and more importantly someone else will be paying their wages. In the meantime, you turn the home-based teams into centres of excellence to bring through the youngsters and expose them to high-class competition. But the SRU had an old-fashioned approach and that proposed pay cut in 1999 was a case in point.

───────────

Jim Telfer was retiring as coach after the 1999 World Cup, and for that reason it was an emotional tournament. Whatever you thought of his administrative skills, the man was an icon in the game and players would have shed blood for him. Sometimes, if there wasn't any blood, he actually invented some. During that World Cup, he took Stuart Grimes aside and instructed him to roll up his sleeves. Grimesy, who had thought he was being dropped, did as he was told and Jim took out a red marker pen and drew slashes on his forearms. Back in the team room, Jim played the opening moments of our game against South Africa, then stopped the video.

'Anyone notice anything?'

Silence.

'Three tackles by Grimesy in the first thirty seconds. If ye'd all done that, we'd a won. Grimesy! Roll yer sleeves up! Put your hands above your heed! Stand up, man!'

Grimesy did as he was told.

'Ye see that! That's blood! Every time he wakes up, he pinches hisself, cos he canna believe he's here! Right, get on the bus!'

He'd worked a similar number a few years earlier before a game in Ireland. We walked into the team room, and he said, 'Right, all of ye on the bus!'

So we headed out.

'No! That bus!' And he pointed to some chairs in the back of the room. He'd arranged them all in two-by-two formation. We sat down.

'Wainwright!' Slap. 'You sit there! Ye're driving!'

Already we were starting to giggle. I was sitting next to Bryan Redpath, who couldn't help himself. I was trying to keep a straight face, 'Will you stop looking at me, Brush!'

'I'm sick of hearing Townsend's name,' Jim continued, 'Logan's name, Hastings, Weir, Redpath. There's one man in this team who's the ugliest man ye'll ever see. Even his mother has to think twice before looking at him.'

The front-row forwards were all thinking this could be their moment. It had to be Kevin McKenzie.

'His face is battered, kicked and bruised. He's the heartbeat of this team. He's the reason we're winning. Ian Jardine! Stand up, man!'

All you could see were shoulders rocking as people tried to stop laughing. Jardy was in shock – he reckoned he was quite good-looking, which I guess he was – but he got to his feet.

'Look at him! Ian Jardine! What an ugly bastard!'

We all turned round to look at Jardy, and the tears were rolling down our cheeks. Jardy didn't know whether to laugh or cry. Praise didn't come much higher from Jim.

'Right, on the bus, the lot of ye!'

I stood up. 'Which bus, Jim?'

Slap.

---

It was a weird World Cup. We were excited, thinking we were in with a chance, but it didn't feel real because it was being played at home. The fashion crimes of the SRU had reached a new low. Our kit was orange. Orange is the new black, they told us. No, it's not. We thought it was a spoof and were expecting the fat man from the Tango adverts to come out and slap us at any moment.

Of all the SRU's failings, their sense of fashion was the most shocking. It happened every time there was a World Cup or a tour. It was a shame, because there was always a sense of anticipation before they handed out the new stash. It was like Christmas, except you'd open the gear up and then just sit there staring at it, the blood seeping away from your cheeks. Oh. My. God. It wasn't just the disappointment, it was the knowledge that we were going to have to wear this stuff. There was a feeling of dread.

After that World Cup, the players took over choosing the kit. Up until then it was as if someone had been doing it through the bingo machine. Up came orange and blue. Bingo! The manager thought it was smart. The manager was sixty.

Our big game was that first one against South Africa. We gave it a good shot and were leading at half-time. It was an exciting game, full of running and errors, but South Africa took the lead early in the second half and kept us at arm's length until they ran in a couple of tries at the end for a 46–29 final score.

That put us on course for a quarter-final with the All Blacks – again. My most distinct memory of that World Cup is lining up opposite the haka on a dark, wet night, with about 60,000 flash bulbs going off all around us in the gloom. Who were they taking pictures of, I wonder? The guys in black doing the war dance? Or the guys in orange socks watching it?

They smashed us in the first half. It was 25–3 at half-time, three tries to nil. But, with our World Cup over, we found our form and outscored them in the second half to lose 30–18.

It felt like the end of an era. We bought Jim a bench for his garden. Saying farewell to him as a coach was emotional. It was the end of a decade, the end of a millennium. We had played to the limits of our ability and won the last Five Nations. Jim had never been on finer form.

He was moving upstairs to be director of rugby, and Ian McGeechan was poised to take over on the training paddock. Not a bad replacement, then, and really the only man who could fill Jim's boots.

—————————

I already knew that I was going to marry Gabby by this stage, barely nine months after we'd met. We'd been through all the rites of passage – I'd met her family, she'd met mine, we'd moved in together, and, probably the most important thing for me, we'd broached the subject of my dyslexia.

I was round at her place only three weeks after we'd met, and there was an interview she'd done in a paper lying on the kitchen counter. She shoved it in front of me.

'Here, have a read of this,' she said casually, as if it were the easiest thing in the world. 'Tell me what you think.'

This was my worst nightmare come true. I'm not really exaggerating when I say that all my life I'd been running from this moment. Up until that point I'd been making do on the reading front, continually avoiding situations where I might be put on the spot, or getting out of them when I had been, constantly bothered by the feeling that this avoidance strategy would one day blow up in my face.

Now here I was, caught in the headlights by someone who already had me by the heart, even if I'd only just met her. The stakes were higher than they'd ever been for that reason alone. I didn't want our relationship to be over before it had begun, but how could I expect this gorgeous high-flier to find me attractive if I couldn't even read a newspaper article?

My stomach tightened and I started to panic. My eyes skipped over the page and all the words. Every now and then one might stand out and make sense, but it was lost in the chaos of letters and spaces. I could feel Gabby standing over me, and the stress became unbearable.

I looked away and said, 'Aye. It's very good.'

Gabby smiled at me in a puzzled way.

'You're a very quick reader.'

'Aye. Do you want a cup of tea?' And I headed for the kettle.

'Hang on. How come you can read so fast?' I didn't answer.

'Can you not read?' she said.

'Of course I can read.'

She brought the newspaper over to me.

'Go on. Read this.'

By now I was agitated. I knew this girl was on to me and I despaired as I thought I saw the end approaching for us already. I held the newspaper and stared at it uselessly.

'You can't read, can you?' she said gently.

She put her arm round me, because the tears were welling in my eyes.

'I'm dyslexic,' I said.

She carried on cuddling me.

'Are you going to finish with me now?'

'What?'

'Well, I can't read, can I? You must think I'm thick.'

I should have known that she was too good to think like that. Instead, she almost immediately started talking about ways of beating the dyslexia, courses I could go on to learn to read, but that sort of talk made me even more emotional. For me, courses meant going back to school. There was no way. So Gabby left it until we went on holiday to Bali that summer, when things were calmer, and we spoke about my problem more fully.

It was the first time I'd properly faced up to my dyslexia, or talked it over. Deirdre Wilson, my tutor after school, had been the first to diagnose me, but I couldn't process any of the things she was trying to teach me. My mum knew I struggled, but I wouldn't let her in and we never really tackled it. I'd told Kirsty, but, although she tried to talk about it, I told her I didn't want to, and that was that. The only other person who knew was Nigel Melville. I'd told him soon after I'd joined Wasps, because I knew, now that it was professional, I wasn't going to be able to keep hiding from team sessions that involved pen and paper. As well as I got on with Nigel, though, he wasn't going to help me get over this. Gabby was the one who forced me to face up to it and she gave me the confidence to do so. I knew very quickly that I'd found my soul mate.

# 13

## Taking the Kicks

Life seemed pretty good. Gabby must have thought that this was how it always was in my life. In the first few months of our relationship, I'd won the Five Nations with Scotland and the Tetley's Bitter Cup with Wasps. I was scoring points at will. From the end of the World Cup to the beginning of the new Six Nations, I'd racked up another couple of hundred for Wasps. Our Premiership campaign was not going brilliantly, but we'd won our pool in the Heineken Cup, and we had cleared the first hurdle of our defence of the domestic cup.

None of us in the Scotland camp, meanwhile, could wait for

the Six Nations to start. We were champions, Ian McGeechan was our new coach, it was a new competition and we were the first to play the new boys in the tournament's new city, Rome. How much more exciting could things get?

It was a lovely sunny day, the Scots were in good voice, everyone was excited, everything was fine. Until these bloody Mitre balls turned up.

Mitre balls are a slightly different shape from the Gilbert ones we were all used to in Britain. We'd practised with Mitre balls all week, but we'd let some of the air out of them until we could locate some sort of sweet spot. They have a very different feel and I am certainly not the only kicker who has had trouble adapting to them – Ronan O'Gara and Jonny Wilkinson have, too.

On the day, the match balls came out, and I broke into a cold sweat when I realised how much the Italians had pumped them up. It is the right of the home team – or the home team's kicker – to decide what pressure the ball should be pumped up to. There is a minimum that has to be satisfied, otherwise it's up to you. Diego Dominguez, their kicker, had gone for the absolute maximum, and it dawned on me that I was in trouble. It was like kicking a stone. Or maybe I just let myself think that I was in trouble. Doesn't matter. I was thrown by it, and that's all it takes to smash the balance of a goal-kicker.

I had a shocker with the boot that day. We all had shockers. John Leslie, who was now our captain, had been rushed back into the team after injury, and he was off within a quarter of an hour. The Italians were mad for it on their championship debut, and we were in no state to handle them. Dominguez kicked everything. He scored a massive twenty-nine points – six penalties, three drop goals and the conversion of their try. I converted the first of our two tries but missed four penalties, three of them badly, and eventually handed over the kicking duties to Gregor. We lost 34–20. Our defence of the title was in tatters, and we'd played only one game.

It was the lowest point of my rugby career to date and the first time I'd felt how miserable and lonely the kicker's role can be. I'd missed kicks at Twickenham the year before, which in retrospect cost us a Grand Slam, but at the time we'd been heroic in defeat, and none of the misses had been as bad as some of these.

Here there was no heroism. We'd been blown away, but I knew the most obvious failure had been mine, which is the way it is for a goal-kicker. I spoke to Gabby on the phone and I was really down. She was presenting the sports on ITV News and had sat through the whole sorry affair in the office. After I'd spoken to her, she said to Katie Derham, who was presenting the news, that she wished she could be out in Rome for me, and Katie told her she should go. She looked up the flights, and there was a late one from Heathrow, so she leapt on it.

Meanwhile, I went out with Gregor, Gordon Bulloch and Glenn Metcalfe, and as I walked down a street, I could see and hear people bitching about me. 'Fucking Kenny Logan. Lost us the game.' That had never happened to me before, and it was horrible. Horrible.

At one point, I was standing at a bar near a fat, middle-aged guy who was playing up to his mates, slagging off everyone in the team and me in particular. He knew I could hear him. I listened to it for a while, then walked out with the others. As I went I overheard him make some comment about me not being man enough to talk to them.

'Just keep going,' I said to myself. 'Be bigger than they are.' But when we got outside I said to Gregor, 'Fuck it,' and went back in. Gregor tried to call me back. He knew what it was like to kick for his country. The guy in the bar was looking pretty pleased with himself, but his mates saw me coming and looked anxious.

I unloaded all my frustrations on him. 'I love playing for my country,' I said. 'Do you think I wanted to miss those kicks? Do you think I did it just to annoy you? I'm really sorry I let you down, but I've let myself down more than anyone. It hurts me more than you can know, and if I've lost us the game, I'll take the blame. But don't you fucking stand here showing off to your mates and slagging off the team, when less than a year ago you were cheering about how proud you were to be Scottish. I'm proud to be Scottish come hell or high water. You're one of those fans who's proud when your team are going well and doesn't want to know when they're not. You're the fucking disgrace.'

There were a lot of Scottish fans in there, and they went quiet as I ranted at him. And as I walked out a few of them started to applaud – not enough of them for my liking, maybe, but a few was better than none. I think I'm right in saying that the guy I was talking to that night was the one who came up to me a couple of years later and apologised. I can't be totally sure, because this wasn't going to be my last run-in with a fan.

Gabby touched down in Rome at about midnight and came to meet us. She and I just walked the streets for hours. I was so in love with her. She understood the highs and lows of being in sport, and I was so moved that she'd come out that night to be with me. In the season after I'd first met her it was all Kenny this, Kenny that. Everything was going so well. Now she was showing how perfectly she could handle the bad times.

We sat down at the Trevi Fountain, one of the most romantic places in Europe. I may have been a bit drunk but I really wanted to marry her, and I thought, 'This is it, I'm going to ask her.' I looked into her eyes, I was about to ask the question.

Then a broad Scottish accent broke the silence. But it wasn't mine.

'Hey, Kenny. Big man. Unlucky today. Let's be honest. You had a shiter. But ye'll be all right, eh? I've got your autograph anyway.' And the fan slapped me round the head and walked off. It could almost have been Jim Telfer.

I felt the moment had passed, so I didn't propose, which is probably just as well. It wasn't the right time. We walked through Rome till five in the morning, went back to the hotel and then had to be up at six for the flight home. By now the alcohol was wearing off and the misery was really flooding in. We got home, went to bed, then went out for lunch. The hangover was kicking in and I had the weight of the world on my shoulders. I spoke to Gavin Hastings, angling for any crumbs of comfort he could throw me.

'My defence was good, though, wasn't it?' I pleaded, but none of that really mattered.

It was a relief to be in London, I suppose, where how Scotland had fared against Italy mattered to hardly anyone at all, and it was a relief to be back at Wasps straightaway. Gareth Rees, who was now our backs coach, got right behind me. He'd always said that kickers can only win you games, never lose them. If you're reduced to blaming the kicker, there's something wrong with the team – and it was true that even if I'd kicked all four of the ones I missed, it still wouldn't have covered the margin of our defeat.

The next weekend I scored twenty-six points for Wasps against Saracens and felt a bit better about things, but our next Six Nations game, in Ireland, was a disaster, if not so much for me. I kicked fine and we were 10–0 up after I'd scored a try, but then Ireland ran away with it for a 44–22 win – their first win over us in twelve years. Brian O'Driscoll was brilliant and Ronan O'Gara was among a few youngsters making their debuts. I became the first player to be sent to the sin bin in the Six Nations, for an incident with another debutant, Peter Stringer. I never even touched him, ref.

We went down to our third loss of the championship to France at Murrayfield, 28–16, and our season was falling apart. I had a pretty good game, finding a bit of space, but I missed a relatively easy kick at goal in the first half, and Chris Paterson took over the kicking. Sure enough, I was out of the team for the rest of the championship, which was salvaged only by a shock win in the driving rain to deny England a Grand Slam.

You can never help feeling bitter and twisted when you're dropped, and I was no different. I'd been dropped because of my goal-kicking, simple as that. I'd never asked to be goal-kicker; I'd done it to help the team out. This was how I was repaid.

It's more complicated than that, though. The truth is that dropping players is one of the coach's most important devices. If a player is struggling for any reason, mental or physical, I would always recommend dropping him. I used to see it as a wall. If you're playing well, the wall's got no holes in it and the bricks are all stable. When you're playing badly, some bricks start falling out and some get wobbly. Sometimes, the only way to fix it is to knock the wall down and build it back up again. When you get dropped, you go back to experiencing that horrible sinking feeling of not being good enough. The honesty kicks in, and you focus on the things you should be thinking about, while weeding out the irrelevant. If you're continually trying to patch up a deteriorating wall, there's no chance for that sort of process to take place. It's better to drop a player altogether. His replacement might not be as good, but you'll get that other player back better and more quickly.

I don't know how many times I was dropped by Scotland – there's a long list of players who won the odd cap here and there instead of me during my career. Sometimes I was furious at what I saw as the injustice of it. But I always came back.

At least I was able to concentrate on Wasps. They, too, relieved me of kicking duties. Kingy took over for the rest of the season. I had no problem with that. I was sick of it all.

Northampton featured heavily in our run-in to the end of the season. We played them in the quarter-final of the Heineken Cup at Franklin's Gardens and were robbed blind. It was Kingy's turn to have an off-day with the boot. Paul Grayson, who didn't have an off-day, nicked it at the end with a penalty that should never have been awarded. Northampton went on to win the whole thing.

Then we played them twice in five days – once in the league and once in the Tetley's Bitter Cup final, which we'd reached for the third year running. They put out a second team against us for the league game, seemingly with instructions to smash us before the final. So we smashed them back and won 54–12.

In the build-up to the cup final, Keith Barwell, Northampton's owner, made some stupidly provocative comments on television, claiming we were iffy and had no world-class players, while they had an abundance. We were seething. With the game hanging in the balance, I scored a try and afterwards ruffled Paul Grayson's hair and said, 'Who's world class now?' It was out of character and I apologised to him later, but I was so pumped up. We all were. It was quite close – 31–23 to us in the end – but it was the usual story. We scored the tries, Grays kicked the points. The Northampton players were furious with their boss for his comments. At every tackle and ruck we made reference to them. Nigel and Lol didn't have to do anything to get us up for that one. And so we won the cup for the second year running.

I pulled out of the Scotland tour to New Zealand that summer. I just needed a break and a proper pre-season. It didn't go down well with Jim Telfer. Margot Wells didn't want me to go, and we both decided I should give it a miss. My back was playing up, as usual, so I used that as added justification, not that it cut much ice with Jim. But you have to listen to your body. The SRU wanted their pound of flesh, and your club wanted theirs as well. Sometimes you had to say no. It wasn't a bad tour to miss, either. The scorelines in the Tests read 69–20 and 48–14 – not to Scotland.

And during that summer I had come to a big decision. I was going to propose to Gabby. I wanted to ask her dad first, though, and I decided to do it when he and I went on a golfing holiday to their place in Spain. Gabby was busy at Euro 2000, so we went off down to the Costa del Sol. Robbie Mailer came along as well. I told Robbie on the plane over what I was planning to do.

Gabby's dad, Terry, is a wind-up merchant. The first time I went to Gabby's family home was about three months after I'd met her. We went to the wedding of a school friend of hers. I didn't know anyone, so I drank lots. At the end of the night, Gabby bundled me into the car and we went back to her parents' place. Terry plied me with more alcohol, and soon I was wondering out loud how nice it would be if we all went out in the garden naked. Gabby was just trying to shut me up; Christine, her mother, didn't know where to look; and Jordan, her brother, who was thirteen at the time, was confused. 'What's happened to Kenny?'

The next morning I woke up with that horrible feeling you get when you've drunk too much in the company of sober people. Yes, you're hung over, but there's also that question hovering over you, 'What did I do last night?'

Gabby was pretty offhand with me that morning, and when I went down to breakfast Christine barely looked at me. Something wasn't right. Then Terry came in and said, 'Kenny, can I have a word?'

Oh no, I had done something. The atmosphere in the house was screaming it. In the hallway Terry turned to me and he didn't look happy.

'I don't mind you getting drunk,' he said. 'What I don't like is you trying to get into bed with my wife naked. Are we clear?'

I was spluttering, 'I'm sorry, I'm sorry, I'm sorry.' This was even worse than I'd feared. I went through to apologise to Christine.

'OK,' she said, not amused. 'But don't let it happen again.'

There was no respite from Gabby, either. She was mortified at my behaviour. I spent the day with my tail between my legs. I was horrifically hung over as it was, but the extra shame had me feeling like a leper.

Terry and Christine were having a drinks party that afternoon, and as I came round the corner I overheard Terry talking to his mates. 'He actually thinks he got into bed with Christine last night!' And they all roared with laughter. I smacked him round the head. Now I knew what I was up against.

More than a year had passed when we went on our golf trip. Terry and I were good mates by then. He'd also met Robbie and got on well with him, and we were taking this holiday for a bit of boys' time.

I planned to ask Terry during our first round of golf, and Robbie subtly suggested that he walk round with a trolley while Terry and I took the buggy.

I was really nervous about asking him. I love him to bits, but when he smells fear he has no mercy. I was waiting for him to have a couple of decent holes before I broached the subject, and it was proving a long wait.

After ten holes, Robbie was badgering me. 'Have you asked him yet?'

'No. I'm just waiting for the right moment.'

'Jesus.'

Eighteen holes came and went, and I hadn't done it. So I decided to ask him at the restaurant that night. We went to De Medici, an Italian restaurant. The owner was a mad football fan.

'Ah! Meesta Yorath! Benvenuto! Meesta Yorath's here, everybody!'

Cue general uproar. While Terry was holding court, I agreed with Robbie that he would go off to the toilet when Terry sat down, and I would ask then.

So Robbie went off, and Terry and I were chatting away. I was just trying to get the right movement into the conversation, but it still wasn't happening. Robbie was soon signalling to me that he had nothing else to do in the toilets. When could he come back? I motioned to him to keep away.

Finally, I gathered all my will power and forced myself to say, 'Terry, I want to marry Gabby.'

He didn't flinch. 'Does she want to marry you?'

'What? Yeah. Well, I think so.'

'I don't know.'

'She does!'

'That's not the vibe I'm getting.'

Then Robbie burst in. He'd had enough of this.

'Look, have you asked him yet? Terry, what you have said?'

I explained to Robbie that Terry wasn't sure Gabby wanted to marry me. The debate went on, as did the drinking, and by the time we left the restaurant I couldn't work out whether he'd said yes or not.

Terry came in for breakfast the next morning and didn't say a word on the subject. This was becoming unbearable.

'I'm going to have to ask him again,' I said to Robbie. He agreed it was the only thing to do. I had no idea that Terry had let Robbie in on the wind-up and had told him to keep it going.

Eighteen holes of golf later and still I hadn't found the moment. It had been another bad round for Terry, but at the end of it he put his arm round me and said, 'It would be an honour to have you as my son-in-law.'

---

So, only one more person to ask now. And only one place to do it. It had to be up at the Wallace Monument, overlooking the farm. The problem with that was that we had another couple of weeks of Euro 2000 to get through, then Gabby and I were going on holiday to Majorca for a week.

I've never been so desperate for a major football tournament to finish. I spent a lot of time wandering the streets of Amsterdam, but I did at least pick up a nice diamond. Then it was off to Majorca, so that Gabby could unwind for a week, even if I couldn't.

Finally, I got her back up to Scotland. The old farmhouse where I'd grown up was being rebuilt because of subsidence, so we spent the morning making the final adjustments to the plans for the new house. Once I'd put that part of my youth to bed, it was time to think about the next step forward.

Gabby had never been up to the Wallace Monument before. 'You'll love it,' I told her. 'I hope.'

We climbed through the woods of Abbey Craig, where I used to play as a boy. Gabby was constantly suggesting we go off to explore down this route or that. 'Can we just get to the top?' I kept saying. If I didn't know any better, I'd say she was deliberately trying to wind me up. Like father, like daughter. She says she knew I was going to propose. No way. I was too subtle for that.

At the top of the hill, a group of Japanese girls were taking in the sight by the monument, and I was desperate for them to go off and leave us to it. When they finally left, I asked Gabby if she loved me. She said she did. So I asked her to marry me. She said she would.

We stayed up there for quite a while after that. Gabby couldn't stop crying. There may even have been a tear in my eye as well.

I'd come back home, and my girl had said yes. Rugby was no longer number one, and the world felt a better place for it.

———————

That autumn it was the usual routine. I wasn't picked in the Scotland squad for the November internationals, despite the fact that I'd scored more than a hundred and fifty points in the first ten games of the season for Wasps. I was brought back for the Samoa game, the third and final Test of the series. Despite my form for Wasps, they gave the kicking duties to Gregor, who had kicked in the previous two Tests, and that was fine by me. They said they wanted a higher work-rate from me, which meant they were still angry that I hadn't gone on tour with them in the summer, but the benefits of taking that summer off were kicking in. My back wasn't bothering me and there was a freshness to my approach. I gave them what they wanted, and I was back in for the start of the 2001 Six Nations.

It was my fiftieth cap, so I led the team out at the Stade de France. After all the times I had been dropped and reinstated and dropped again, I'd wondered if it was a milestone I would ever achieve. Certainly, I'd been far from sure less than a year earlier, when they dropped me on forty-eight caps after my kicking problems in the Six Nations. I wasn't convinced I would ever see a Scotland shirt again. That broke my heart, because playing for my country was everything to me.

Now, not only was I playing, they had also given me the kicking duties again. I was happy with that. It made sense. I was kicking better than I ever had for Wasps – my strike rate for that season was eighty-four per cent. Ian McGeechan kept pointing this out to the sceptics in the build-up to the game, as well as the fact that, despite the misses against Italy that had attracted so much attention the previous season, my strike rate for Scotland was actually higher than any other player's in the previous thirty years.

Geech was probably the only guy in the Scotland coaching set-up at that time I felt any connection with, but the goal-kicking had been blown up into a big issue, whether it was by the press, the perception of the public or any genuine failings on my part, and Geech looked as haunted by it as anyone else. He was quoting these statistics about my goal-kicking so as to back me, but it was also saying in public, 'Hey, he's really not as bad as you think he is,' which was meant well but didn't exactly add up to a ringing endorsement. I'd never felt as if I'd had the full support of the Scotland regime at any stage, certainly compared to the support I felt at Wasps, and when I ran out to receive the acknowledgement of the crowd on my fiftieth cap, I took it alone.

Another reason I was kicking was that Gregor wasn't comfortable doing it. The other option was our full-back, Chris Paterson, who would go on to break all records for consistency as a goal-kicker but at the time couldn't kick his own backside. Sometimes I wish he'd started kicking earlier. In fact, I blame him for the whole sorry affair. If he'd let us know that the best goal-kicker in the world was all the while hiding inside him, I might have been spared the lowest moments in my career. Twat. 'Mossy', as he's known, is actually president of our kicking club. The rule is that you have to have missed a kick from in front of the posts or scuffed one along the ground. We're all in there – Big Gav, Gregor,

Craig Chalmers, anyone who's anyone, but we're proudest of Mossy. He's a good lad, too.

After three minutes against France, Gregor was off, so Duncan Hodge came on. He's another in our kicking club. Hodgey was the only other guy in the squad who kicked regularly in those days. The game was going pretty well for us – we dominated the first half, and I kicked my first two penalties from an angle without any bother. The first brought up my two hundredth point for Scotland. I had a chance to kick a third, from the most acute angle of the lot. I struck it well, but it drifted just wide.

It was 6–6 at the break, but we were in charge. Nothing was said about the kicking question in the changing room. When we were awarded a penalty just after France took the lead with a try at the start of the second half, I stepped up to take it. Confusion reigned for a moment or two when one of the fitness guys brought out Duncan Hodge's kicking tee.

'This isn't my kicking tee,' I said.

He shrugged. 'They want Hodgey to take it.' Hodgey came over. He was as confused as I was. So was Andy Nicol, our captain.

'Why do they want me to kick it?' said Hodgey. I was bewildered; Hodgey was bewildered; Hodgey missed the kick.

Christophe Lamaison kicked a penalty at the end to make the final score 16–6 to France. We had missed a load of try-scoring chances and we were gutted. I was particularly unhappy about the way the kicking duties had been taken from me. Apparently, it was once again my nemesis, Jim Telfer, who'd been on my case. Director of rugby he may have been, but it never stopped him muscling in on team policy, even when Geech was coach. He was screaming from the box to have me removed after my miss in the first half. Jim had vowed in public after I'd been dropped the season before that I would never again take a kick for Scotland, so maybe he had a bee in his bonnet about that. Either way, his bee got out of control in the fortnight that followed.

I asked Geech afterwards why I'd been taken off the kicking, and he said I'd looked tentative.

'What the fuck does tentative mean?'

'Nervous.'

I reckoned he was the one looking tentative over all of this, and the chaos continued in the build-up to the next game against Wales. In between times, I went back to Wasps, where they know how to handle a goal-kicker, and I kicked two conversions and three penalties in the mud and rain at Kingsholm, and we beat Gloucester on their own patch, 28–3.

So I reported back to the Scotland camp in decent spirits, but Geech and Dougie Morgan, now the kicking coach, were not committing on who was going to kick against Wales. Gregor was ruled out, and Hodgey was an option as his replacement at fly-half. They told us to have a kicking competition every day for the week. I kept winning it, and even Hodgey was happy to admit that I was the form kicker, but by Wednesday there was still no news. I told Dougie and Geech that they needed to make up their minds. Whoever it was going to be needed to know. They said they hadn't decided yet, so I told them if they wanted me to do it, they had better decide by the end of the day, because after that I would refuse. Twenty minutes later they came and found me and said they wanted me to kick the goals.

They also said they wanted me to keep it a secret in the press conference the next day. I was at my wit's end. This was obviously a very clumsy way of trying to protect me from the pressure of the press. Well, a) how was it supposed to make me feel, knowing that they thought I needed protecting, and b) what possible benefit could there be from letting the press continue with their speculation over who would kick? And, boy, did they continue with it.

I played along and pretended at the press conference not to know who was kicking. All the coaches needed to do, though, was what Wasps would have done. They just needed to say at the start of the week that I was scoring freely for my club, I was the best kicker they had and that I would therefore be kicking for my country. Taking me off the kicking duties in the France game because of one kick from the touchline that narrowly missed was their mistake.

After all that, I wasn't in the best frame of mind when we arrived at Murrayfield on the day of the game, but that was nothing compared to my state of mind when someone showed me the programme. In it, one of the newspapers had taken out an advert featuring a picture of me kicking in front of a mocked-up set of goalposts. 'Kenny Logan: will he kick it?' ran the headline, and there were balls going off in every direction but through the posts.

This, I stress, was in the match-day programme as produced by the SRU. This was the SRU publishing a piss-take of the very man they expected to kick goals for them that day. 'Have you seen this, Kenny?' the boys kept saying to me. My reaction was borderline violent. 'Get these fucking books away from me!' All the humiliation of my schooldays came crowding in again. I was hot and agitated and felt as if the world were peering in on my failings – only now, they actually were.

Then one-time headmaster Jim Telfer came stalking the changing rooms.

'Hey, Logan, have you seen this?' he said, thrusting the advert in my face for the hundredth time. 'Make sure you kick better than that today!'

Winding up a rugby player is the best way to get him to perform on the pitch, but things are different for a goal-kicker. Goal-kicking is the only skill in rugby that is performed in absolute isolation. The rest of the team can do nothing for you. You are on your own. As a result, what works for the rest of the team, or even what works for you as a part of the team, is not necessarily what will work for you as a goal-kicker. Wasps understood this so well. As a player there, you constantly had people in your face, defying you, winding you up and challenging you. As a goal-kicker, you had a mentor listening to you, talking things through with you, boosting your confidence and putting an arm round you. No one in the Scotland regime seemed to understand the difference, not even Geech – or if he did, he never acted on it round then.

I was boiling over by the time I got on to the field. It was a crazy, windy day with tickertape and debris whipped in every direction round the stadium. In general play, it was one of the best games I had in a Scotland shirt. I thrived on the confrontation and anger. However, it'll be remembered for the kicks I missed. Anger is not good for a kicker.

Neil Jenkins made things even worse by kicking everything in sight. He was amazing in those conditions. By half-time I'd missed two, one an absolute sitter, and kicked two, but Jenks had kicked six for an 18–6 lead. Gabby had hightailed it up from London and arrived at half-time. She sat down next to Robbie.

'He's having a shocker,' he told her. 'I don't know if he's ever going to recover from this.'

The score became 25–6 just after the restart when Mark Taylor intercepted John Leslie's pass for the first try of the game. We couldn't believe it. We weren't playing badly, but we were staring at a nineteen-point deficit in front of our home crowd with less than half the game to go.

I was becoming more and more wound up, so that I was playing better and better but kicking worse and worse. I made a break and Mossy finished it off brilliantly for one of the tries of the season, and we were back in it at 25–13. I actually landed the conversion! Then I missed a penalty before managing to get my head together to kick my third out of six, but Jenks slotted another, so we were still twelve points behind with time running out. The game was frantic by now, and we were piling on the pressure, running at them from all angles.

With five minutes to go, Jim McLaren went over to make it 28–21, and I had a sitter of a conversion from in front to get us within range. I hooked it horrendously, and the crowd started booing me. My head had gone now. Emotionally, I was all over the shop.

Still we pressed on, and with two minutes to go, Tom Smith sprinted over like a centre. The conversion would draw us level, and Andy Nicol realised I was in no state to take it. He chucked the ball to Hodgey. I was glad. I just walked back into position. My mind was numb. My body was numb. I could still hear the booing. Hodgey slotted the kick for a 28–28 draw. It had been an amazing comeback, but if I'd kicked even half as well as Jenks, who walked off with twenty-three of Wales's points, we'd have won.

I felt completely alone, just as I had all week. I couldn't wait to see Gabby after the match; I couldn't wait to get back to Wasps, where I felt loved. The Scotland guys were great after the game, but the damage had already been done.

I remember sitting next to Tom Smith in the changing room afterwards. Tom, Gregor and I had come up together through the ranks with Scotland. He was never one to say much, but when he did it hit home all the harder.

'Nobody else wanted to take the kicks,' he said to me in that quiet way of his. 'You're the only one brave enough to do it.'

It summed him up, really. It wasn't his job to make me feel better, but as a friend and team-mate it came naturally to him anyway, and it was something for me to cling to when I thought I was drowning. He'd just saved the team with a piece of skill and pace that any of us in the three-quarters would have been proud of. He and Shawsy were the most skilful forwards I ever played with – you'd never think twice about passing to either of them in open play – but he was so humble. He was as embarrassed about scoring the match-saving try as I was that I had missed so many potentially match-winning kicks. He felt the scrums hadn't gone so well and preferred to blame himself for that.

I took my boots off and headed to the warm-up area out the back of the changing rooms. I sat down in the corner and wept. It's the only time I ever cried after a game. It was the lowest point of my rugby career.

Only one person could have come in then. Jim Telfer. I looked at him and I wanted to kill him.

'Unlucky,' he said. 'Happens to the best of us.'

And I thought, 'You fucking old bastard. Why couldn't you have been like that before the game? I wish you'd give me the bollocking now, not then.' If he'd been positive to me before-hand, there may not have been the need for the bollocking anyway. If he could have just reversed his psychology and said, 'You'll dominate today, Kenny, like you do for your club.' Just to have heard that from him before the game would have made a world of difference.

Soon the texts and phone calls were coming in – Craig Chalmers, Reesy, Gavin Hastings, all the guys who knew what it was like. Gav was a great friend to me then. 'Don't let them get to you,' he said. 'They did the same to me.' I don't know who he meant by 'they' – the SRU, the press, the public – but I knew it felt as if 'they' were everywhere.

Reesy told me I had a decision to make. Did I want to carry on kicking or not?

'I'm never kicking again,' was my initial reaction. Why would I? I'd never sought it out. It was only four years earlier that I'd even started doing it properly at my club. I'd been doing it for Scotland for just two years, and I was already their third highest points scorer of all time, so I can't have been that crap.

Soon Reesy had me thinking differently. I knew I was never going to kick for Scotland again but I still had points in me.

'You know what?' I said to him. 'I'm going to show them how good a kicker I can be. I'm going to win the Golden Boot in England.'

'Good man,' said Reesy. 'See you on Monday.'

And that's just what I did. I scored four hundred and seven points in twenty-six games for Wasps that season. We won all but one of our remaining fixtures and came second to Leicester in the Premiership. I scored nine tries and a hundred and thirty-two points in the seven matches remaining after Scotland dropped me. I felt they'd been wrong.

That night, though, Welshmen were singing in the streets of Edinburgh, 'There's only one Kenny Logan.' I didn't want to know what the Scots were singing.

It had started to rain, and Gabby was wearing open-toed shoes, so she jumped on my back and we set off up Princes Street for the hotel, passing a drunk who was wearing Scotland gear on the way.

'Oi, Logan, you're a disgrace!' he slurred.

'Just keep going,' Gabby said. 'Just keep going.'

I carried on, but I couldn't let it lie. 'No. No, I'm not.' I put her down and went back to have another rant at a fan.

'Say that to my face!' I said. 'Do you think I woke up today and decided I was going to miss those kicks? "I know what, I'll really piss off the entire nation today. And I'll make myself feel shit for the next fucking however many weeks, months or years." Don't ever say that to me until you've kicked for Scotland yourself.'

I lifted Gabby out of the puddle I'd left her in and we headed off again.

'Feel better now?' she asked.

'Yeah.'

I never kicked for Scotland again.

# 14

## First Dance

I didn't make the cut for the Lions tour to Australia in the summer of 2001. I was gutted. Actually, I think I'm more gutted thinking about it now than I was then. It was as if I was only semi-aware that there was a Lions tour. Normally, I'd be right up to speed with who was in the running and where I was in the pecking order, but this time it all passed me by. Until the plane left without me. Then it kicked in.

I realised it was almost certainly my last chance to play for the Lions. What made it harder to bear was the unknown role my goal-kicking had played. If I had been picked for the squad, I probably wouldn't have kicked anyway, but when the world is laughing at you as a kicker how can that not affect any assessment of you as a player?

The truth is, if you took out my kicking for Scotland – in fact, if you took out my kicking for Scotland just in the Wales game – I was playing as well for club and country as I ever had. But I chose to have the worst day of my life with the boot in front of Graham Henry, the Lions coach. He was Wales coach that day, so was probably very grateful for my kicking collapse, but he certainly wasn't going to be impressed by it.

How can you talk about these things without sounding bitter? Well, if a professional sportsman with any pride is being honest, he is bitter when he doesn't get picked for things he thinks he should have been picked for. I looked at the wingers Henry took on that tour. I'd played against all of them countless times in the Premiership, in Europe and at Test level, and there was nothing any of them had that I didn't, with the exception, maybe, of Jason Robinson, but even he was a wildcard selection, having only just converted from rugby league. England supplied three wingers and two full-backs to the party, but that was the best England team we'd ever seen. They were scoring tries for fun and would have cruised to a Grand Slam had it not been for the foot and mouth outbreak that disrupted that year's Six Nations. Who wouldn't look good on the end of that team?

I think I would have thrived on a Lions tour. I was a good tourist and I'd always been dangerous when given decent ball.

How great it would have been to have played in an environment like that. I thought I should have gone in 1997 and in 2001, but I would say that. It's also true that I seemed to be in my best form between Lions tours. If there had been tours in 1995, 1999 or even 2003, I would probably have gone. It just wasn't to be, and I'll always feel something is missing from my career. That's the only thing, really. A Grand Slam would have been nice, as well, I suppose. Winning the World Cup wouldn't have been bad, either, but that was never a serious possibility. Otherwise, I'm pretty happy with my stash.

———————————

Luckily, I had something even bigger than rugby lined up for that summer. Gabby and I were getting married, and it was to be at Logie Kirk, my local church back home, where Dad and Hamish are buried. I was so chuffed – all the strands coming together for what would be the best day of my life.

First, though, came the serious matter of my stag do. A three-day mystery tour on a bus round Scotland kicked off with a game of football in Stirling on the Friday afternoon. The only rule was that you had to have a beer in your hand or you couldn't play. If you finished it, you had to run to get another. The game went on for about two-and-a-half hours. Scotland (my Scottish mates) were losing to England (my English acquaintances) 7–1. The call went up for last goal wins when I saw in the distance a man in black approaching, and I thought, 'Ah, my secret weapon.' It was Ally McCoist.

He took to the field, and the game went on for another half-hour or so in a stalemate (it was roughly fifteen on each side). Then the ball comes over, Coisty takes it on his chest, controls it with one knee and volleys it with his other foot into the top corner. He threw his arms in the air, shouting, 'Yes! The greatest moment of my life! The Castle on one side, the Monument on the other, a beer in my hand and the winner against England!'

That was the start of a brilliant three days – Robbie, my best man, pulled out all the stops – but it nearly came at a severe cost. That Friday night we went out in Stirling. Some of the party came back to stay with me at my mum's house, the rest went to stay in a hotel. One of the boys brought a girl back to the farm – there were about ten of us crashing there, bodies strewn all over the place. I crashed in a room with Robbie, and this girl came in. 'Oh, it's Kenny Logan!' she said, and ripped my covers off. I told her where to go, but she came back with her friend and jumped on me. I lashed out with my leg and again told her where to go. So she left with her friend, but as she went out she said to Coisty, who was sleeping in the living room, 'I'm selling my story to the papers.'

'On you go then,' he said.

I thought nothing of it, but a few days later I was tipped off that some girl was trying to sell her story about me to the *Sun*. Apparently they were planning to run it the day before the wedding.

I was straight on to my agent, who put me on to his PR man. I told him everything, and he told me this girl had signed an affidavit saying she'd had sex with me. I was stunned. And terrified. I told Gabby, and she hit the roof. As if we hadn't got enough on our plate with our wedding round the corner.

'You're sure nothing happened?'

'Nothing! It was at Mum's house! Mum was next door! She could hear me tell the girl to fuck off! My mum is a witness!'

'We can't get married with this hanging over us, Kenny!'

That left me with about three weeks to sort it out.

Next, I heard there were pictures. I just couldn't understand it, and you do start to worry and to question yourself. I think when you're innocent you believe you're guilty and when you're guilty you believe you're innocent. You start racking your brains for any grounds she might have had for going down this road, for anything she might have on you. Robbie was in the room with me that night. He said the only thing that could have got me into trouble was the way I'd kicked out at her. If I'd connected, she might have been knocked out. But I hadn't connected.

So the PR guy told the girl to produce the pictures and very quickly their story went from naked photos to no photos to we kissed to we didn't kiss to he groped me on the dance floor. Gabby really knew she was lying then – as if I'd have been anywhere near the dance floor. Finally, the whole thing disappeared. I'd lost nearly a stone through the stress.

---

At least I was looking trim for the big day. I knew things were going my way when I got a hole in one on the fifth at Loch Lomond Golf Club two days before. I hit a beauty heading straight for the green. It landed out of sight, and when we couldn't see it on the green we thought it must have rolled off.

'Not as good a shot as you thought,' said Robbie. Then I casually looked in the hole. 'There's a ball here, lads!'

Terry moved in like a shot. 'Step away from the hole!' He looked in and there it was – my Famous Grouse ball, which is now framed at home.

The next day we had a tea party at Gleneagles, followed by a barbecue at Hendy's house. Everyone was assembling, and there was a lot of banter about kilts. I was going to be wearing Logan tartan, and, yes, Gabby married a man wi' nae pants on, as is decreed by ancient lore. Robbie wore a kilt, too, and so did my ushers – my brother James, cousin Ally, Hendy, Gavin Carlin, Gareth Flockhart, Big Gav, Kingy and Shawsy – but I think only the Scots wore them properly, not that anyone was checking. A few of the other boys wore them – Scrivs, Jonny Ufton, Dallaglio. Lol was on crutches after the knee injury that had ended his Lions tour early, and he was telling everybody about the cool Paul Smith lounge suit he'd bought for the occasion.

'Sounds great, Lol,' said Kingy, 'but you'll not look so cool when everyone else is in black tie.'

'What?'

We managed to find him a kilt instead.

Jaguar had lent us a fleet of cars for the day. Gabby turned up in a cream SS Airline Saloon, and I drove the first ever green E-Type. Two hundred and fifty people came to Logie Kirk. It was too many, really, for such a tiny church, but the service was beautiful. We had a gospel choir, and most of our relatives were in tears – my mum, my brother Andrew, Gabby's dad, Gabby's sister Louise, Gabby, me. Both families had lost people who would otherwise have been there – Gabby's younger brother, Daniel, had died suddenly of an undiagnosed heart condition at the age of fifteen, nine years earlier. That morning I had spent a few moments at the graves of Dad and Hamish. I was probably more emotional about Hamish not being there. If Dad had been alive, he would have been well into his eighties, but, like Daniel, Hamish should have been there.

Gabby arrived – slightly late – and as I looked round I wondered what I'd done to deserve her. She looked amazing, as always, but looks only go so far. She's intelligent, caring, passionate, hard-working and we share so many interests, not least, sport. When she came to watch me play, it wasn't just because she wanted to watch her man, she was genuinely interested in the game. I don't ever have to feel guilty about watching sport on TV, because Gabby's either watching it already or she's presenting it. It's as if I sat down, dreamt up the perfect woman and, hey presto, there she was, walking down the aisle towards me in a stunning ivory dress.

Most of all, though, we're best mates. From the word go, it was as if we'd known each other for years. The boys loved it when Gabby came out for a drink. She'd just naturally fit in. I didn't have to worry about leaving her talking to any of them. She had them eating out of her hand. They were charmed. 'Is she blind or something?' they would say to me. 'What's she doing with you?' Dunno. She just is. And here was proof.

Outside the church a couple of hundred members of the public had gathered, including some sweet old ladies who were saying, 'Och, he's done really well!' The media were there and were great. We chose not to sell the rights to the wedding, although *Hello!* made their usual offer, and the photographers were very respectful of the occasion. None of them tried to follow us to the reception at Gleneagles.

After Gabby and I had stopped in the Ochil Hills for photographs, we joined the guests at the hotel for drinks on the lawn and things went with a swing. I got my speech out of the way early. Gabby constantly interrupted me throughout it. Start as you mean to go on . . . Later, Terry made a beautiful speech – he's a very emotional guy – and Robbie brought the house down with his.

Then after fireworks on the lawn came the part of the day I had been dreading most – the first dance. And it literally was our first dance – she'd never got me on to a dance floor before. My avoidance strategies for dancing were as developed as those for reading and writing. I was terrified of this first dance, and the boys knew it. Huge rugby players elbowed their way past the old folk to stand on the edge of the dance floor, arms folded, waiting to be entertained. The gospel choir from the church had turned into a twenty-strong soul band. Gabby had chosen 'As' for our first dance, but they started playing 'Lovely Day'. Gabby thought it was some kind of intro, so she just stood there waiting for them to break into 'As'. They could have broken into 'Humpty Dumpty' and I wouldn't have known any better.

'Why aren't we moving, Gabs?' I whispered to her. 'Let's just get this over and done with.'

For the next couple of minutes I hopped from one foot to the other as if I had a stone in each shoe. I would stand still only to lift my hand up and let Gabby do a couple of twirls under it. The minute we were finished I headed straight to the bar. Later, Shawsy grabbed the microphone, and this 6ft 8in white guy spent the rest of the night singing with this amazing choir of black singers. To be fair, he didn't sound too out of place, even if he might have looked it.

And so the best day of my life went on until the staff politely asked me in the small hours if I could help them remove one of my guests from the front steps of the hotel. Kevin McKenzie was sprawled out asleep with a beer in his hand and the contents of his kilt dangling over one of the steps. It was time to call it a day.

***

Gabby and I went on honeymoon to the French West Indies and then to a retreat in Vermont. It was beautiful, even if I was having to train every day. Wasps were in the middle of pre-season, and after our exploits at the end of the season before, when we came through to finish second, we reckoned we were ready to take the Premiership by storm. All the more so, when Craig Dowd, the mighty All Black prop, arrived at the club.

Unfortunately, it didn't turn out that way, or anything like it. We had a shocking season. At least, we had a shocking first half of the season, which was becoming a habit. We won three of our first eleven Premiership games, lost four of our six Heineken Cup pool games and were knocked out of the Powergen Cup in the first round. In December we were four points adrift at the bottom of the table. Relegation was staring us in the face if we didn't get our act together.

Then, as was becoming just as much of a habit, we blitzed the second half of the season. Eight wins followed in the next eleven Premiership games, but it was only good enough to get us up to seventh place, and for the first time we were looking at playing in the European Challenge Cup the next season. The Challenge Cup was the Heineken Cup's little sister, rugby's equivalent of the Uefa Cup.

It may have been a flop on the field, but that 2001–02 season at Wasps will be remembered for the changes in the coaching panel, with Shaun Edwards and Warren Gatland joining the club and setting up a new regime. It would mark a change in culture and finally push Wasps up the last rung of the ladder, turning us from an excellent trophy-winning outfit into the side that would topple Leicester as the standard-bearers of English rugby.

A look at our results suggests that the influence of the new regime had an immediate effect, but it wasn't as simple as that. We spent the first half of that season battling an injury crisis. Lawrence missed the first eight months of the season, recovering from the knee injury he'd picked up on the Lions tour. By the time he'd returned at the end of March our revival was under way. Meanwhile, Nigel had been as busy trying to find us a new home for the following season as he had been working on our rugby. Fulham Football Club were moving into Loftus Road, while their Craven Cottage ground was renovated, which meant we had to move out. We all suffered with the uncertainty.

What Gats and Shaun brought was that hard edge we hadn't had previously. Nigel had laid the foundations – most of the people who formed the bedrock of the squad that was about to dominate the English game were signed by him. Gats and Shaun came in and raised the bar again.

It wasn't all sweetness and light. When Shaun first arrived we all thought he was a nutter. Ask me now and I'll tell you he is the most enthusiastic guy I've ever known, but at the time he was a nightmare. He just wanted to do everything, including play. He was constantly stepping into our training sessions to take part, and it used to wind us up.

Part of the problem was how brilliant he was. He had a bad leg and couldn't run properly any more, which didn't help his credibility when he joined in, but his skills were breathtaking. He could send out a grubber kick and say, 'Jump,' and it would bounce up on cue, and he could vary the point at which it did that. His passing skills were amazing too. It didn't do a lot for the players' self-esteem, having this guy showing us how to do it. The way he would muscle in on our routines made us wonder who was coaching and who was playing.

Reesy started to take offence at the way Shaun was taking over. He was now meant to be backs coach, but we would all go in at the end of one of his sessions, and the next minute he would look up and Shaun had got us back out again to do another. The camp started to split, which didn't help results on the field. I was obviously on Reesy's side, since we had become so close and he had been such a rock to me as a kicking coach. Shaun rubbed him up the wrong way. Team meetings were called – we had to get rid of this guy.

In the end they got rid of Reesy that November, along with the forwards coach, John Lambden. We felt terrible, because we were letting Reesy down on the pitch, and it was a personal blow to me.

Then Shaun changed very suddenly. It was easy to forget that not only was this his first job in coaching, it was his first job in rugby union. What we hadn't seen was the amount of video-watching he'd been doing. He doesn't do things by half, and that enthusiasm of his stretched to watching hours and hours of union, so as to get up to speed, which he did very quickly. His overbearing approach at the start was probably just his way of making a mark in a new environment. Almost overnight he took a step back and started giving us a bit more space. He started listening to us – Kingy and Rob Howley had his ear, so did Fraser Waters, who was becoming another senior figure. How that bloke didn't play more times for England I'll never know. For years Fraser was the best centre in the Premiership. He was also phenomenally posh. Not many people know that he was expelled from Harrow School for streaking at Lord's and knocking the bails off with his todger.

Anyway, we soon started to buy into Shaun's approach. He

had us doing endless drills on the simplest skills. For example, he wanted us to score tries with a minimum of fuss. Get it down as soon as you cross the line. No showboating. Once Fraser pushed his luck when scoring a try, getting it down just before he reached the dead-ball line, and Shaun went for him afterwards. Fraser had to do extra sessions working on his touchdowns, literally putting the ball down over the line about a hundred times. 'Good try, Fraser. Now, pick the ball up and score another one.'

The following season, Shaun's little brother was killed in a car crash. It rocked the club – Billy-Joe was an up-and-coming league player and had trained with us in pre-season. His death had an enormous impact on Shaun and he changed again after that. It brought us even closer to him.

I would go so far as to say he was the best coach I ever had. For me, he was fantastic. The video-watching extended to him studying my next opponent so that he could tell me his strengths and weaknesses. 'Eh, Kenny,' he used to say in his broad northern accent. 'Come out here. You've got Marcel Garvey this weekend. I've been watching him. He doesn't like it when you cut inside and fend. So I want you to do that all day.' There and then he would get me cutting inside and fending against no one over and over again. To a normal person it would have looked ridiculous. He even briefed me about my opponents in up-coming Six Nations matches – nothing to do with Wasps. He did more than anyone to get me through the last years of my career. Even when I left Wasps altogether and went to Glasgow, he kept on helping me.

Halfway through that 2001–02 season Nigel was feeling the pressure, as we were bouncing along at the bottom of the table. That was when he went out and signed Warren Gatland as forwards coach. Gats came up to sample a Wasps game for the first time when we travelled to play Newcastle in January. If we'd lost, the feeling at the club was that Nigel would have been sacked. Martin Offiah scored in the corner with the last play, and I had a conversion from the touchline to win it on a windy day.

Apparently, Gats shook his head and said to Nigel, 'It's a tough kick.'

'He'll get it,' said Nigel. 'It's the ones in front of the posts you need to worry about.'

Nigel kept his job for another week.

But by March he had gone. Again, it was a personal blow to me. Nigel had been a key figure in helping me to settle in London. When I came clean to him early on about my dyslexia problems, it had elevated him into a tiny circle of people who knew about it. I think Nigel was ready to leave, though. He had recruited Gats, and you don't recruit someone like that just to fill a role as assistant coach. He was paving the way for his own departure.

It was the right time for Nigel to go. We'd come as far as we could under him. It's hard for a side to improve when you have the same boss saying the same things to the same people. When Gats succeeded Nigel as director of rugby, it changed all that at a stroke. I wouldn't say Gats was the best coach in the world, but he was very good at getting a team to play in a certain way and to do it consistently. He kept everything very simple and he could switch between good cop and bad cop at will, which he used to do very cleverly.

Mainly it was bad cop in the early days. He reckoned we were nowhere near fit enough, and he put us through the wringer, even though it was midseason. I couldn't do any training with Margot, I was so knackered. The following pre-season, he brought in Craig White as fitness coach, and that really turned things round. He brought the ice baths with him, and he took us out to Poland to train at a cryotherapy unit. It was all state of the art. Craig was the most sophisticated fitness coach we'd had. He was a Margot for the whole club. He personalised training regimes for each of us, and he understood the value of rest. Before Margot, all the fitness coaches I came across had one simple solution to any problem – get in the gym. They were continually suspicious that you were trying to get out of a gym session. 'No, I've got a bad back,' I wanted to say, 'and, what's more, you're the reason I've got it.'

Craig, like Margot, was too clever for that and soon we were the fittest side in the country. I'm ashamed to say that it was when Craig arrived that I finished with Margot, and it did feel as if I was splitting up with a girlfriend. It was the hardest thing in the world. Fitness at Wasps was so good now, and Gats had warned us that he didn't want anyone training outside the club. She understood.

Wasps were about to move to the next level in their journey. The second half of the 2001–02 season was the limber-up to that high point, even if, results-wise, it did nothing more than steer us clear of relegation. The 2002–03 season was when we made the breakthrough. And it was when I made a breakthrough, too, that would not only improve me as a player but as a person.

# 15

## Double Vision

Gabby had never let the issue of my dyslexia lie. She doesn't believe in letting things fester and she doesn't believe in not facing up to challenges, but this was awkward because she knew it was the one thing in the world that truly upset me. My response to her promptings was always aggressive and defensive. She couldn't understand why I wouldn't face up to this. I'd played rugby for my country, and my profession required me to face challenges constantly just to survive in it. If my tackling wasn't up to scratch, say, I would work relentlessly at it. How many times had I been dropped, only to come back and prove people wrong? So why could I not take on this challenge?

I had no answer, other than to point to the little boy still inside me. He was too scared – too scared to reveal himself and too scared to go back to the classroom, the place that had arrested his development in the first place. He didn't want people to think he was thick.

Gabby could see what this attitude was doing to me. My secret had become a dark, festering sore, and my insistence on hiding it rather than facing up to it was affecting me deeply. I was constantly worrying about being exposed, and because I was having to compensate for it by, for example, talking a lot more than was normal and running from certain situations, I could never achieve the balance that would enable me to handle the world on my own terms. It was like a rugby player who was nervous about his dodgy back – attempts to compensate for it led to problems elsewhere. Then there was the question of what it could mean for the rest of my life. Now that we were married, the rest of my life meant the rest of Gabby's as well. So she kept working away at me.

She had seen a Trevor McDonald programme about a new treatment for dyslexia, and she'd recorded it. As usual, I refused to watch it, but I knew she was right, and I knew if she'd had my condition she would have overcome it by now. I look up to my wife and trust her. My stubbornness was wavering.

One night I put the tape into the video and watched the programme. On my own in front of the television, I found myself starting to come round to the idea. The treatment described involved no books. It was based on physical exercises. Well, I could do that, all right. Maybe . . .

Gabby later asked me if I'd watched the programme.

'Yeah.'

'Well? What do you think?'

I shrugged. 'Phone up and get me an appointment.'

'You should do it.'

'No, you do it.'

'OK. I will.'

'Good.'

She went for the phone and I called after her. 'Don't tell them it's for me, though.'

'As if they're going to know who you are.'

'No, don't. They might think I'm stupid.'

That's how I found myself in a pretty basic church hall in Chelsea, the sort of place you'd find a children's playgroup, which was quite appropriate since the other people enrolling were children. I hoped they might think I was a parent or something. I did the tests and the people in charge confirmed that the programme could help me. One of the tests tracked my eyes as I tried to follow text on a page. Usually, your eyes follow smooth lines, but mine were all over the place, jumping here and there, moving at different speeds. There was no focus to my efforts. I knew my concentration was appalling, which they confirmed with bells on, but this business about my eyes I hadn't realised. It made so much sense when it was pointed out.

I signed up to take the programme, which was called Dyslexia,

Dyspraxia and Attention Deficit Treatment (DDAT), in autumn 2002. It was pretty straightforward stuff, about ten minutes twice a day of simple exercises in balance and coordination using Swiss balls, wobble boards and bean bags. The exercises were not anything special, but taken together, they are designed to stimulate a particular area of your body, the cerebellum. It's like the gearbox of your brain, and if it's working efficiently, your brain's processing powers are dramatically improved, which has repercussions for all sorts of different areas. I was doing the course for my reading and writing, but it also had a major impact on my rugby and my relationships with people.

Nothing much happened to begin with, but after about four weeks of the programme I started to feel a bit strange, as if something wasn't quite right. I went very quiet, which was definitely not right. In training I couldn't catch the ball. It came to a head in a Powergen Cup game against Bath, a few days before Christmas 2002, about six weeks after I'd started the programme.

Wasps had left Loftus Road and this was our first season at Adams Park in High Wycombe. The game was broadcast live on the BBC, which was unfortunate, because we were awful. We gifted Bath two tries and we were all dropping the ball. I don't know what everyone else's excuse was, but I was starting to think this treatment I was taking, far from resolving my reading and writing problems, was in serious danger of costing me my job. At one point in the game, I was running down the touchline with the ball and suddenly I just ran into touch. Inexplicably. The place went quiet. On the TV, the commentators were wondering out loud what I was doing. Gats was staring at me in an intimidating way, and I stood with the ball under my arm, staring at the line I'd just crossed for no reason. Whoa! What had just happened?

We mounted a late comeback but lost 20–17, so we were out of the cup and, although we were in touch with the new play-offs that were going to decide the Premiership champions for the first time, we were proving inconsistent in the league. Gats was furious with us, telling us that we thought we were better than we were when actually we were fly-by-nights who learnt to do something properly then got bored with it and moved on to something else. He accused us of thinking too much outside the box when we'd be better off if we concentrated on doing what we knew.

His words cut particularly deeply with me. He didn't know I was taking this programme, but I felt as if he was talking directly to me. Later, he did talk directly to me, and it wasn't nice.

'Kenny, that's the worst I've ever seen a winger play,' he said. 'What's wrong with you?' I had no answer. 'You better sort it out, because if you don't it's bye-bye.'

I was on the phone immediately to the DDAT people. 'I've got to stop. This treatment is messing me up. I'm going to get sacked.' They were adamant I had to carry on. This disorientation I was suffering apparently meant my take-up had been excellent. My spatial awareness was going to suffer in the short term, but it was a good sign. The theory goes that when you do the exercises it starts to stimulate your neurological pathways and, basically, they have a little fight as they try to work out which way they're going. I was in this stage of confusion.

It continued over Christmas, and Gabby was convinced I was

depressed. She was right. I glazed over and became very quiet. I was 'glaikit', as we say in Scotland. What's more, I couldn't be bothered to do anything about it. Gabby and I went to a New Year's Eve party, and I just didn't contribute. I sat in a corner all night.

I took to wearing gloves in training because I knew I had to do something about not being able to catch the ball. Then it all changed. It was exactly as if someone flicked a switch in my head. Suddenly I could see things on the field. I'd always thought I had good peripheral vision. I didn't. I'd been suffering from tunnel vision all my life. Suddenly I knew what having peripheral vision felt like, and a new world opened up.

I started communicating properly with Kingy and the others on the field. Information was starting to stick in my head. I was remembering moves all of a sudden, which was a massive transformation. All my rugby career, I'd been like a stuck record. 'What's the call? What's the call? What's the call?' I used to run around the pitch saying it over and over again. I must have been so annoying. The boys used to take the piss out of me constantly for it. Now suddenly it stopped.

And I was catching everything in training, off my toes, one-handed. I remember Shaun Edwards shouting at me, 'Eh, Kenny, ever since you put them gloves on, ye're like fookin Soopaman!'

For a while I thought it might be the gloves, so I wore them to training every day, but when I forgot them one time, it made no difference. Craig White and Mark Bitcon, our conditioning coach, sat me down and asked me what I was doing differently.

'What do you mean?'

'Well, you're a different person.'

'I'm fine, honestly.'

'You're sure you're not taking anything stupid?'

But the thing was, I *was* a different person. I was thirty years old and I'd played nearly sixty times for my country, yet I'd never been on a senior players' committee. That changed very quickly – with Wasps and Scotland. Ian McGeechan was stunned at how I'd changed – Gregor, too. My friendship with Gregor, in particular, took off after that. We'd played together for years but we'd never really understood each other till then. He, more than anyone, noticed differences in me. I had mellowed a bit and become wiser, or at least less headless. As a result, I was more on his wavelength, able to anticipate where his next pass might be coming from. Gregor had vision on a rugby field like no one else, which sometimes got him into trouble, because no one else could see what he was trying to do. Suddenly, I felt as if I could see some of it, and it did great things for my game. Since the 2001 Six Nations, I'd had one start for Scotland, so patchy had been my form and so dodgy my ageing body, but I was back in for the 2003 championship and I played fourteen times that year.

And my kicking felt totally different. I'd handed over the duties to Kingy by then, but I still took the long ones and I was hitting the ball better than ever. I'd known I was not a pedigree goal-kicker when Jonny Wilkinson once said that every kick should feel the same. 'Shit,' I thought, 'not one of my kicks feels the same.' Now, though, I knew what he meant. One of Jonny's exercises, which we adopted at Wasps, was to kick at the goalpost from the corner flag, so that you are perfectly side on to the goal. If you get within a couple of feet of the post, it's a good kick. I hit the post once, and Kingy challenged me to do it again. I hit it three times in a row. The tragedy in the context of my career till then was that I was even hitting the ones in front of the posts without any bother. It all felt different. Those missed kicks that had blighted my international career – I would never have missed them feeling like this.

Since that Bath game before Christmas, I'd been dropped to the bench, but I was back in for our home-and-away double-header against Stade Francais in the European Challenge Cup. I played a blinder in both, kicking three penalties from long range, two from inside our half, scored a try, set up another couple. Twice we beat the team that were about to become French champions. We were starting to motor again.

And it was around then – at the age of thirty – that I finally learnt my vowels. It is no exaggeration to say that I consider it an achievement to rank with any in my rugby career. The sense of pride was overwhelming. When I looked at words, they no longer leapt about in front of me. They started to sit more neatly on the page, and I didn't panic when I saw them. The people at the programme told me it was because of the effect the exercises were having on my cerebellum. I'll take their word for it. All I know is that everything written on a page seemed to calm down all of a sudden.

The next time I went on holiday with Gabby, I read Paul Gascoigne's autobiography from start to finish. Thoughout it, I kept turning to Gabby to ask her if she knew such and such a fact about Gazza's life. I think it was my way of confirming for myself that I had taken in what I'd just read.

It felt as if I was being admitted into normal society at last. I'm never going to be a speed-reader and I'm not going to challenge the output of Shakespeare, but to be able to fill in forms on my own and to be able to read a newspaper article over a cup of tea, rather than to work long into the night on it with a marker pen and a sore head, these are pleasures I never thought I'd enjoy. Never again did I hide in the toilet when I saw pens and paper laid out for us in the team room. I went around the place looking for opportunities to read and write, to show off my new skills, not to anyone else, just to myself.

Perhaps the most important thing it did for me was to make me feel comfortable talking about my problems and the years of shame I'd secretly suffered. To speak about your failures and your weaknesses makes you feel better. The little boy who had cowered inside me was able to come out and announce himself. In so doing, he was able to grow up at last. Now I have no problem admitting I can't read something. I'll ask for help, and I'll learn. I'll quite happily ask Gabby how to spell a word, and, what's more, there'll be a decent chance of me remembering it the next day. What the programme did was to fill all the holes in my bucket. Now I am in a position to learn, and I am adding a little more to my bucket everyday.

When I left Wasps a year later, I came out about my dyslexia. I was bombarded with phone calls from team-mates and friends. 'Is that why we always had to pay the bills?' said Kingy and Scrasey, my two flatmates in the Logan Lounge. 'Is that why

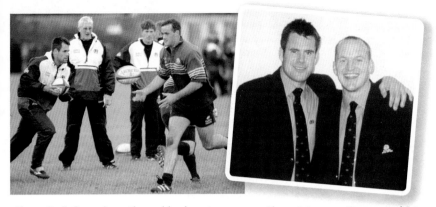

*Above*: Back from the strike and back trying to impress Jim Telfer.

*Above*: My mate Gregor and I in our 1999 World Cup blazers.

*Inset*: Kicking for goal in the big game against the Springboks. We were leading at half-time but went on to lose 46–29.

*Above*: Facing the Haka in orange socks – our orange shirts hidden by our tracksuits.

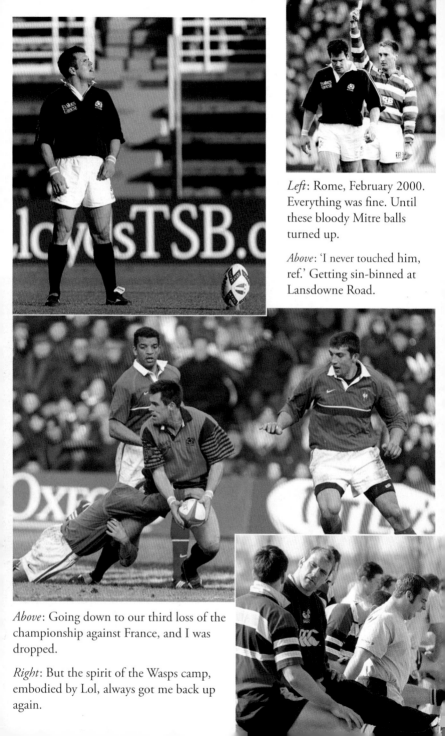

*Left*: Rome, February 2000. Everything was fine. Until these bloody Mitre balls turned up.

*Above*: 'I never touched him, ref.' Getting sin-binned at Lansdowne Road.

*Above*: Going down to our third loss of the championship against France, and I was dropped.

*Right*: But the spirit of the Wasps camp, embodied by Lol, always got me back up again.

*Above*: Back to winning ways in the Tetley's Bitter Cup final against Northampton in May.

*Right*: From the moment I met Gabby I knew my life had changed. I would ask her to marry me that summer.

*Above*: 2001 Six Nations against Wales. Anger is not good for a kicker.

*Right*: My mind was numb. My body was numb. I never kicked for Scotland again.

*Left*: The best day of my life.

*Below*: The new-found joys of reading. Gabby was the one who forced me to face up to my dyslexia and she gave me the confidence to do so.

*Below*: My best man and ushers: Robbie Mailer, James Logan, Jordan Yorath, Gavin Carlin, Simon Shaw, John Henderson, Alex King, Gareth Flockhart, Gavin Hastings, Ally Logan.

*Top left*: After starting treatment for my dyslexia I was all over the place against Bath in December 2002.

*Top Right*: But soon, Shaun Edwards would be calling me 'Soopaman'! Making a break against Gloucester in the Premiership final.

*Right*: We smashed them, 39–3, to be crowned champions of England.

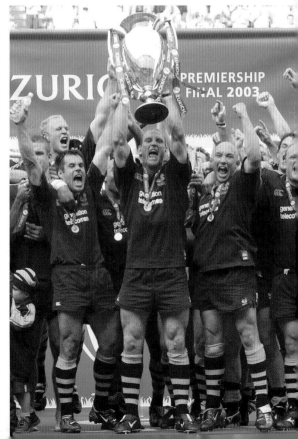

*Above*: I was back in favour with Scotland for the 2003 Six Nations, scoring a try against Italy…

*Above*: …and being awarded Man of the Match. I saw a chance to announce my retirement and I took it.

*Above*: There was only one place to end my Scotland career. Playing Australia in Brisbane in the quarter-final of the 2003 World Cup.

*Right*: Brush and I were inconsolable. Playing for my country meant the world to me.

*Right*: I told Gabby there was absolutely no way I was doing *Strictly Come Dancing*.

*Below left*: Getting kitted out by Bill, the dresser.

*Below centre*: I saw the panic in Ola's eyes as it dawned on her what she was taking on.

*Below right*: But it ended up being the time of my life.

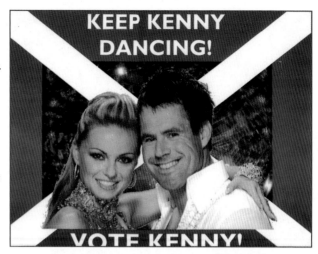

*Above*: A pack of All Blacks couldn't have stopped me from joining 'Strictly Come Dancing: The Live Tour!' – a riot from start to finish.

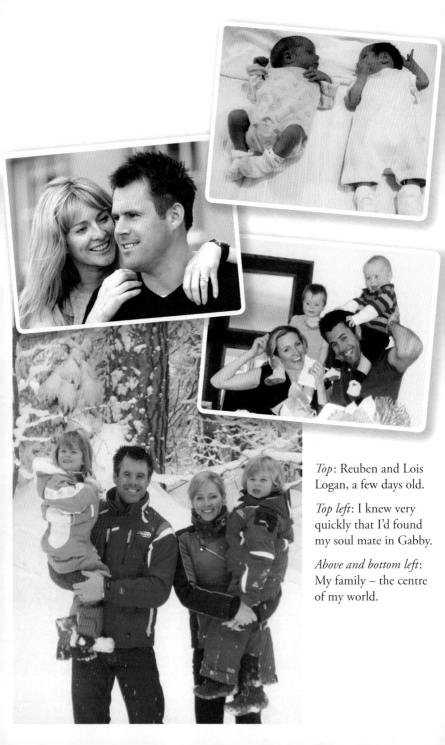

*Top*: Reuben and Lois Logan, a few days old.

*Top left*: I knew very quickly that I'd found my soul mate in Gabby.

*Above and bottom left*: My family – the centre of my world.

you never used to do this? Is that why you used to make me do that?' And the one thing so many of my friends said independently of each other was, 'Why didn't you just say something, you twat?'

I'll never really be able to answer that. It's not something that can be rationally argued. It was a deep-rooted, gut instinct that I just couldn't overcome. The thing about learning to read and write is not so much what it did for me on a practical level – it's more about how it enabled me to overcome the shame. To feel a better person basically. It came too late to do much more for me as a rugby player than give me an Indian summer at the end of my career, when I played some of my best rugby. But I know the second part of my life is going to be so much more manageable and enjoyable than the first part. I've never felt so balanced and so happy as I do now. It is making me a better husband and a better father, which is what matters to me from here on in.

———

And it was making me a better player. Wasps was the place to be in the second half of that 2002–03 season. Those two wins over Stade Francais signalled the start of us going into overdrive, and proved how well Gats, Shaun and Craig were managing our season. The idea of Wasps storming the second half of the season was not new, but usually it was because we all seemed to be injured in the first half. This time there was something more controlled about it. Shaun had always been big on this point. You don't win trophies at the start of a season. True, you can play so badly that it costs you your chance of winning anything, but if you're not playing well come the end, you don't have any chance.

From this season, that was even more the case because the authorities had decided that the champions would not necessarily be the team that finished at the top of the league. The championship would be decided by a play-off. This was controversial because some people thought that consistency throughout the season should be rewarded more than the ability to win a couple of knock-out games at the end of it. On the other hand, champions are supposed to be able to handle the pressure of a big occasion, and with so many squads giving up so many players to the internationals over the course of a season the side that finishes top of the league may well not be the best in the country. For example, we often had more than ten players away with their countries for long stretches. With a handicap like that, how could anyone say that the team who finished top were without question better than us? They weren't, as we went on to prove.

That year, Gloucester finished top. They'd beaten us at Kingsholm in a tight, ugly match at the start of January. After that, we won fourteen of our remaining fifteen matches, finishing second in the league, which meant a play-off against the third-placed team, Northampton, to see who would play Gloucester for the title.

We beat Northampton, and the next week it was the European Challenge Cup final. We had defeated Pontypridd home and away in the semis to set up a final with Bath at the Madejski Stadium in Reading. We smashed them, 48–30.

The most memorable thing about that game was the way Lawrence wound up the Bath boys. He was brilliant at it. At one point he said to Steve Borthwick, 'You know your problem, Borthers? You train like Tarzan, but you play like Jane.' Lol kept at them all afternoon and eventually Danny Grewcock flipped and rained punches on him at the bottom of a ruck. He was going off for that, and everyone knew it, including him.

Then it was the Premiership final against Gloucester. They'd won the league by a mile, but we didn't care. If anyone had read the rules at the start of the season, they would have known that winning the league did nothing other than get you to Twickenham. We smashed them as well, 39–3, to be crowned champions of England.

God, there was a lot of moaning. They're still bitching about it today in the West Country, which is precisely why they didn't deserve to be champions. They thought they were the moral victors before they'd even taken to the pitch, but they were kidding themselves. They'd played some fantastic rugby that season, nearly all in the first half. But to quote Shaun once more, you don't win anything in the first half of a season. Since Christmas we'd been the best side in England. As far as we were concerned, we were the best side in Europe as well. That year Toulouse beat Perpignan in a poor Heineken Cup final, but the champions of France were Stade Francais, and we'd beaten them twice on the way to winning the European Challenge Cup.

We made no apologies for being champions and headed to the Orange Tree in Richmond for the mother of all piss-ups. We were a group of guys who had been together for a long time by this stage. There had been the odd addition and the odd departure – Rob Howley and Craig Dowd had arrived and played massively important parts – but we were basically the same bunch of boys who had won the league six years earlier and then taken a wee while to grow up in the years that followed, partying a bit too much and picking up just the odd cup here and there.

We still partied in 2003, but only when we won. Gats liked a bevy. I remember him nodding off at the back of a team meeting after one too many, but it meant he was happy to be one of the boys after a good win, and that only helped the team spirit. Shaun didn't hold back, either. Champagne was his tipple.

That season was the start of a new era. I was getting on and had just one more season at Wasps, but I'm proud to have been part of the beginning of the Wasps dynasty that dominated English rugby for the next few years – and became champions of Europe twice.

Getting on I may have been, but I was playing as well as I ever had – maybe I wasn't quite as quick as I used to be but I was a more rounded player. It meant there was more work to be done. The next morning I dragged myself out of bed and headed to the airport. Scotland were on tour in South Africa, and we had a World Cup to prepare for.

---

I knew this was the last chapter for my Scotland career. After a bit-part in the 2002 Six Nations and my usual exclusion during the autumn internationals, I was back in favour and played a full part in the 2003 championship. It wasn't a vintage year for us – we hadn't had one of those since 1999 – but we beat Wales and Italy to finish fourth.

After the Italy game I was awarded man of the match. I'd scored a try, set up another and made some important hits in what was a tight game. Italy beat Wales that year and were causing problems. John Inverdale was interviewing me after the match on the BBC and mentioned that it was a great way to finish the Six Nations. I suddenly saw a natural chance to announce my retirement and I took it.

'Yes,' I said, 'and it's a great way for me to finish my international career. That was my last Six Nations game at Murrayfield.'

I hadn't planned to say it then, but I just thought, 'What the hell, I've got man of the match, I've already decided I'm retiring at the end of the World Cup, why not?' No one had expected the announcement, but it wasn't a massive surprise to the team.

When I joined up with them all for two Tests in South Africa, I was on cloud nine, after the double success with Wasps and the feeling that I was uncovering new powers following the DDAT programme. I had officially completed the course, but I kept it going for fear that my run of form might stop.

It didn't. In the first Test in Durban, I had one of my best games for Scotland. We all played superbly. The Springboks were massive – a stone a man heavier than we were in the pack – but we ran rings round them. The only problem was, in true Scottish fashion, we lost. Heroically. We scored three tries, all of them brilliant, but the best was the third, about ten minutes into the second half. I broke from our 22 off Gregor's pass, made it to their 22, then the ball went through God knows how many more pairs of hands, before Andy Craig flipped it up to Chris Paterson for one of the best tries we'd ever scored. It won try of the year, and I collected the award in Sydney at a dinner the night before the 2003 World Cup final. It left us 25–12 up going into the final quarter, three tries to nil.

But we let them in for a soft try. Then in the last ten minutes they hit the post with a penalty, it bounced back out, their man clearly knocked it on, but he pulled it back in, and the ref didn't notice. They scored again seconds later and we were trailing for the first time, 29–25. We hammered away at them in the last five minutes, and Nathan Hines lost the ball as he tried to ground it over their tryline with the last play of the game.

It was agony. I'd rather have been hammered than to be so cruelly denied a game we should so obviously have won. There was nothing more we could have done. Gregor was outstanding, Tom Smith, Bryan Redpath, Glenn Metcalfe – the old boys in perfect harmony – but it was no compensation.

The second Test was at altitude in Johannesburg and we didn't play quite as well, although we were leading at half-time before the effects of the thin air took their toll and we lost 28–19. Despite that, it was a good warm-up for the World Cup.

Everyone was desperate to know my secret. How was it I was not only playing so well but was seemingly a different person – more intuitive, more mature? Suddenly I was full of things to say, which was nothing new, but now the things I said were actually worth listening to. Geech immediately recruited me for the senior players' meetings. Sixty-odd caps it took me, but better late than never. I'd walk into the room, look around and nod to my old mates. 'Gregor, Brush, Tom. So, this is what you get up to in these meetings, is it?' It was as if I'd finally been released from remedial class and was able to go to the same lessons as the boys I played rugby with.

They put it down to whatever Gabby was doing to me. Life was good, and I didn't fear the coming day when my international career ended. My reading was getting better, the little boy inside was relaxing and finding his feet at last. My business, Logan Sports Marketing, which had started life as a little sideline under the name of Exclusive Scotland in the late nineties, was thriving, and I took on a partner, Paul Sefton, who now owns half of it, to help ease the load. Doors were opening in my head, and I could now get a proper view of these amazing big rooms. For years I'd been locked up, but at last I could go through and have a proper look at it all.

In that kind of mood I was ready for the last leg of my eleven-year Scotland career, back in the land where it had all started, the World Cup in Australia. But the day before we set off, there was one last thing I needed to do. We'd been training at Murrayfield, and Chris Paterson, Duncan Hodge, Glenn Metcalfe and I were gathering the balls together at the end of the session. I took one last look round the old place. Then I dug my heel into the turf where the halfway line meets the touchline and plonked a ball in the dent, an angled sixty metres from the posts.

'This is it, boys,' I said. 'My last ever kick at Murrayfield.'

Amid the jeers, I ran up to the ball and swung my boot at it.

It was a perfect strike, and in the same movement I turned round and walked down the tunnel with my fist held triumphantly in the air, not once looking back.

'I don't believe it!' I heard Mossy cry behind me.

In the changing room a few minutes later he confirmed what I knew already. My last kick at Murrayfield had sailed perfectly between the sticks.

# 16

# A Fine Ending

There was only one place to finish my Scotland career, and that was in the city where it had started. I apologise now to all the Scotland fans – and to my team-mates at the time – who had hoped we might win the World Cup in 2003. Unfortunately, the scheduling of the tournament had set the final for Sydney, whereas my Scotland debut had been in Brisbane. For me to have scored the winning try against England to win the World Cup in Sydney would have ruined the symmetry of my international career. So, instead, it had to be defeat by Australia in the quarter-final in Brisbane. Sorry, everyone.

It was not a good World Cup for us, but it was a dramatic one. I don't know why we couldn't recapture the form of that summer tour, just a few months earlier. A big blow was the loss of Andrew Mower, our openside, who had been a star in South Africa. He was the only genuine openside we had, a relentless tackler who took no prisoners at the breakdown. As we were preparing for our first game in Australia, he broke down with the knee injury that would end his career, and we lost a vital piece of what had given us our zip on the South Africa tour. If we'd played like that again, we would have given anyone a good run, but we never really got close to it, and at times we were a million miles away from it. Rumours were circulating in the press about a rift in the camp. I've no idea where they came from. If only there had been a rift. We could have done with one to spice things up. Everyone got on too well, if anything. We were all too nice.

We won the first two games, against Japan and the USA, but we didn't play well in either. Then came our low point – a 51–9 hiding against France in Sydney. It was a wet night and we gave as good as we got for the first half-hour. Then France scored a try towards the end of the first half and another at the start of the second, and we collapsed.

We had one more pool game to go after that, against Fiji, and a lot of people reckoned they could turn us over. We were petrified of being the first Scotland team not to make the quarter-finals, and only when faced with that prospect did we come up with anything that might qualify as a rift.

There was a mass punch-up in training that week. The first team were training against the second team, and the second team were making life difficult. There was no referee, so they were just niggling away, pushing the boundaries. It's what you do when you're not in the side. If you can disrupt everything that the first team are doing – if you can make them look crap – there's more chance of changes being made and therefore more chance of you getting into the team.

Tom Smith, who is not a man to speak out unless he's really, really pissed off, gathered the first team in and laid down the law. The next time one of the other lot took a liberty, he said, it was time to pile into them. Sure enough, one of them grabbed someone's jersey or something – I don't know what it was that kicked it off – and before we knew it the two packs were laying into each other.

Tension was running high. There was a strong feeling of the end approaching, and it was unnerving us. Bryan Redpath and I had already confirmed we were retiring, so had Jim Telfer (you guessed it, he was back again, now as forwards coach, but this time he was retiring from rugby altogether). Ian McGeechan was finishing as coach to become director of rugby, and a whole load of other players, including Gregor Townsend and Glenn Metcalfe, would never play for Scotland again after that World Cup.

Geech and Jim had between them dominated Scottish rugby for decades. Their achievements are legendary, rightly so, but the flipside is that it becomes harder and harder to keep things fresh when you have been part of the furniture for so long. Gregor and I told Geech before that World Cup that we felt his team meetings were going on too long. The man had a lot of insights to pass on – all of it good stuff – but players don't like sitting through forty-five-minute lectures. It's not only dyslexics who suffer from overload. The mark of the man, though, was the way he took our feelings on board. Geech listens to people and when he sees something isn't right he changes it immediately. There aren't many coaches who are so welcome to the input of others, and there are barely any with Geech's ability to handle so many points of view and turn them into something that makes sense. It's what made him the coach he is, and knowing how well he understands people, I just wish I'd told him early on about my problems.

Jim's style was different – his talks were more heart on sleeve and less technical. But his talk before the Fiji game was the first time we had ever looked round at each other as if to say, no, that hasn't hit the mark. Bryan Redpath was captain, and with Jim still in the room he stood up and outlined a different version of how we should play. Brush was a brave captain like that. More interestingly, Jim may well have agreed with him. He seemed happy to let Brush do it, and after the game he came round to shake everybody's hand, which was a noble thing to do.

It was a crazy game, one of the best of that World Cup. Rupeni Caucaunibuca (don't ask me to spell that again) was the star of the tournament – and he played two games. In his first, against France, he scored a brilliant try, then laid out Olivier Magne and was banned for the next two games. That meant he returned for our final pool game, and for forty minutes it was the Caucau show. He scored two more brilliant tries and we were 14–6 down at half-time.

The changing room was like a morgue. I remember looking round at my team-mates, unable to believe we were about to go out. Brush, Gregor, Tom, Glenn, Stuart Grimes, Nathan Hines,

Simon Taylor, Gordon Bulloch, Jason White, Chris Paterson – there were some seriously good players there. Could this really be it? Was this going to be my last game for Scotland? Marooned on sixty-nine caps and the shame of going out at the pool stages? We had to do something. We had to find a way of turning it round. In short, we had to stop Caucau.

Late on in the first half, Caucau had forearmed Simon Danielli, his opposite number, in the face, and he was out cold. So James McLaren had come on at wing. Big Jim was no winger, and for his second try Caucau had gone round him as if he hadn't been there, just moments after Jim had come on. Now Jim had another forty minutes to face. As the only specialist winger left in the side, it was obvious I had to switch wings to mark Caucau.

Geech and Alan Tait, who was now defence coach, came over to me in the changing room.

'Kenny,' said Geech.

'I know,' I said, cutting him short.

'We want you to go up against Caucau.'

'I know. I'll do it. Don't say anything.'

I didn't want any advice or lectures. It had gone beyond that. This could be my last forty minutes of international rugby.

I moved over to Caucau's wing for the second half. Gregor was playing at outside centre, with Chris Paterson having moved in at fly-half for this game. Gregor had not been having a great time at stand-off, and this switch was designed to take some of the pressure off and give Mossy his head at No. 10, a last attempt to get the formula right.

Taity, Gregor and I sat down together and drew up a plan for what we had to do. I said we had to adopt Wasps' style of blitz defence for this next forty minutes. I would rush up on Caucau from out to in, but it needed Gregor to come up with me, so that we left no holes in the wider channels. Andy Henderson was playing inside Gregor, so Taity briefed him.

I've never taken more of a battering than I did in that second half. I was in Caucau's face for all of it, and he was getting frustrated. He got me on the deck, smashed me in the face and fore-armed me. I was constantly winding him up, bantering in his ear – doing all the things Shaun Edwards had taught me at Wasps. I took a high ball and he lifted me up and speared me into the ground. 'Is that your best?' I taunted him. He was raging, but he didn't score again. Chris Paterson had a great game at fly-half, and he chipped away at their lead with his goal-kicking. Then Tom Smith rumbled over for a try and the conversion won it for us with four minutes to go, 22–20.

The world was shaken by the brilliance of Caucau, and there was more talk about him after the game than there was about us, the team that had won. We weren't apologising. We'd won ugly, which made a nice change from losing gallantly. And that was an outstanding Fiji team – four years later, without Caucau, they beat Wales to make the quarter-finals of the World Cup, where they very nearly beat the eventual champions, South Africa. There was no shame in beating them by a mere two points.

It set us up for a quarter-final with Australia in Brisbane. Public expectation was that we would lose by thirty or forty points, but we didn't buy into that. The pressure was off now, yes, but Brush and I wanted the last leg of our international careers to go on for as long as possible. We wanted to match Gav's lot in 1991 and make the semi-finals at least. A lot of the guys felt the same way.

It was another dramatic day. And the fun started before kick-off. We were out on the pitch limbering up when Ben Hinshelwood, who used to spend this time practising his torpedo kicks across the field, shanked one and it hit Mossy slap in the middle of the forehead. He was knocked out cold. No one could get a peep out of him. When the boys finally got him to his feet, he was all over the place.

We went back to the changing room as the medical staff worked frantically on him. Gregor and I were sitting on the bench, head in hands.

'You're going to have to kick at goal,' he said to me.

'I know,' I replied. 'And you're going to have to play fly-half.'

At that point, Mossy came in, and Gregor and I ran over to him. 'Mossy, Mossy, you're all right, aren't you? Say you're all right!'

He can't have been after the state he'd been in, but he played, and he played a blinder, landing a drop goal from practically the halfway line for a 9–9 scoreline at the break. We were all over Australia in the first half, and it was a travesty that we weren't ahead at half-time. Just a few minutes earlier, we had sucked in the Australia defence, and I saw Gregor get his hands on the ball. What followed was an example of when two players read each other perfectly. I took off and at the same time Gregor sent out a cross-kick into the wide-open space. It landed on their 22. I caught it and had a clear run-in with nobody in sight, but the referee blew his whistle. I couldn't believe it. What had we done wrong? Foul play? Off-side? Not Australian enough? If only. He was blowing his whistle because *Australia* had infringed. He awarded a penalty to *us*. One of their players had punched Nathan Hines. Big deal. What about the advantage? What about our try?

It was one of those times when you're so angry it takes your breath away. His decision was more than unjust, it was illogical and insane. The referee's name was Steve Walsh. I've heard he has since been stood down; if only he'd never been stood up in the first place.

Then, just after half-time, we had the ball at a ruck, and Phil Waugh, the Aussie openside, blatantly waded into it from our side and picked up the ball. We looked to the referee, which was obviously pointless, and he just shrugged and let play go on. They broke away and scored for the game's first try. The guy just didn't want us to win, simple as that. I'm not saying we would have won, because Australia took it away from us then and ended up winning 33–16, but if our try had stood, as it so clearly should have done, and theirs hadn't, which it so clearly shouldn't have, it would have been a mighty close game. I'd have backed us.

As it was, the final whistle sounded, and it suddenly came crashing in on me that that was it. The end of my Scotland career. I couldn't help myself – I just started crying my eyes out. Brush was the same. We were inconsolable, not that it stopped anyone trying. We went from one hug to another. It was overwhelming. And it carried on after we got off the pitch. My mum sent me a text, and I replied: 'I love you so much, Mum. Thanks for being such a huge support. I know Dad's with us.'

It had been eleven years since he'd died, eleven years playing for

Scotland. What a rollercoaster. There had been great times and bad times. I must hold some sort of record for the most comebacks by a Scotland player. I won't list all the players who were capped on the wing instead of me during my career, but it must run to at least a dozen, and the two main reasons for that were my going to London and taking on the goal-kicking. If I'd stayed in Scotland and kept my hand down when the cry went up for a goal-kicker, I could have won a lot more than the seventy caps I took away.

But I don't regret any of it – except not playing for the Lions. I wish I'd gone on that Scotland A tour to South Africa in 1997. When Ieuan Evans picked up his injury on the Lions tour, I would surely have been called up, but my back was playing up badly (injury cost me a fair few caps as well) and I stayed at home. I also wish I'd made more of an effort to get to know Geech, when he'd invited me to do just that early on in my career.

Otherwise, I'd do nothing differently. If I could talk to the guy who put his hand up when his country asked who was going to kick the goals, I would tell him to go for it. Goal-kicking caused me my two deepest lows as a player – the Italy game in 2000 and Wales game in 2001 – but otherwise I loved it, never more so than in 1999, when we won the last Five Nations. I'm proud I stood up to take the kicks and I'm proud that I ended up third on the list of highest points-scorers for my country, behind my two great heroes, Gavin Hastings and Andy Irvine. Mossy, though, has since overtaken all of us.

Most of all, though, I was passionate about playing for my country. It meant the world to me. Every time I was dropped, marginalised or written off, I just worked even harder, and every time I came back. By the end, I was playing as well as I ever had, which allowed me to go out on my own terms.

I wish it could have gone on for ever, but you know it can't, and that's what makes it so emotional when it's over. I was just chuffed to retire with Brush, who had become one of my best mates. We tried to convince Gregor to retire with us, but he wanted to carry on – he was only thirty – and the first thing Matt Williams, the new coach, did was to drop him. Gregor never played for Scotland again. After eighty-two caps he deserved better than that, and I wish Brush and I could have persuaded him.

That wasn't Matt Williams's only controversial call – he also asked me to come back. No one had ever done that before – defied me to, yes; invited me, no. I went to watch Scotland in the following Six Nations and it was a shocker – we lost every game and collected the wooden spoon. After the second game – a defeat by England, now the world champions, at Murrayfield – Matt approached me in the foyer and asked me if I wanted to put my boots back on. I laughed, but he took me aside and said, seriously, he wanted me to come back. The team needed my leadership. I laughed again. It was flattering, but my mind was made up. Later that season, he rang to invite me on the tour to Australia that summer. He wanted me to captain the midweek team and he promised me a role in the Tests if I wanted it.

But that wasn't how my rugby career had ever been with Scotland. It had been a fight from start to finish. A mad, glorious, desperate, beautiful fight. I'm happy that I will remember it like that for ever.

At the end of the 2003 Six Nations, Brush had warned me of the next fight I would have on my hands.

'I'm telling you this as a friend,' he said. 'I've heard that Warren Gatland has said he wants to offload you.' Great.

It's difficult to know with Gats when he's just trying to get into your head and when he genuinely wants to get rid of you. He'd made life hard for me during that season, but I'd made it harder for him to drop me. Now, in 2003–04, which I knew was my last season at Wasps, with my contract up at the end of it, I was up against it.

Like any player, I'd had my fair share of injuries, but the problems with my back were by far the biggest. They never really went away. A standard joke on Scotland tours was the way I threw my mattress on the floor if the bed was too springy, which it usually was. Gabby used to get frustrated if we went away to some swanky hotel, only for me to insist on sleeping on the carpet.

In the 2003–04 season, though, the problem became really serious. My back had been niggling throughout the World Cup, and I came very close to quitting altogether when I got back, but Kevin Lidlow was able to work his magic, so I kept going. When I got back to Wasps afterwards, the combination of my back and Warren's attempts to wind me up meant I didn't get many opportunities. I played eight games from the end of November, when I returned from Australia, to the end of that season. He couldn't accuse me of not taking those opportunities, because I scored seven tries and always played well, but he made a point of picking on me. I scored a try in my first game back and he complained that I hadn't scored two. I scored four tries at Calvisano in the Heineken Cup and got man of the match, and he dropped me for mistiming a tackle.

I got my head down, though, and continued working away but I was missing a lot of training sessions, which made it easier for Gats not to pick me. In fairness, I was costing them a lot of money, and I wasn't goal-kicking any more. Part of the problem was that I was bringing in a lot of commercial deals for the club through my sports marketing company, and the commission for those had to be included as part of my pay and therefore part of the wage bill. It was adding another forty or fifty grand to my salary and putting pressure on the wage cap.

I was told around then that Gats said in a board meeting he wanted to get rid of me, but Chris Wright, the owner of Wasps, had said there was no way they were offloading me before my contract had run out. I'd been too successful for the club. I can't say for sure if that conversation ever took place, but if it did, Gats really wouldn't have liked it. I had always had the support of the board, and when my contract did run out at the end of that season, Chris and director Charles Levison, who's sadly no longer with us, offered me the post of chief executive. That would have been an interesting challenge, but the timing wasn't right and I wanted to have one more season back in Scotland.

There was no arguing with what Gats was achieving with the squad, though. The previous season had been the most successful in the club's history, and this time we went one better, winning the Premiership again (having come second again) and the Heineken Cup. I'd played such a limited part on the field that I could share in only part of the glory, but, even if Gats hadn't wanted me there, the rest of them knew the part I'd played in the club's journey.

When I didn't make the twenty-two for the Heineken Cup semi-final against Munster at Lansdowne Road, I made the trip to Dublin anyway.

'Kenny, you're a true club man,' Shaun Edwards said to me. 'You've every right to be pissed off with us, but you're here, and that speaks volumes.' Shaun knew as well as anyone the work I'd been putting in that season and the pain I was going through.

But it was nothing compared to the pain of leaving. My time had come. If I'd stayed another year, I would have played even less and I would have been paid an awful lot less. Geech rang to see what I was doing. He was director of rugby in Scotland now, and when I told him I'd always wanted to finish in Scotland, he made it happen. There was some question of whether he'd place me in Glasgow or Edinburgh, but I was pleased when it ended up being Glasgow, where I'd played regional rugby in my youth. So with the next year of my future secure, it was time to say goodbye to my home for the past seven years or so.

The annual end-of-season club dinner was, predictably, the scene of more tears. Five of us were leaving. In front of about six hundred people, Lawrence handed out the end-of-season awards and presented shirts to the leavers. I saw Paul Volley and Peter Scrivener welling up as they were about to collect theirs. I was last up and Lawrence made a little speech. By the time he had described me as a guy who had come down from Scotland seven and half years earlier and captured everyone's hearts I was crying like a baby. I managed to get a speech out between the tears and was given a standing ovation. Gats shook my hand and said I was a credit to my family.

When you've loved being somewhere for so long, there's no easy way to leave. It had been such a big decision for me to leave home and come to a place like London in my mid-twenties. In the intervening years I'd become a husband, learnt to read and write, won seven trophies and scored more points (1,376) and tries (79) than anyone in Wasps' history. And I'd grown up.

There's always a special bond with anyone you grow up with. Wasps had become another family to me. and I can say with honesty that there was not one person I came across there that I wouldn't call a friend. Some became best friends. We were proud of our saying 'Once a Wasp, always a Wasp'. It's an easy slogan to come up with, but I don't believe there are many clubs that can lay as true a claim to it. So many players left Wasps to go somewhere else and were disappointed by what they found.

I will always be a Scotland player, first and foremost, because it is my homeland and my passion, but the Scotland set-up was, and still is, light years behind the set-up at Wasps, in terms of professionalism, spirit and the way they looked after their players. At Wasps they struck the perfect balance between pushing players to their limit and providing support and sympathy when it was needed. They developed a culture of winning that in British rugby could be rivalled only by Leicester.

In 2007 I was one of eight players from Wasps' history to

become the first inductees to the Wasps Hall of Fame, along with Rob Andrew and Rob Howley from the modern era. To be picked out from some of the legends who have played at the club over the years was a massive honour. But it was an even bigger one to pull on that shirt and play alongside so many mates throughout the best days of my career.

# 17

# Twin Achievements

It had always been an ambition of mine to finish my career in Scotland. For a while it looked as though I wouldn't get the chance, until Kevin Lidlow sorted out my back. So it was with real excitement that I headed north. Gabby and I bought a three-bedroomed flat in Glasgow, which was my base. The two of us clocked up some airmiles that year, flying back and forth from London.

It was an exciting new venture for me. I was looking forward to working with my old Scotland team-mate, Sean Lineen, who was in charge of Glasgow's backs. I had heard a lot about his potential as a coach. I also had opportunities to work with the commercial department in the SRU, trying to bring in sponsorship and investment. I couldn't have been more chuffed with the way it had worked out.

Maybe my expectations were too high. What followed was such a letdown. The first thing the chief executive of Glasgow, David Jordan, said to me was, 'I hear you're going to be working in the commercial department. We need a new sponsor.' The second thing was to tell me he was off on holiday for two weeks. I wasn't impressed, either by the fact that they didn't have a sponsor or the fact that he was going away before we'd got one. By the time he'd got back from his holiday, however, I'd secured a deal with Highland Spring.

The problems didn't stop there. The stadium at Hughenden was inadequate and there was no shop to sell merchandise.

Then there was the coaching. Hugh Campbell was the head coach and a nice guy, but niceness isn't enough on its own. He was to be sacked the following year and Sean, his assistant, was only too happy to take over.

I was really disappointed by Sean. Again, I'd probably had my hopes raised too much by the hype surrounding him, and I'd been lucky enough in my career to have had some of the best coaches in the world. Against all of that he was going to have to go some to live up to expectations. He didn't.

The drills were poor, with lots of emphasis on touch rugby and no exposure to game conditions. He asked me to take a defence session once. We were playing the Ospreys and I had the boys operating a blitz defence.

'What are you doing?' said Sean. 'You're ruining the session.'

'What do you mean?'

'We're trying to do some backs moves here, and you're blitzing.'

'Well, you're doing loops and moves that are going to play into their hands. The Ospreys aren't just going to sit back and watch.'

'I'm the coach. I'll decide what moves we're doing.'

So we went back to a drift defence, ran through all the moves, and we got tanked at the weekend.

'They're good at blitz defending, aren't they?' I said to Sean afterwards.

The atmosphere was all wrong. There were some good players there, but there was no snap or energy. I've never been afraid of talking, but I'd never done so much of it on the pitch as I did that season. No one ever said anything. At Wasps we were constantly talking to each other.

Mark Bitcon had come up with me from Wasps to be conditioning coach. He told me that Sean had asked him, 'How did Wasps cope with Kenny?'

'In what way?' replied Mark.

'He's always pushing us and questioning everything we do.'

'Well, at Wasps there were fifteen of them. If you want the players to raise the bar, they expect you to as well.'

It was true. That was what Warren Gatland and Shaun Edwards did at Wasps. It was what Ian McGeechan and Jim Telfer did with Scotland. If they wanted you to raise your game, they raised theirs. There was no sitting back and expecting players to jump when they were told to. They were as proactive as they expected us to be. The same old story doesn't wash with good players. They'll see through it. Talk is cheap. You can cajole and criticise all you like, but, if you're not actively doing things to show that you're improving as a coach as much as you ask your players to improve, you'll get no response.

It was disheartening to go back and see the foundations that had been laid for Scottish rugby. Not a lot had changed since I'd left nearly ten years earlier. Part of the problem was the lack of edge. The Celtic League, it has to be said, has become a much better competition since, but at the time it was weak. We knew we had no fear of relegation, and making the Heineken Cup was easy. Our main aim that season was to finish above Edinburgh in the table, which we did, by a point. Overall, we came sixth. The celebrations weren't exactly crazy.

I don't think the district coaches are under enough pressure in Scotland. Alan Tait, Stuart Grimes, Carl Hogg and Bryan Redpath are examples of guys who have gone to coach elsewhere, and they are really finding out about pressure. There's no comfort zone. The threat of relegation stares them in the face, and the struggle to qualify for Europe is intense.

Glasgow came bottom of the Celtic League the following season, during which Hugh was sacked and Sean took over. If you come bottom of the league in England or France, that's it. You're gone. Heads roll, revenue plummets.

I worry about Scottish rugby. I seethe when English people take the piss out of it and see us as a second-rate nation, but the truth is we're the only rugby country not improving. What have we done since 1999? We've gone backwards. Where have England gone? Forwards. New Zealand? Forwards. Italy? Forwards. Japan?

Forwards. Uruguay? Forwards. We're the only ones going back-wards.

---

For me, though, in May 2005, I'd reached the end of the road. I was thirty-three when my last season drew to a close. As a winger at that age, it's all over, red rover. You're doing well if you're thirty and still cutting it. In 2004 Austin Healey and I were the two oldest wingers in the Premiership at thirty-two and thirty-one.

It was time to call it a day. Maybe a disappointing final season wasn't such a bad thing after all. It might have made it easier to finish. Rugby had been my salvation. Without it I don't know how I would have coped with the first three decades of my life, but I was ready now for the rest of it. It was time to move on to a new challenge – fatherhood.

---

Gabby and I had assumed, like most people, that we could pick and choose when we got pregnant. We started trying in 2002, within a year of getting married, and two years later there was nothing doing. We were both tested time and time again. I was convinced it must be me, I'd been kicked in the balls so many times on the rugby field. But, no, we were both fine. Apparently, we were one of the twenty per cent of couples for whom it just wouldn't happen.

It was hard, because people were always asking if we planned to have kids, and often these people were journalists. So we were constantly having to put our childlessness down to busy schedules, but the joke was wearing a bit thin.

After two years of that we decided to try IVF. There was no fuss over it and we didn't think twice. We'd each suffered tragedies in our lives. I'd lost Hamish; Gabby had lost her brother, Daniel. This was no big deal. We'd tried the natural way, but when that wasn't happening, we tried something else. Now when I look at our children, I don't care how we got them.

I'm proud we went through IVF, and I'm proud to talk about it. I don't understand why people get so squeamish about it. Let's face it, if you try to get pregnant for years and years without any luck, then suddenly you succeed, you've probably had some help somewhere. We didn't talk about it at the time, because you don't talk about your attempts to get pregnant, but once we'd succeeded we wanted people to know. There were so many doctors and nurses who helped us on our journey. Aside from anything else, we didn't want to brush their contributions under the carpet.

We'd have rather done it naturally, but when that wasn't happening the practical sides of both of us took over. I remember when Gabby lay on her back in a room full of doctors and nurses, and the main man did what he had to in order to get her eggs back in. I took her hand. 'This wasn't how I'd imagined it,' I whispered.

It worked first time. We were pregnant, and it was a fantastic feeling. Gabby was scanned regularly and at eight weeks they heard a heartbeat. Oh! And there's another! We looked at each other, amazed, but it was too early to say we would be having twins. Most people don't get to see an eight-week scan, and some start with twins without ever knowing it, because by the twelve-week scan only one has made it. At twelve weeks, though, ours were still going strong. We'd already broken the news to our families that we were pregnant, but now we could tell them the full news that we were having twins.

Gabby's mum, Christine, has an amazing network of friends. She sent out a text with the news to everyone on her phone and in no time at all the first phone calls came through. The whole world seemed to know. We had to decide there and then how we were going to handle the IVF question, and we immediately chose to be open about it.

The pregnancy went smoothly. Gabby was amazing throughout – you'd barely have known anything was different, other than by the size of her. At twenty-eight weeks she presented the Champions League final. That was the one where Liverpool, 3–0 down against AC Milan at half-time, came back to win it. I nearly went into labour during that one, but Gabby remained cool throughout.

At thirty-seven weeks, Gabby went into Queen Charlotte's Hospital in Hammersmith to be induced. The midwife told me to go home and get some sleep, ready for a long day ahead. While I was gone, Gabby started to feel uncomfortable. She told the midwife she thought she was giving birth.

'That's why you're here, dear,' responded the midwife.

Gabby became more and more unsettled and wrestled with the dilemma of whether she should phone me. At about one in the morning she rang and I went back to the hospital. She was already into her breathing routines, so I sat down and we swapped motivational stories throughout the night – you're Lance Armstrong on the incline, Steve Redgrave on the water, Ellen MacArthur in the middle of a storm, anything we could think of.

During the following day, Terry and Christine, who were now separated, came down from Leeds with Jordan, Gabby's brother, but nothing was really happening. Gabby was only three centimetres dilated, and by eight o'clock the next evening the doctor said he was going to have to perform a caesarean. It was a blow to Gabby, because she'd decided at an early stage that she wanted a natural birth and she'd tried to do everything during the pregnancy to achieve that. The twins were not happy, the doctor told me. It had been twenty-four hours and he just wanted to get them out. I'd delivered countless calves in my life, but I bowed to his superior knowledge when it came to delivering humans. After I'd rationalised this decision, I talked it over alone with Gabby. Just as we'd got our heads round it, the doctor came in and performed his checks. Suddenly, she was eight centimetres dilated. I don't know if it had been the crying that had done it, but she'd progressed so fast that the doctor said he could deliver them naturally after all. It was such a high. Gabby was in agony and joy at the same time. There was whooping and hollering in the room. Come on, babies!

At 11.40 p.m., Reuben McKerrow Logan was born. I saw the whole thing. I'd watched calves being born, but seeing your own child emerge for the first time is like nothing else I've known. His little face was screwed up and he was screaming for all he was worth. He was healthy and loud and everything was fine.

Gabby gathered her strength for Reuben's sister, while I took the little man out to introduce him to Gabby's folks. The high of meeting your first-born child was one thing, but this was a double high because there was still another one to come. Reuben had been in the right position, head first, but his sister was breach, the wrong way round. We'd hoped that once Reuben had been born, she might turn in the womb. Nobody wanted to rush her out, because of the stress it might place on Gabby. Minutes passed, but she wasn't coming. Jordan was getting agitated outside. 'Oh my God!' he said, looking at his watch. 'The other one's going to be born past midnight. They're meant to be twins. They can't have different birthdays!'

In the end, other concerns hastened her delivery. Her heartbeat was starting to race so they had to act. The doctor literally reached in and grabbed her by the legs.

Sixteen minutes after Reuben and four minutes before midnight, Lois Maya Logan was born. Reuben's head had looked like a biker's helmet, a sort of flattened cone, because he'd been squashed up against the wall of the uterus. It was amazing the way it reshaped itself over the next few days. But Lois had been floating, so hers was perfectly round. They were both gorgeous. Everything was perfect. The nurses were performing their checks and there was general hubbub in the room.

In the excitement, though, we suddenly realised that Gabby was in trouble. The doctor, Professor Fisk, called out for assistance. The lights in the room came up and there was chaos.

'What's wrong?' I shouted.

Gabby's uterus hadn't retracted. Blood was pumping out of

her. She was being drained of it. Her face and ears were white, and she looked as if there was no life left in her. They tried to stop the blood but couldn't – it was like a hosepipe. The doctor shouted out that they needed a blood transfusion. I took Gabby's hand and clenched it, but she was drifting away. I looked at her and then at these two tiny babies, then back at her. Panic was rising in me, panic and confusion. They managed to stem the blood at last, and prepared her for a transfusion. There was blood everywhere. The floor was covered in it. People were rushing back and forth through it.

They wheeled her through to the theatre. Outside, Gabby's folks had been waiting for more news. Instead, they saw her being rushed past on a trolley covered in blood, the wheels leaving red tracks as they went. There was more panic.

'Is she going to die?' I said to the doctor when we got to the theatre.

'No, she's not going to die,' he replied. That made me feel better for a moment until it occurred to me he was bound to say that. He's not going to say, 'Oh yeah, she's had it. Enjoy your last few moments together.' So I was back on the balls of my feet.

A few minutes later, things were under control. The blood transfusion had taken, and Gabby had been stitched up. She was confused when she came round. I leant down to her and said, 'We've got two kids. They're fine. And now they're just finishing off your designer vagina.'

We laughed, and the kids were rolled in, bawling their eyes out. Within forty-five minutes, Gabby was feeling fine and breast-feeding them. It was amazing to see. She'd just lost forty-five per cent of her blood, and there she was, straight into the next stage of motherhood.

By now it was the early hours of Friday. Gabby wasn't leaving hospital until Monday, and Christine was staying at our house. That afternoon I said to Gabby I was going to wet the baby's head. She agreed I should, so I rang up the boys, and we went out in Chiswick that evening – Shawsy, Scrivs, Damian Hopley, Jamie Redknapp, Shaun Edwards. Going out with that lot is bad enough at the best of times, but I hadn't eaten or slept since Wednesday.

The vodkas were flowing even before we'd left the pub. One of Jamie's mates, a guy called PK, had just opened a nightclub in the West End, so we all went there and found champagne waiting for us. Finally, PK told us he had a room at the Dorchester, where we could have some beers and some food. By now it was about 3 a.m., and I was all over the place. I threw up in the lift at the hotel. PK got his driver to take me and Jamie home, but Jamie was worried about leaving me on my own, because I'd been sick, so he took me back to his place.

When I woke up the next morning, around eleven, I felt terrible and had no idea where I was, but I remembered I was now a father. I tried to focus. It was somebody's bedroom. Carefully, I made my way out on to the landing. Still didn't recognise anything. I got to the stairs and heard women's voices drifting up from below. 'There are women down there,' I said to myself. 'I'm a father and there are women down there. What have I done? Where am I?'

I went back into the room I'd woken up in. There was a bucket by the bed. I couldn't find my mobile phone. The curtains were still closed, so I opened them and looked out. That was when I knew I was at Jamie's house. I recognised the garden.

Meanwhile, Gabby hadn't been able to get hold of me. She'd rung her mum at our place, who had to tell her I wasn't there. My mum was coming down from Scotland that day – she'd been in touch with Gabby and didn't know where I was. Scrivs could only tell her that we left at about three in the morning. I was in big trouble.

Down in the kitchen, Jamie's wife, Louise, congratulated me on becoming a dad.

'But don't you think you should be at the hospital with Gabby?' I nodded sheepishly. 'You're a disgrace,' she said, and I don't think she was joking.

'Yeah, you're a disgrace,' said Jamie. I think he was.

Louise rounded on him. 'And you're in even bigger trouble. You should have been looking after him. You know what it's like being a dad.'

'Yeah,' I said.

Jamie's phone rang, and it was John Vincent, who had also been out with us the night before. He's Katie Derham's husband and a good friend, as he was about to prove. Gabby was really worried about me, he said. Jamie told John I was with him, so he came round to pick me up. He drove me home and I tried to pull myself together. It turned out I'd left my phone in the car the night before, so I rang through for my messages. There were lots of them. My mum had left a bad one.

'You're a father of two now. What do you think you're doing? This is disgraceful.'

Her flight was due in at 1 p.m., so John drove me to Heathrow to pick her up. She was torn between the pride she felt at having two new grandchildren and the shame she felt over her son. With my mum in the back of the car, John had to pull over on the M4 so I could be sick. It was so embarrassing. My drinking days were long behind me. I hadn't even drunk that much the night before, but the lack of food and sleep and the adrenaline of the previous twenty-four hours had taken their toll. I wanted to shout out between chunders, 'Mum! This really isn't me!'

John dropped me and my mum off at the hospital. Gabby had been furious with me, but John had managed to smooth things over a bit with some diplomatic words on the phone. The atmosphere in the hospital was awkward, with Gabby and me and our two mums trying to enjoy the kids and forget about my disgrace. That was when John burst in, full of cheer. He'd been to the local garage and bought flowers, Mr Kipling cakes, cuddly toys and sweets. He was full of banter, and the ice was finally broken.

A couple of days later, Gabby and I brought Reuben and Lois home for the first time. We each put one in the car. After we'd driven off, Gabby said to me, 'Did you strap Reuben in?'

'No. Did you strap Lois in?'

'No.'

That was a good start to our life as parents.

But we took to it. Gabby's a brilliant mum, and Reuben and Lois were good babies. Feeding them throughout the night was an ordeal, though. Each one could take an hour. You'd barely got back to bed before you had to get up again.

I'd never been more pleased to be retired from rugby. Dragging myself away to go training or travelling would have been a real trial. I still had the occasional meeting, but my business partner, Paul Sefton, was able to look after most things. For the first five or six months I could enjoy seeing the kids grow up. So many fathers don't get to do that, which makes me very lucky. I do think you bond with kids when they're that age, even if the kids don't realise it.

These days Reuben and Lois are little people in their own right. They can walk, talk, do their own thing and tell you what's wrong, which means Gabby and I have a bit of our independence back as well. They're not identical twins, but they're great mates, and they touch your heart strings in so many different ways.

Reuben's a big boy, full of heart and very kind and loving. Lois is kind, too, but she's not afraid to tell you if something's wrong. She's bubbly and extrovert. And they're showing signs of inheriting some sporting talent. Lois could swim at three and Reuben could ride a bike without stabilisers at the same age. They each show a turn of speed as they chase each other round the house.

Most importantly of all though, they can both sing 'Flower of Scotland'. And I make sure they do it over and over again.

———

For a while, though, there was something important missing from their lives – a grandfather figure. From the age of two, Reuben and Lois saw very little of Terry for about two years. We're delighted that he seems to be coming to see us a bit more now, but for a while there we thought he might be drifting away from us.

We don't know why he withdrew, but since he and Christine divorced towards the end of 2007 that's what he did. There didn't seem to be any animosity from him towards us. There was contact – text messages were exchanged, the odd phone call, cards, Christmas presents for the kids. But that was as far as it went.

I know it sounds selfish, but I'll say it anyway. He has been the perfect father-in-law for me. When I first met him, I couldn't believe my luck. I'd met this perfect woman, and now I was meeting her perfect father, her perfect mother, her perfect family. From the word go when he tricked me into thinking I'd got into bed with Christine he was a brilliant laugh. He is a sportsman, and, by God, does he know his sport. He spends hours reading newspapers and books, not just about football. To have someone like that as a father figure was so good for me. He has so much advice to give on sporting matters. And no one has a bad word to say against him in those circles – Gabby's interview subjects are always asking her how her dad is. He and I got on like a house on fire from the start, playing golf and socialising. But the more I got to know him and love him, the less I saw of him. It should have been the other way round.

It's not for me to try to second-guess why he withdrew, but one thing's obvious – he's had a hard time. Gabby's whole family were sent reeling when Daniel, her younger brother, died in 1992. Terry took it the hardest. I can't imagine what it must have been like for him, the way it happened. Daniel had just signed schoolboy forms with Leeds United, the club Terry had played at for nearly ten years. Terry was so proud of him. They were having a kick-around in the garden at home one day, when Daniel suddenly fell to the ground. Terry thought he was larking about, but when he didn't get up Terry went over to him, and Daniel died in his arms of an undiagnosed heart condition. He was fifteen years old.

They battled on as a family. Gabby was at university, and Louise, her younger sister, was away modelling in Japan. Jordan was only six. Terry and Christine had always had a feisty relationship, but the arguments started to outweigh the good times after Daniel died. They held it together for another eleven years, but on Gabby's thirtieth birthday in 2003 Terry moved out of the family home. The hope was that time away from each other would be a good thing.

It didn't turn out that way. Just over a year later, Terry was driving home when he mounted the pavement and hit a pedestrian, who suffered a broken pelvis and head injuries. Terry had been more than three times over the limit and was lucky to be spared a jail sentence.

We'd hoped that the accident might mark the bottoming out of his troubles. He was banned from driving for three years, and he hasn't reapplied for his licence since. We don't think he'll drive again. But it appears he didn't give up drinking. Two years later, towards the end of 2006, he was taken into hospital with pancreatitis and put on a drip. Only then did he stop – on medical advice.

It seemed that that might be the turning point. For about six months from the following January he spent a lot of time with us in London. They were happy days. He got to know his grand-children properly.

Since that summer, though, he stopped coming down. The divorce came through, and maybe that hit him harder than he thought it would. However much they had grown apart, Christine had been crucial to so much of what he had achieved in his career and to developing the personalities of their children. While he showed them what was possible through his own achievements, she was responsible for helping them grow their wings. She is a phenomenally positive person, and if it's true that a girl grows up to be like her mum I know I've chosen well. The independent streak that marks out the Yorath family is as much down to Christine as it is to Terry. She is a successful businesswoman with her own property-development company, and she'll think nothing of working until two in the morning. Jordan is part of her team now and is a really impressive guy. You could say he was hit the hardest of all by Daniel's death. Not only did he lose his brother, but he had to grow up on his own while his parents dealt with the tragedy. Gabby and Louise had both flown the nest.

But they've all found a way through. Terry and Christine are on good terms, and now we are starting to see more of Terry again. I don't know why he went away, and I'm not going to ques-tion it. We're just so happy that he seems to be coming back round again.

# 18

# Murder on the
# Dancefloor

My wife has always loved to dance, and she's always been bloody good at it. She could dance for England. In fact, she has. Well, it was for Wales, but that still makes her pretty good. She came eighth in the rhythmic gymnastics at the 1990 Commonwealth Games.

I'm the exact opposite. I've never been able to dance in my life and I always hated it. When we were out on the town, or at a wedding or something, I learnt pretty quickly to recognise that look in Gabby's eye that says, 'I want to dance. Where's my husband?' It was my cue to vacate the building, or at least get involved in a deep conversation with someone at the bar. 'But, sweetheart, I can't dance. I can't even tap my foot. Please, the boys and I are having a really profound discussion here.' I used to hate going anywhere with Gabby that had a dance floor.

She knew it was a weakness in me, but she doesn't let things lie, my wife, and, just like with the reading and writing, she had plans for me to face up to it. I could never have imagined just how far she was going to go with this one. Learning to read and write was one thing – at least I could do it at my own pace and in the privacy of my own home – but the programme she got me to tackle to address my dance problem was to take place in front of ten million viewers on primetime Saturday night television. Thanks, Gabs.

My wife had been a fan of *Strictly Come Dancing* for a while. I'd never got into it. I was aware of the show. I'd seen Matt Dawson on the previous series. I think I may even have voted. Anything to get him off.

Gabby was supposed to have been on the show for that 2006 series. She was still with ITV, and they had agreed for her to do it, but Gabby's relationship with ITV was falling apart. Mark Sharman, the head of ITV Sport, appeared to be on her case without ever having the grace to confront her about it. She was being marginalised from the big sports events in favour of ITV's new signing, Steve Rider, and then the day before the university boat race, which she was presenting live, a story appeared in the *Daily Mail* that Steve Rider was to front the World Cup and that

Gabby's future at the station was in doubt. It was obvious that Gabby could not stay at ITV. She was a peripheral figure during the World Cup, Sharman ignored her calls, and then at the end of it David Pleat rang her when we were at home one Sunday afternoon to say how sorry he was to hear that she wouldn't be presenting any more football at ITV. It was the first Gabby had heard of it.

So things were bad. And then they blocked her from appearing on *Strictly* at the last minute, literally the day before she was due to film the promos. They had suddenly decided that she couldn't go on the show because she was synonymous with ITV – the channel that it seemed were all the while trying to get rid of her. It was an obvious attempt to get her to walk out of her contract a year early as far as we were concerned.

The BBC signed her up at the beginning of 2007, so she was free to do *Strictly* that year. She met Charlotte Oates from the Beeb in the Orange Pekoe, a café round the corner from our house in Barnes. I went along to meet them, innocently enough. The three of us talked about Gabby doing the show and there was a lot of banter. Are you sure about this, Gabs? What if you get knocked out in the first round? I suppose I should have noticed that something was going on, the way the two of them were exchanging glances, but I didn't. Then Charlotte suddenly turned to me and said, 'We want you to do it as well.'

I looked at them both and burst out laughing. They looked at each other again and then at me, and it started to dawn on me that they were being serious. An icy shiver ran down my spine.

'No way,' I said. 'Absolutely no way.'

'Look, you don't have to make a decision now,' said Gabby.

'Oh, don't worry. I've made my decision, all right.'

'Let's not rule anything out, darling. I'm doing it anyway. I reckon it would be fun for you to do it as well.'

Deep down, I already knew I was going to lose this one.

We went home and discussed it with Philippa and Bernie, our PAs. They were raving about the idea of the two of us doing it, and another little piece of resistance in me died.

This was in May, so the show was far enough away for it not to seem real. I was wavering. Two weeks later, Charlotte called and said they definitely wanted me to do it. Was I in? What the hell, I thought. Let's just see how I get on. It can't be that bad. So I said yes, whatever, and promptly forgot about it.

As the time got nearer, I noticed people mentioning the show in everyday conversation. '*Strictly Come Dancing*?' I would remark casually. 'Yeah. What do you think of that show?' And people would say how much they loved it, and I would think, 'Shit. This programme's massive.' Still, I blocked it out of my mind. Even when we signed the contracts, it didn't really sink in that I was actually doing it.

Then, with about two weeks to go, I started looking at YouTube, and that was when I began to think, 'Oh my God, what have I done?' With a week to go, I was waking up in the middle of the night, dripping with sweat. The first time I thought I must have a fever, but then I was waking up shouting, 'No!'

'What is it?' Gabby asked, turning on the light.

'I'm not doing it. I'm not doing it. I'm not doing it.'

'Doing what?'

'*Strictly Come Dancing.*'

'Oh shut up and go back to sleep.' And out went the light.

It sounds funny when I describe it, but it wasn't funny. I was deadly serious. You don't wake up in the middle of the night in that sort of condition if you're only joking. I may have got over my dyslexia, but this was taking me back to the bad old days at school and the gut-wrenching fear I used to suffer every day. Forget about the fact that I couldn't even clap in time with music, how was I supposed to memorise all those moves? My memory had improved massively in recent years, but that fact flew out of the window in my panic. I'd forgotten how well I could remember, if you see what I mean.

Suddenly, in September 2007, it was happening. Each contestant was taken to meet their partner. I was meeting mine in a studio in Chiswick. On the way, I got a call from Gabby, saying she'd met her partner and knew who mine was, but she wouldn't tell me anything more. Then I walked into a room full of cameras and saw Ola Jordan. I knew who she was. The fit one. She didn't know much about me, other than that I was a rugby player. That's when I discovered that Gabby's partner was James Jordan, Ola's husband. I had to smile. They're clever, those BBC types.

We got going immediately. Ola taught me the most basic step of them all. It's called the box, and you just have to step forward, to the left, back and to the right. I couldn't do it. I saw the panic in Ola's eyes as it dawned on her what she was taking on. God knows how much panic she saw in mine.

We tried some more easy steps – from the cha-cha-cha and the jive. It was hopeless. The messages from my brain just weren't getting to my feet. Don't ask me why my feet could do what I wanted them to on a rugby field but not on a dance floor, it was just the way it was. I think I was in a state of shock. As for trying to make it look graceful and in time with music – forget it. I left thinking only one thing. 'How can I get out of this? I've got to get out of it. This is just ridiculous.'

Back at the office, Philippa opened the door, because I had no keys with me, or I had forgotten how to use them. I don't know. I was in a daze.

'What's happened?' she said when she saw me. My face was grey. I sat down with that horrible nervous feeling I had at school surging through me. 'My God,' I thought to myself. 'I'm not putting myself through this again.'

When Gabby got back that evening, she was flying.

'Oh my God! I love it, I love it! It's brilliant! I love dancing!' She had her whole routine done already. She'd sailed through it.

'You're making me sick,' I said. She actually started dancing in front of me in the evenings. 'Just go somewhere else and do that, will you!' She was on cloud nine; I was in the depths of depression.

I racked my brain to find a way of getting out of it. The Rugby World Cup had just started, and I had a contract with ITV to be a pundit for the Scotland games. Surely, there would be a clash.

'Right,' I said to Gabby, 'if any of the *Strictly* dates clash with the World Cup, I'm not doing it.'

'You don't really have to do the World Cup,' she said.

'Whoa there!' I replied. 'Rugby's my life. Dancing isn't. Of course the World Cup takes precedence.'

So I rushed off to look up the dates and would you believe it?

Not one of them clashed. My only hope was if Scotland won their pool, in which case they would have had a quarter-final on a Saturday night – the first Saturday night of the show. The main problem with that lifeline was that Scotland had the All Blacks in their group, so there was no chance.

I was kidding myself, though, because by then it was too late anyway, and if Scotland had beaten the All Blacks, I would actually have been in deep shit – I had signed contracts for *Strictly* and for the World Cup and I couldn't have got out of either of them at that late stage. Mind you, not even the lawyers were worried about the potential clash when I signed for both – that's how much of a chance Scotland were given.

Then a funny thing happened. I went along to rehearsals the next day, and I noticed myself get a wee bit better. The same thing happened the day after that. By the Friday, I was actually feeling a bit confident. That feeling of nerves and fear that I'd had every day at school had started to fade. Something else had taken over now – a gradual increase in optimism and a sense that I was making progress. It was called learning, apparently. If only I'd come across it at school.

All of a sudden, I was quite enjoying myself. Ola and I were getting on well. We met at 9 a.m. every day and didn't stop rehearsing till twelve. We broke for forty-five minutes for lunch and then it was back to work till 4 p.m. – no breaks, no cups of tea, only the odd sip of Red Bull to keep us going. I lost nearly a stone over the course of the programme.

It wasn't until we all came together for the Friday rehearsal for the first show that I was able to put my progress into perspective.

I didn't like what I saw. I may have been improving, but I was still way behind. Sitting there watching the others and realising how good some of them were was a real comedown. And Gabby was brilliant, which didn't help. She'd already done two dances by the time I'd even done one. She coasted through the first week.

I walked into that first show on the Saturday night like I was walking into a head-on collision with a train. I was all over the place. Never have I known nerves like it. Forget the stuff I had to go through at school – those were debilitating nerves that bubbled away the whole time and brought on illness and depression. This was like fire consuming me and it brought on a kind of paralysis. Sweat was pouring from my hands. My mouth was like the Sahara. It didn't help that Ola was, if anything, even more nervous than I was. She was shaking. I think she generally gets nervous before performing anyway, but it was obvious that this was worse than usual, and it was obvious why. She knew how shit I was. I tried to make a joke about how her nervousness really wasn't helping, but neither of us laughed.

The waltz was our first dance. We stood backstage like the condemned, waiting to go on, and we could hear them showing the video of us training together. I imagined all those people sitting out there enjoying a nice evening's entertainment, and all the people in their homes doing the same.

Then the announcer introduces you. And you have to go on. There's no getting out of it. You walk on and you hear the audience cheering, but all you can see are the lights, bright spotlights in your face. About a hundred things are going through your head. 'Focus on the steps,' I kept saying to myself, 'just get the steps right. Just get through it. Without physically harming Ola.'

In focusing on the steps, I forgot about posture and about smiling. Later I watched the recording of that first dance, and I looked like Jack the Ripper. I looked like a serial killer on the dance floor. There was maybe a bit of the Joker in there as well, my 'smile' was so set in stone. As far as I was concerned, each dance step was nothing more than one step towards the end of this torture. Which is not what dancing's meant to be about. But Ola and I got through it, and it felt exactly as if I had crossed a tightrope without falling. All I knew was that it was over, the music had finished, and I wasn't dead. The relief was overwhelming.

Then I was introduced to the judges, and they didn't like me, but what did I care? They were nothing compared to Jim Telfer. I could handle these judges. Over the season, they were good fun – I knew that they were there to entertain first and foremost. Arlene Phillips and her little pre-rehearsed lines were hysterical – 'You took the T out of Tango and trashed it.' I didn't understand what she was talking about most of the time. I'm not even sure she did. My main gripe with them was that they spent too much time slagging you off and not enough giving constructive criticism. A couple of weeks or so after my first dance I made that point, which went down well with the audience. To be fair, I think the judges made more of an effort to help me out after I'd said it. After the waltz, though, they were all agreed that I had looked rigid and terrified. And they were right.

Sure enough, I ended up in the dance-off that week with Brian Capron, an actor from *Coronation Street*, and I really wanted to win it. Just a few weeks before, I would have been screaming at myself to lose. Getting out at the first opportunity would have sounded like the perfect result, but I was now hooked on the show. I could see hope for myself, and I could see that I was improving. I really didn't want it to be cut short. My fellow sportsmen, Willie Thorne and John Barnes, had already been bombarding me with banter – it's great having Kenny here, they said, as long as we beat Kenny we'll be happy. And I never said anything. I just swore to myself that I would beat them. Didn't know how, hadn't got a clue. Barnesy had rhythm. When Ola asked me to clap in time with the music on our first day together, it was like I was trying to catch a fly.

I came through that first dance-off. Brian and I had both been given a waltz to do that first weekend, while the others had the cha-cha-cha. The judges said that the waltz was far harder for novices to pull off. I smiled a bit more naturally and that seemed to do the trick. Craig Revel Horwood was the first judge to vote. He went for Brian and his partner, Karen, and I thought my time was up, but Arlene and Bruno Tonioli went for Ola and me, which left Len Goodman with the casting vote. I knew I was in with a chance then, because Len had been the most positive about me and he was a big sports fan. He's a passionate West Ham man, but he also loves his rugby. Sure enough, he came through for me, so I lived to fight, sorry, dance another day.

It had been a lucky escape. Those judges were on my case. My only hope lay in winning over the public. I didn't think I would survive another dance-off, so I had to make sure I was never in one again, and that meant winning the public vote.

The dance-off went out on BBC1 on Sunday evening, and, by some miracle of teleportation/TV scheduling, fifteen minutes later I was in Paris for ITV at the Scotland–Argentina quarter-final. Of course, we had actually filmed the dance-off straight after the live show on the Saturday night.

Robbie, meanwhile, had phoned me on the Sunday morning. Throughout my rugby career he had been the one guy who was always totally honest with me about my performances. It looked as if it would be no different with *Strictly*.

'Kenny, what were you doing last night?'

'What do you mean?'

'That wasn't you. Just relax. Be yourself.'

It may have come too late for the dance-off, which we'd already filmed, but it was the best piece of advice I had. I'd been so terrified that first night. Now that I'd got through it, I just needed to loosen up and try to let my personality come through.

The following week it was the girls' turn, and all the boys had to do was take part in the group dance. Arlene picked me out from the crowd as having improved, which gave me a massive boost of confidence, and by the following week something had clicked. I no longer cared about looking an idiot. I was here to enjoy myself, and that was what I did. The public, God bless them, went along with it, and their votes kept me out of the clutches of the evil judges for week after week after week.

Meanwhile, Gabby was going through a rough patch with

her partner, James. He can be pretty chauvinistic – 'I'm the man. If I tell you to jump, you ask when and how high,' that kind of thing. It's the way things are in the dance world. The man leads on the dance floor, and that usually extends into rehearsals. This was never going to go down well with Gabby. She's been brought up in a man's world, and she knows how to stick up for herself.

They had a huge argument, and James stormed off. Gabby came home very upset. She'd stood toe to toe with James, but when she got home it all fell out of her and she broke down. I should say before I go on that I love James to bits, and he and Ola are now really good friends of ours, but we didn't know them so well at this point.

James rang me soon afterwards and asked if Gabby was all right, and I told him she wasn't.

'I would never treat your wife the way you treated mine. If I spoke to Ola like that, you'd want to kill me. I would advise you to ring Gabby up and apologise.'

Which he did. This alpha male role he likes to play up to is a bit of an act, and it's something that dancers get away with, because in their world they are always leading. He toned it down a bit from then on. Gabby had confronted him, and he wasn't used to it. They got on like a house on fire after that. Sometimes you need that conflict for your relationship to move on to the next level.

Gabby has since complained that I wasn't much of a help to her in the build-up to their first dance, and I suppose it's true. She'd helped me through the preparation for my first dance. Apart from anything else, it was so obvious I needed help. Desperately. But I'd just assumed she was fine, and if she said she was nervous, I didn't think she really meant it.

This was the problem for Gabby and *Strictly*. Everyone reckoned she was fine – public, judges, pro dancers, even her own family. In a weird way, it meant she had more to overcome than the rest of us, and she was the only one who realised it. By the time the rest of us had, it was too late.

The judges' comments were mixed about her first dance, which was a quickstep. She wasn't very happy with her performance, either, and the judges had her fourth out of the seven girls. James had always said that mid-table on the leaderboard was the most dangerous place to be, because the public might not vote for you, so Gabby thought she would be dancing off that night. She was worried about it, and so she didn't look ecstatic when the judges gave her their scores. In the end, she was OK, and Stephanie Beacham lost out in the dance-off to Letitia Dean.

Gabby had her eighty-year-old granny in the audience, as well as her mum and a few of her school friends from Leeds. It was 11 p.m. by the time we'd finished filming the results show and the audience had been in the studio since 4 p.m., without anything to eat. Rather than make her starving granny climb a set of stairs to get to the lift to go to a crowded bar, she decided to have a little party in her dressing room and treat the seven or eight of them to champagne and food. Alesha Dixon popped in for a glass, and so did Kelly Brook, two of the other contestants. I had a drink with them and then went up to the bar. Gabby needed to be up at half past four the next morning to catch a flight to interview Martina

Hingis, so at midnight she went home, while I went on to a club with some of the others.

On Monday morning there was a story in the *Sun*, claiming that Gabby had refused to leave her dressing room after the show because she was so upset at the judges for putting her in fourth place. Obviously, it was rubbish, but what was even more distressing was that the story seemed to have come from someone associated with the show, who knew that Gabby had stayed in her dressing room. Gabby rang the press officer, but she just shrugged. I suppose, for them, it's all part of the clippings file.

So Gabby now had a reputation of being competitive and a sore loser, and it was too late to do anything about it. If she'd leapt around with joy at the judges' scores, maybe the leaked story would have led on lovely Gabby looking after her dear old granny in her dressing room. That's the power of spin and in this case Gabby was the innocent victim of it. However, it made me realise that I had a chance of not being completely humiliated in this competition. It appeared that being a good dancer was not what it was all about. I decided it was up to me to milk that for all it was worth. All the same, the idea of playing to the audience was soon to be taken to a ridiculous extreme.

# 19

# Time of My Life

By week four of *Strictly Come Dancing*, I was as surprised as anybody that I had survived so long. Ola and I were doing the samba, and I was torn to pieces by the judges. Bruno said I had the grace of a vacuum cleaner, Craig called it a dance disaster, Arlene said I needed to start praying. Even Len had to admit it was 'bloody 'orrible'. They gave me eighteen out of forty, which was the worst mark I would get in the show. It was a setback after a decent showing the week before in the tango.

It wasn't the worst score of the weekend, though – that was the sixteen that Kate Garraway was given for her samba. Kate's competition had been dominated early on by the injury she had picked up in training. She had sat out the group dance in week one, and in week two, the girls' first individual dances, she arrived at the studio on two crutches, rehearsed on one and performed on none. She said she had tendonitis in both feet. Now, I'm no physio, but I think it was more likely that she had some muscle soreness from all the training as tendonitis takes a long time to clear up. All the same, it was a clever move on her part as she managed to get the sympathy of the public. People love all that soldiering on in the face of adversity, and she did even better than I did to keep avoiding the dance-offs. She kept getting the worst score from the judges, and she was all over the papers because of it. It was all good fun. Then she hurt her back in week seven and started blaming her performances on that, and the public had had enough. She was voted off.

Anyway, back to week four. Kate and I were rock bottom, she'd got sixteen and I'd got eighteen. We were way off the pace. The next one was Barnesy on twenty-two (Willie was already out by now – one down!) and the others were all in the thirties or high twenties.

Gabby had danced a brilliant samba and scored thirty, which still seemed a bit harsh I thought. Still, it should have made her safe, but she could feel something in the air. She's very intuitive. There's no point trying to lie to her, because she just knows when things are right or wrong. She felt something was wrong that night, and she turned to Penny Lancaster and said, 'I'm going home tonight. This is the end for me.'

We all lined up for the filming of the results. They told Kate and Anton early on that they were safe, and I knew something wasn't right. Eventually, we were left with three couples. Ola and me – fine. Penny Lancaster was still there, and so was Gabby.

I just assumed it was the BBC playing around, ramping up the family tension by waiting to the end to tell Gabby she was safe. My only hope had been to dance off against Kate, so I was preparing to leave the competition, because there was no way I was going to beat Penny. Apparently, James whispered in Gabby's ear, 'Poor Kenny.' We all just assumed my time was up. All of us, that is, except Gabby. She was standing just behind me, and when I turned to look at her, I could see the nerves on her face. She just knew.

They kept us all standing there, building the tension, before they announced the last couple to stand down. I heard the K when Bruce Forsyth said, 'Kenny and Ola,' and I was rooted to the spot. Stunned. Ola said, 'Oh my God,' and held her hands up to her mouth in shock. We didn't even celebrate, because it blindsided us so completely. I didn't know whether to laugh or cry. Of course, I was chuffed, but I just couldn't understand how it had happened.

Still, I thought Gabby would win the dance-off. I know I'm biased, but it was clear to me that she was a better dancer than Penny, and I still don't understand how the judges decided that Penny should stay. Penny danced to 'These Boots Were Made For Walking', and to my mind she did actually walk round the stage. Gabby, on the other hand, danced. Len, who had the casting vote, confessed to me later that it was the most difficult decision he'd ever had to make on the show. It was actually Craig, the hardest judge to please, who voted for Gabby, but the others went for Penny.

I was devastated for Gabby, because I know how much she loved being in the show. She was devastated, too, but showed it only when we got home. That night, we were first out of our dressing rooms and into the bar. Even then the press stirred things up the next week about there being a rift between Gabby and Kate. There wasn't, and why would there have been? Just because Kate wasn't as good a dancer? Well, neither was Gabby's husband.

I remember my mates phoning me that night, before the results show had been screened, asking who was out.

'Are you still in, are you still in?' They'd all been texting like mad for me.

'Yeah, I am.'

'Who's out, who's out?'

'You'll never believe it. It's Gabby.'

'No way. It can't be!'

None of them had even thought to vote for her, because she was so good. She didn't need their votes like I did. They were genuinely shocked. It felt as if the entire nation was shocked, there was so much press about it. That mid-table curse that James had talked about had done for her. People don't tend to vote for you if you're looking comfortable; it's the no-hopers like me who get all the sympathy votes. The judges were furious that they had been put in the situation of having to choose between two of the best dancers, and that old argument over the virtues of the public vote went into full swing.

Gabby knew she had a talent for dancing and it was cruel that she wasn't going to get a chance to work on that any further. I felt awful, because I was still in. By then I was loving it, it's true, but not so much that I wanted to carry on at the expense of my wife, who had pretty much forced me to do the thing in the first place.

I grabbed my phone and called Charlotte at the BBC.

'What are you doing?' said Gabby.

'I'm phoning the BBC.'

'Don't be stupid.' The phone was ringing. 'Kenny.' Still ringing. 'Kenny! Put the phone down!'

It was too late. Charlotte answered, and I told her I wanted to resign and let Gabby take my place. I liked the show and everything, but I wasn't that fussed. Gabby not being there was a joke. But Charlotte charmed me with all this talk about the sanctity of the democratic process, and Gabby was by now fighting to get the phone off me. So I let it go.

Instead, Gabby and I had to sit down together and come to terms with the fact that we had got it so wrong. Our world was being turned upside down, because, contrary to what we had always believed to be an obvious truth, it had turned out that I was actually the best dancer in the house. Yes, on the surface it appeared that she was more graceful than I was, that she had more of a sense of rhythm, but it's like an ugly golf shot, isn't it? It's not what it looks like, it's where it ends up. And I was going further than my wife. Ha!

In fact, the whole thing had made me determined to go as far as I could. Ola and I would do it for our other halves. Gabby and James became our number-one fans. James was a massive help to me, giving me tips and advice. Every time we avoided the dance-off in the weeks that followed, James would be the first to come running through to give me a big hug. Ola would just be standing there. He was a great support and became a really good mate.

I knew more than ever that it was time to come up with some extra touches to win the public vote, since being able to dance was so obviously just one part of it. I decided to wear a kilt for our next dance, the paso doble. If I'd danced my first dance with Gabby at our wedding with nothing on underneath my kilt, as tradition demands, surely I could do this one open to the elements as well. The BBC insisted that I couldn't. Either I did it with my pants on or I couldn't do it in a kilt at all.

By now, my dancing was beginning to split opinion among the judges, which was progress from when they were agreed on how bad it was, but they didn't go for our paso. Their combined marks came out at twenty-one and had me bottom of the leaderboard, which was actually the only time I was bottom, other than the week I was eliminated. The public saved me from the dance-off – the kilt seemed to have gone down well with them at least. So the next week we danced a Viennese waltz to 'Flower of Scotland' and I whipped out a thistle at the end of it and gave it to Ola. The judges gave me my best mark so far, and I was safe for another week.

And so it just kept going, no matter what the judges said – and they said a hell of a lot – hot air most of it. Len and Craig practically came to blows over our cha-cha-cha. Len stuck up for me again. Every week the others seemed to change their mind on whether I was any good or not. The only constant was the support from the other contestants and the pros. And the public.

I was still there in week eight, and that was when I started to feel I was really getting somewhere. It helped that I'd found a dance-related skill that I could do better than anyone else, and it just happened to be the most important one of the week. As a group dance in week eight we performed a tribute to *Dirty Dancing*, which centres round the famous lift that Patrick Swayze pulls off in the film.

The show built up the question of who was going to do the lift on the night, and we boys were getting a bit competitive over it. I knew by now that I was good at them, because that week I'd been practising the American smooth with Ola, and that weekend we were going to do the first one-armed lift ever tried on *Strictly*.

As we were in the middle of arguing over who should do the lift in the group dance, I stood in the middle of the studio like some kind of twenty-first-century warrior of dance – or Conan the Barbarian, as Bruno had called me after one of my dances – and I cried out, 'I could lift anyone in this room!' Brendan Cole, one of the pro dancers, said, 'All right, lift me then.' Brendan weighs around fourteen stone.

He ran at me like Baby in *Dirty Dancing*, and I hoisted him in the air as if I were changing a light bulb. Nae problem. Just to reinforce the point, I started lifting him up and down over my head. 'Yeah, baby.'

'All right,' said Brendan. 'Kenny can do the lift.'

So it was decided that I would lift Ola in the group dance. Before we got down to rehearsing, there was a slight delay. All the girls had formed a queue. They wanted to know what life was like up there in the stars above my head, so obviously I had to show them. One at a time, girls.

Matt Di Angelo and Gethin Jones had been calling me 'Dad' throughout the show, because I was a wee bit older, but now they could only stand at the edge of the room and watch as I showed them that I really was the Daddy. Poor old Matt could barely lift his hand above his head, let alone a dancer. Barnesy was skulking in the corner with them. His banter had suddenly dried up as well.

On the Saturday night, Ola and I did our American smooth, and it was our best dance yet. The one-handed lift went down a storm. Even Craig thought it was all right. He gave me six out of ten. The others gave me eight, for a total of thirty, my best yet by far. I was on a high and felt as if I could do anything.

Just before we went on for the group dance I said to Ola that I wanted to practise the *Dirty Dancing* lift one more time. Thank God I did, because this was the first time we'd tried it with her in the silk dress she was due to wear. The dress she'd worn for the rehearsal was deemed too big and had been changed at the last minute for the one she was wearing now. Whenever we'd done the lift before that, she'd been in lycra or a tracksuit. I tried to lift her in this new dress, but I couldn't get any purchase. For the lift you have to place your hands on the girl's pelvis before you hoist her, but my hands just shot up her body. Wearing silk, it was as if she had covered herself in grease.

We turned to James, 'We can't do the lift, we can't do the lift.' And soon everyone was in a mad panic. We were due on in about two minutes. The wardrobe girls are amazing, the way they can turn things round in seconds. They checked what Ola was wearing underneath and decided simply to cut the dress off her. She ended up doing the dance in just the underskirt. It was made of a kind of net fabric, and worked fine, but throughout the dance we were worrying. Then the moment came and I lifted her high into the air. The roar from the audience was incredible.

That night I understood why these performers put themselves through it all. I suppose it's a similar buzz to playing in a big game, except you know there's going to be a set climax and you know that it's up to you – there isn't any opposition to worry about or to blame if things go wrong.

To cap it all, Ola and I avoided the dance-off once more. This was getting ridiculous. It meant I was now in week nine. Barnesy was voted out that night. I was sorry to see him go, because he'd been priceless throughout and is a good mate, but there was no denying it now – I'd seen off him and Willie. I was the last sportsman standing!

Kelly Brook had faced Barnesy in the dance-off and had not been particularly good that weekend by her standards, and we soon found out why. It turned out her dad had been ill with lung cancer and he died the following Tuesday. Kelly initially said she was going to carry on with the show, as her dad would have wanted, but by the end of the week she had withdrawn, because she was just too upset. It put everything into perspective – all the hoopla surrounding the show over the previous few weeks in the media and on the streets. It was just a dance show, after all, and half of us weren't even dancers.

In the grand scheme of things, our little ups and downs were so insignificant. All the same, in my personal story those few months will count as massively important. It was only a dance show, yes, but the whole experience had transformed my life almost as much as learning to read and write. That process had given me the tools, but this was the first time since I'd been at school that I was trying to tackle something I really didn't want to do. Rugby had always come naturally to me, so learning and improving were easy. It was something I was good at anyway and I loved doing it. Even there, though, I'd found learning easier after I'd got over my dyslexia, and I'd made my most rapid improvements only then.

With dancing, I'd had no such talent or desire. I was dragged along to it kicking and screaming, just as much as I had been at school, but this journey was one I never experienced in the classroom. It obviously helped to have a teacher as patient, caring, enthusiastic and, let's face it, gorgeous as Ola, and the support from Gabby and James and everyone else on the show helped enormously.

When I was at school, if you were struggling in lessons, you were made to feel it. There was no encouragement, and so the vicious circle began. In *Strictly*, tiny little things like Arlene not slagging me off for just a moment to mention that I was starting to dance in time to the music gave me a massive boost. I know I was no Fred Astaire, but by the end I felt I could hold my head up high.

Come week nine, I knew I couldn't lose. I'd come so far, I was a winner whether I went out that weekend or not. As we were down to the last five couples (six if Kelly and Brendan had still been there), we had to dance twice now. Ola and I did the foxtrot and the rumba. The rumba was the hardest for a rugby player. There are not a lot of steps – it's all about intensity, passion and acting. James tutored me in how I should basically ravish his wife.

'You've got to be all over her,' he said.

'OK.'

In truth, I found it difficult. I knew how to be passionate with Gabby in the privacy of our home, but this was different. I gave it my best shot, though.

'Right, that's enough. You don't need to grope her boobs that much.'

'But that's what you just did!'

'Yeah, but I'm her husband!'

'You can't show me what you want me to do to her, then complain when I do it!'

It got confusing at times.

The judges liked our foxtrot and gave it thirty, but they didn't like our rumba, giving it only twenty-three. There was more arguing between them. Len and Arlene nearly came to blows this time. Everyone backstage was really positive, though. The pros said it was one of the best rumbas they'd seen on the show. Slight exaggeration, maybe, but it was nice of them to say it.

Letitia and I ended up in the dance-off, and the judges decided it was time for me to go. That was fine. I'd had a hell of a run for my money. I would have taken one more week if I could, but after that it would have started to feel embarrassing. Alesha, Matt and Gethin, the three left in after Letitia, were so much better than I was, and I would have been found out eventually. That's why John Sergeant's decision to withdraw from the competition the following year was so unnecessary. He worried that he was actually going to win the thing. No, he wasn't. However popular he was, at some stage he was going to be left at the mercy of the judges, and they would have voted him off in a shot.

So it was back to reality for me. It had been three months from the start of rehearsals to me leaving the show – three months in a bubble. You don't have much time for anything other than rehearsing. You're aware of what's being said about you in the media, but there's not a lot of time for reading papers and watching TV, so there's no real sense of quite how big the thing is.

There had been glimpses of how big it was getting. I took Ola up to Scotland one week during rehearsals. I was already quite well known in Scotland, but now everyone was stopping me in the streets wishing me well, while back in London, lorry drivers shouted out their support.

But it was only when I returned to the real world that I realised how much it had seized people's imaginations. I suppose it shouldn't come as a surprise, but the truth is I am far better known now for my dancing than I ever was for my rugby. I get recognised a lot more, by women in particular. Sometimes I have them screaming at me. But I've told Gabby to pull herself together.

Some people might find it depressing to be better known for something you were crap at than for something you were good at, but I don't think anything of it. I find it funny that some-body can be a rugby player all their life, then do a TV show for three and a half months and be more famous for that. It's the nature of entertainment these days. The fact is that Saturday night mainstream television is always going to reach a far larger audience than Saturday afternoon rugby on Sky Sports. The exposure was horrendous to begin with, because I was so bad at dancing, but I got better and now I'm quite happy with it. It's a different chapter of my life, a different chapter of this book, and I've always said that I didn't want to be known as just a rugby player all my life. So, if nothing else, at least I've achieved that.

Alesha Dixon went on to win the show, which was a popular choice. She was brilliant – a beautiful dancer and a beautiful person. Matt and Gethin, who came second and third, became great friends, too. Experiencing all those ups and downs together in the goldfish bowl could only pull you together. It was a bit like being on a rugby tour – only with make-up and sequins.

It had been an emotional few months, from the fear of doing it, through the farce of Gabby's early exit, to the pride at learning a new skill – and now, when I see Gabby and a dance floor in the same room, I no longer run a mile.

# 20

# What Goes
# on Tour . . .

If the hard work and team spirit of *Strictly Come Dancing* made the show feel a bit like a rugby tour, it was nothing compared to 'Strictly Come Dancing: The Live Tour!' That's right. My dancing career was not over just yet. If you'd told me at the end of the 2003 World Cup that not only would I tour again but that the next one would be a dance tour, I would have laughed in your face.

But when I was asked the following year to appear on the 2009

*Strictly* tour, I didn't need anyone to talk me into it. A pack of All Blacks couldn't have stopped me.

The 2009 version was the second live tour of the show, the first having taken place in 2008, the January after our show had finished. Matt Di Angelo and Letitia Dean from our series went on it, and apparently it was not an entirely happy camp. The chemistry didn't work.

I can't speak for that tour, but I can say that the exact opposite was true of ours. I'd love to be able to tell you lots of juicy tales about what bitches the girls were and how precious the boys were, but the truth is I loved absolutely everyone, from the celebs to the dancers to the make-up girls, the cooks, the techies – even the judges. It was a riot from start to finish. The only tales I do have are of drunkenness, camaraderie and side-splitting comedy.

It helped that the star of our show was Julian Clary, one of the funniest men I have ever met. He was very quiet to begin with, because that's the way he is, and the rest of us were probably a bit too loud for his liking. Four were there from the recently finished series, including Tom Chambers, the winner, and Gethin and I were there from the series before. We were all outgoing and liked to party. Julian didn't know any of us well, but by the end of it we all loved him – a brilliant guy. He was very different from the people I was used to. You meet so many people in your rugby career who are raucous and full of banter, which is great, but it was a pleasure to get to know a comedian who was very shy. I think a lot of comedians are shy, but once they put on some make-up and go out on stage they're totally different. Julian is a private person. He was writing a novel during the run (one of the characters is called Kenny, apparently) and otherwise often had his head in a newspaper – the kind of guy who would probably know the answer to any question you might have. We had him downing vodkas by the end, though.

When you're doing the TV show, you see the other contestants just twice a week and it's quite competitive. On tour it's a different dynamic. You're performing in a self-contained competition every night. Sometimes we'd head out after the show to unwind, but more often than not we would stay in the hotel bar. I spent hours with Tom Chambers and his wife, Claire, and it was good to get to know him. 'One more for the road,' Claire would say to us at about midnight, sitting on our bar stools, and then, come four o'clock, it would be, 'Right, this one is definitely it.'

I already knew Gethin pretty well from the TV show, but our friendship deepened on the tour. He used to take me out shopping, which is another thing that didn't tend to happen much with my mates in rugby. Funnily enough, Gethin is actually a rugby player – he nearly turned pro.

During the TV show, Alesha and a few of the others were convinced he was gay. I didn't buy it, but I promised her I would find out. I asked him one day if he had a girlfriend and he said he didn't, and I started to wonder whether the rumours might be true. Then, about five or six weeks into the show, Gethin and I were having a bite to eat in his dressing room, and he said, 'I've got something to tell you.'

'This is it,' I thought. 'He's going to tell me he's gay.' I was poised on the edge of my seat, and then someone knocked on the door.

'We're not in!' I called out.

'You're needed on stage.'

'Just give us a couple of minutes! Please!'

But the moment had gone, and Gethin got up to leave, so the gossip continued.

About a week after that, he said to me, 'You know that thing I was about to tell you?' I nodded and concentrated on looking all caring and sympathetic. 'Well, you asked me if I was going out with anyone. I am.'

'Who was it?' I was thinking. One of the dancers, maybe? Could he have fallen in love during the show?

It turned out to be Katherine Jenkins, the beautiful opera singer. I was impressed. I'd recently met her for the first time myself. Katherine often sings the Welsh anthem before matches at the Millennium Stadium. I've got to know her a whole lot better since through Gethin. She was often with us on tour.

For a heterosexual ex-rugby player, Gethin was a very enthusiastic shopper. He chose a load of trendy clothes for me. Gabby was stunned when I returned home between legs of the tour, I was looking so cool. I had to tell her she'd lost the gig. 'I'm going shopping with Gethin from now on. He knows how to dress me.' It was all part of the new me. Not only was I a dancer on tour, I was going out shopping for clothes with my new mates.

In touch with my feminine side or not, I was shocked on the first week of the tour when everyone was booking in for spray tans. 'No way,' I said, 'What's wrong with make-up?' It was pointed out that we were performing every night and doing matinees twice a week, and if I was going to do my kilt routine, which involved bare arms, putting on and taking off make-up every day was going to be a nightmare. So I gave in to the spray tans in the end, and Gethin gave me a lot of stick about it for a few days. Until it turned out he'd been sneaking in sessions on the sun bed.

This wasn't the kind of thing we used to banter about on rugby tours, it has to be said, but dancing and rugby came crashing together spectacularly one night in Newcastle – only the second night of the tour. I'd organised to meet up with some of the boys from Newcastle Falcons, who'd been playing Brive that evening in a European game, and the Brive boys came as well. They had a few Brits in their side – Steve Thompson, Andy Goode, Ben Cohen and Alix Popham to name but four. None of the dancers wanted to come except Gethin and James Jordan. James fancied locking horns with some real men. 'Yeah, I'll take all you rugby boys on,' he said. Stuart Holden, the show's warm-up man, came as well.

Alan Tait was drunk already when we turned up at the night-club in Newcastle, where we'd arranged to meet. Upstairs we joined the Brive lot. Steve Thompson was the ring leader, and he called me and my new dance friends over to drink Grey Goose vodka with them, which became our favourite drink on the tour. They'd put a funnel on the bottle and Thomo was busy squirting it down the throats of his Brive team-mates.

James couldn't resist the challenge. Among the dancers he's the alpha male and he wasn't going to let any rugby players start thinking they were harder than he was. Now, Thomo was England's hooker when they won the World Cup in 2003 and he must tip the scales at eighteen stone, if he's an ounce. He was quite happy to pour the vodka into James's mouth. Normally, it's sensible when you're downing vodka to fill your mouth and then swallow. James wasn't having any of that. He was gulping like a mad man – glug, glug, glug. He'd taken about a quarter of the bottle. Thomo and I were looking at each other, and I grabbed his elbow.

'I think that's enough,' I said.

But James disagreed.

'Come on, give me more of that, you fuckers!'

We practically had to restrain him. Stuart was next and he was soon ready to throw up. Then it was my turn. So I downed the first couple of gulps, but then I put my tongue in the funnel – the oldest trick in the book. Thomo could see what I was doing and played along.

'Go on, Kenny! Keep it going!' he encouraged.

Anyway, James was pretty soon flying. He said to me, gesturing at Thomo, 'I could take that big bloke on!'

'James. He'd just have to look at you and you'd fall over.' I suggested he go over and ask him for a fight, but James wasn't quite that pissed just yet.

By now, Gethin was refusing to drink any more vodka. Thomo agreed to let him off drinking any more if he bought another bottle. So Gethin stumped up the £90 (it was quality vodka), and the first thing Thomo did, of course, was make him drink some of it. He made me drink some too, whispering in my ear that he would blow my cover if I used the tongue-in-the-funnel trick again.

Then it was James's turn, and he gulped like a madman again. He must have drunk half a bottle of vodka, all in all, and that through a funnel, which makes you even drunker. He was gone, away with the birdies. So Gethin and I decided to take him back to the hotel, but on the way James insisted on having another drink somewhere. Which we did.

By the time we finally got him back to the hotel, he was so drunk he couldn't get his room key in the lock. I had the room next door to him and Ola, so I helped him open his door and pushed him into his room. I could hear him bounce back and forth a couple of times between the wardrobe and the wall opposite. Then he finally fell into bed.

James didn't make it for our daily session in the gym the next morning, and he only just made it to lunch, before the matinee performance. He could barely communicate. Ola wasn't too happy with me.

'I'm disappointed in you, Kenny. Look at the state of James.'

'Look, I can't stop him drinking. I was the one who got him home. I put him to bed.'

'No, you didn't!'

'Well, I put him into your room.'

She gave me a bit of a bollocking, but nothing compared to what James got. Funnily enough, Ola and I didn't dance too well in the matinee that day, but James . . . he was on fire. They gave him eighty out of eighty – his best dance on tour – which just goes to show.

More evidence for the benefits of vodka was to be found in Manchester. Kristina, the Russian dancer who'd been John Sergeant's partner on the 2008 TV show, organised a night out for us at a club. When we arrived, we were told we had free drinks, so I immediately ordered a bottle of Grey Goose.

'I'm out of here,' said James, but the rest of us cracked on, getting through a fair few bottles. It turned out, though, that only the first bottle had been free, and as we left, Gethin and I were presented with a bill for £580. He still grumbles about it now.

It turned out to be money well spent, because the next day all those who had not been on the vodka the night before were sick as dogs. The rest of us were right as rain. Ola hadn't had any and she was having a terrible time, throwing up throughout the show. There was a pail backstage, and people were coming off from their dances and either running off to the toilet or, in really bad cases, lurching towards the bucket. It was hilarious. As I told them all, if they'd only been on the vodka the night before, they wouldn't have caught this bug. It cleans out your system.

At this stage, all the shows were being won by Rachel Stevens and Vincent Simone. It got a bit ridiculous – they won the first nine shows on the bounce and, in total, twenty-six out of forty-five, which was a bit tough on Tom and Camilla, since they had won the TV show the previous Christmas. Mind you, Tom was planning on an acting career in America and was learning lines the whole time. He would come up behind me and say in his best American accent, 'If you got the money, I can get you outta this mess. But you better have the money.' God knows what these films were that he was trying out for, but I hope he makes it big, because he's promised to take me to Cannes on his yacht if he does.

In the end, Tom and Camilla won just one out of the forty-five shows, but Tom was always very supportive of Rachel. It summed up the mood on the tour. It was like a big, happy family.

Of course, energies sagged sometimes, particularly during rehearsals, when around twenty people all had something to say. In that respect, again, it was just like a rugby tour, and the only thing you can do is ban all talk and focus on your own role. Afterwards is the time to analyse.

Even if Tom hadn't been such a good bloke, it would have been hard for him not to be supportive of Rachel, because she is so adorable. She has a heart of gold, and it was impossible to begrudge her the complete domination she had over the tour, or to begrudge Vincent his success. He was such a good tourist, an excellent team player, keeping everyone's spirits up with his banter.

All the same, we'd been through Newcastle and Liverpool and were four shows into the Manchester leg before anyone broke Rachel's run. By then we'd each devised personal touches to try to win over the audience, because on the tour, it was purely down to them. We each did two dances, and the judges' marks and critiques served merely as guidance. The winner was decided by the audience alone, who texted their votes. Most of the time, they would agree with the judges, but it was possible to get them to break rank, as I discovered in Glasgow.

Jill Halfpenny was the first to win a show ahead of Rachel. Of all the celebrities, she had come the closest to being a professional dancer. She had an eight-month-old baby, so she couldn't come out as much as she would have liked – and she really would have liked. She doesn't stand on ceremony. She's always up for a laugh, and if you're being an idiot she'll call you an idiot – just what any good tour needs.

Gethin then won a couple of nights on the trot. He milked

the Manchester vote. He went to university there, so he made out it was a return home for him. Yeah, and I played down the road at Sale a few times, so Manchester was like a second home for me, too.

The master at playing the audience, though, was of course Julian. None of us got much time on the mikes, because we were there to dance and be judged. But Julian got as much time as he liked, because he was a comedian. He had them eating out of his hand.

'My mum's very ill,' he would say. 'I'm expecting a phone call any minute. All I want is to be able to ring her up and say, "Mum. I've won." Nothing would make me prouder. As a twenty-eight-year-old man. From Manchester.' We were all shouting out backstage, 'There's nothing wrong with his mum! He's from Surbiton!'

He'd casually asked me for a few typical Scottish phrases and it was only when we got to Glasgow that I realised why. 'Nothing would make me happier than to be able to tell my mum . . . I'm from Glasgae, ye ken. From the Gorbals, just across the water. Och aye, wee man.'

Glasgow was where I felt the most pressure. We'd done the show in front of some amazing audiences of up to 10,000 – there were 15,000 at the $O_2$ Arena – but all along the pros had said, 'Wait till we get to Glasgow.' They said to me, 'Kenny, you'll win Glasgow hands down.'

But what if I didn't? Jill and Darren hadn't won in Newcastle, and Jill's a Newcastle girl. Darren's from Sheffield, and they won just one night and a matinee when we went there. So I was nervous for the Glasgow run.

Whatever city we were in, every night when you were back-stage you could hear the cheers when the names were announced, but at the SECC in Glasgow they roared the place down. We were all buzzing before we'd even gone on. I hadn't felt goose bumps since my rugby career had ended, but I did on that dance floor in Glasgow. Our first dance was the Viennese waltz to 'Flower of Scotland'. The music started, but Ola and I didn't move because we just couldn't hear it over the noise. Then we caught the 'Scotland' of 'Oh, Flower of Scotland' and had to jump to that part of the routine. A piper appeared at the top of the stage, and the noise went to another level. I've never experienced an atmosphere like it. In sports stadiums the noise can be deafening, but it escapes up into the air. Here, the acoustics were such that the sound made by the 4,000 people in the auditorium battered into the stage. It was amazing, and the same for all of the contestants. Each couple came off raving about it. 'Kenny,' they said, 'there's no way you won't win this.'

I did win in Glasgow – all six of the shows, the only ones I won all tour, I'm sorry to say – but I was so proud of the reception they gave all of us. Those audiences loved everyone and were passionate about every dance. I was proud of being Scottish and proud of being part of the tour and proud that I could be feeling such a buzz beyond my rugby career.

To win a clean sweep in Glasgow was great, but, then again, Ola and I were dancing to 'Flower of Scotland' and I was wearing a kilt, so if we hadn't, there would have been something wrong. The only night I didn't really want to win was when Ola and I were in the last two with Cherie Lunghi and James. Cherie was like a sexy mum you had a crush on. She was gorgeous and wise and a brilliant dancer. She and James got full marks for one of their dances that night, and I actually wanted them to win.

Ola and I were never in danger of getting full marks, not least because Craig was on the panel. It was funny watching him try to cope in Glasgow. He just had to give up talking sometimes, because the audience booed so loudly at him when he started having a go at me.

Another good thing about the tour was getting to know the judges better, and Craig is all mouth when he plays the hard man in the judge's chair. The truth is he's a big softie, and he likes to party – he especially loved Grey Goose – so we got on very well when he wasn't slagging me off.

There was a lot of downtime when we really had little more than each other's company to wile away the hours. These are the times when you either form bonds or fall apart. A sign of good team spirit is when everyone is happy just to stay in the bar at the hotel after the show. Going out was difficult anyway, because of paparazzi and autograph hunters. After the Glasgow shows, particularly, there was no chance of anyone going to sleep with the kind of adrenaline that was pumping through us, so we just sat in the bar. Like on a rugby tour, it's when it's an unhappy ship that people tend to go out. The happiest touring parties never venture very far from the hotel.

The Six Nations was on during the tour, and I had a column in the Scottish edition of the *Sunday Times*. This meant I was supposed to watch the games and provide reasoned analysis for tight deadlines. The problem was we had matinees and evening shows on Saturdays and Sundays, so we were performing during the matches.

Luckily, Gethin was willing to help, and so was Jodie Kidd – again, what a great girl, a riot from start to finish, and she loves sport. Jodie, Gethin and I would be glued to the games when we weren't on stage, along with a load of the production team. Len Goodman had to be on stage all the time, but he kept darting back during breaks, mainly to find out the West Ham score.

I told the producer we needed a TV set back there. 'I can't dance without a TV,' I said to him. We would be watching the match, and I'd nip off to do the paso doble, get my marks from the judges, then leg it back and ask Gethin what had happened while I was away. He was my eyes and ears. He should have had a joint byline with me, really.

Gethin was a scrum-half in his playing days, and he's not mad about Mike Phillips, Wales's scrum-half. I agree with him to an extent, because Phillips's pass is slow, but Phillips is probably not that keen on me either. When I played against him once for Glasgow against Llanelli, I scored a try in the corner and I leapt up to celebrate and accidentally smashed him in the face with my fist. Even the referee laughed.

Anyway, whenever we were watching Wales, Gethin was constantly saying, 'Look how slow Phillips's pass is! Look at it! Look at it! He's got to go!' Each time the team was announced, he'd be saying, 'I can't believe it! Phillips is in the team again!' I told him he had to get over it, and it developed into a bit of an argument between us on the tour. One time, we were driving north from London with Rachel in the back of the car. Rachel,

Gethin and I did a lot of travelling together, going to and from London whenever we had days off. I was on the car phone to Gabby, and Phillips had been picked again.

'You've got to say something on one of your shows, Gabby,' said Gethin. 'This can't be allowed to go on. They've got to pick Dwayne Peel.'

Rachel had been sitting quietly in the back – God knows how many hours she'd had to sit through Gethin and me arguing about rugby. Suddenly, she pipes up, 'I don't think they should play this Phillips guy, Gabby. His service is way too slow.' So we'd even brainwashed Rachel by the end of it.

Rachel was still winning the vast majority of the shows, but the big question was who was going to win on the night the DVD was filmed. Whoever won that would be forever preserved on film as the winner. Gethin nicked it. Katherine had come up to watch him, and whenever Katherine came up Gethin seemed to win (apart from when she came up to Glasgow, obviously). It was as if he found her mere presence inspiring. Gethin and I had a lot of heart-to-hearts on the tour about what it was like not being as famous as your other half. I told him Gabby didn't mind it too much.

After Glasgow, there was only one more stop on the road – Birmingham. The journey down was hilarious, drinking wine and playing a card game called shitface in the back of the bus. Julian Clary, in particular, loved shitface. The bonds between us all were being strengthened by the fact that the show was nearing its end.

We had our last big party after the Wednesday night show in Birmingham, which was a few performances short of the end, the following Sunday. Everyone was there – dancers, judges, producers, backstage crew, cooks and so on – and out came the Grey Goose. But it backfired on me. We had all the judges funnelling – Arlene included. Vincent kept tapping me on the shoulder, saying he wanted more. The production guys said they would drink if I did. I pretty much had a shot of vodka every time anyone else did. By one o'clock I had Jodie Kidd up on my shoulders, lifting her to the ceiling. By two o'clock I was comatose. I went to bed, and they tell me I was at lunch the next day, but I don't remember it. I must have gone back to bed because I woke up in time for the show the next evening. That was my drinking over for the tour.

All that adrenaline still had to be got out of the system every night, so for the remainder of the week the casino came to the rescue. I can see how drink and gambling take over the lives of some performers.

James Jordan knows what he's doing in a casino. He was winning a fair chunk a night on blackjack and poker. He brought back his winnings after one really good night, and Ola went off the next day and bought six pairs of shoes with the money.

'Yeah, but . . .' says James.

'No. There's no yeah buts. You go out all night to the casino, I'm going out to buy some shoes.'

She came back like Julia Roberts in *Pretty Woman*, weighed down with shopping bags, but it meant she was happy for James to go again.

On the second last night we were in the bar after the show, and Len Goodman came down. We sat around talking for a bit, then after about half an hour Len suddenly said, 'Who wants to go to the casino?'

James was up for it, obviously, and Vincent said he'd go. I was about two hundred quid down from my previous visits, but I thought, what the hell. We set off, and all the way there Len was grumbling that he'd been in his room and put the kettle on, only to find it was broken. So he'd come down to have a cup of tea with the rest of us, and now he was heading out to the casino. If only his kettle had been working . . .

At the casino, Len started negotiating like the geezer he is, trying to get us a table to ourselves, but the manager wasn't having any of it. 'Do you know who these people are, son?' said Len, pointing to the rest of us, who were standing there like lemons.

He pulled it off, though, and we settled down to play blackjack. The minimum bet at our private table was £25, which meant I had enough for four, and it wasn't long before I was trudging off to get some more money – 'Another £100,' I said, 'and that's my lot.' James was loads up, Vincent was doing OK, Len was down, and the game went on. Suddenly I found myself £500 up, and I was thinking, 'That's cleared my losses and left with me a hundred quid profit.' Happy days. James was still up – he walked away with a tidy sum that week.

Len was having a bad night. He decided to cut his losses and cash in what he had left. My winnings were down from £500 to £400 and I was ready to go to bed, but since I was having a good night, I decided to put that £400 on one hand. The dealer dealt me a four.

'That's not a good card,' said James. Thanks. The dealer had a six. Then he dealt me a king, so I was on fourteen. James told me to stick.

'What? That's never going to win.'

'Stick, I'm telling you,' James insisted.

The dealer has to keep twisting till he's got seventeen or more. He got a ten next for sixteen, so he had to twist again, and it was an eight. The dealer was bust. Eight hundred quid. Thanks, James. Thanks, lads. I'm off. I cashed in my chips and headed back to the hotel with Len.

James ended up having breakfast at the casino.

---

The last night, everyone was quite emotional. Vincent and Rachel were crying, and most people seemed to think I was sure to do the same.

'If you go, I'll go,' said James.

'I'm not crying. Don't be daft,' I responded.

As anyone who has read this far will know, I've been known to cry from time to time myself, and I could easily have gone then. It was really sad. The tour had been the most amazing experience, and for me it's probably one that I will never have again. I'd enjoyed it even more than I'd enjoyed the TV show. It hadn't been as much of a personal journey, but in terms of the camaraderie and fun it couldn't be beaten.

As well as that, I was a much better dancer at the end of the tour than I had been at the beginning. Everyone improved massively over the two months, although our marks never did. We all had our places in the judges' eyes, and they had to stick to that. Julian and I, for example, were always bottom of their leaderboard, which was pretty much the role we had been hired for. 'Your Viennese waltz is better than a six now,' Craig told me, towards the end. He tried to explain why my marks never improved. 'I've got a reputation to live up to, Kenny. I'm meant to be the bad guy.' For the paso doble he always gave me three. But everyone understood that it was a bit of a pantomime.

After the final show came the prize-giving. Rachel won the prize for the most wins on tour hands down with twenty-six. Believe it or not, I was second on six. I thought Gethin had won six as well, so I found myself saying, 'No, hang on. Gethin's won the same number as I have.' It was not like me to let my competitiveness slip and try to share second place with Gethin, but the tour did strange things to you. It made you want everyone else to do well. The producers insisted that Gethin had won five (I still reckon they got it wrong), so it was confirmed that I was officially a better dancer than he was. Thanks to Glasgow, obviously. I never won anywhere else.

There were no egos on that tour. Celebrities helped to attract audiences, but so many people behind the scenes made it tick, and they were all good people. It was quite horrible when it ended. We all just went our separate ways. Emotions were bubbling away. There were tears in everyone's eyes and lots of hugs. Then home.

The whole thing may have had its similarities with a rugby tour, but it wasn't much like one when it came to the goodbyes. I was feeling the pain as much as anyone. Had I changed again? I'd been an illiterate farmer in my life, an international rugby player, a businessman and a dancer. This was something new again. Was I now a drama queen?

Pull yourself together, I said to myself. What would Jim Telfer think? I slapped myself round the face and walked away scratching my balls.

# Epilogue

I sometimes think of that wee lad running in the fields below the Wallace Monument in the late seventies and early eighties, and I wonder if he could have guessed what was lying in store for him – the trophies and the glory and the heartache of his rugby career, the amazing places it would take him and the personalities it would introduce him to. There is the life he would find in the bright lights of London. The craziness of the battles he would fight both on the rugby field and on the dance floor in front of an audience of millions. What sense would he have made of any of it? Would it have frightened him? Or would it have made him feel better about himself?

Because that wee lad didn't feel good about himself. One thing he would definitely have recognised about the life he was to go on to lead was the panic when it came to letters and words, the lapses in concentration and the inability to absorb information. If only he could have known why it was happening and that one day he would find a way to beat it. That one day it would all come good.

There's no doubt that it has all come good. That young boy knew the importance of family. Little did he know that he was to go on to strike gold with the girl he would marry, and the family they would start is now the centre of his world, just as the wee boy's family meant so much to him when there was so little comfort to be found at school.

I know all kids have their crosses to bear, and most of us make our way to some kind of stability in adulthood where things seem a little less scary. But a lot of people don't find that. I was just the kind of confused kid who could have gone down the wrong path, but I had a good family and I had sport. I was lucky.

It breaks my heart that so many children don't have those things. All you want at a young age is a pat on the back every now and then. If you don't get it you can quickly lose your hope and enthusiasm. When I was at school, Norrie Bairner breaking ranks and keeping his PE class going during the teacher strikes, made that difference for me. Otherwise, I would have had no sport and I would have had no pats on the back. That was just the sort of time I could have dropped out altogether. Not everyone is into their sport, of course, but everyone is, or could be, into something, and the role of education is to help to identify that and to develop it.

I despair of the education system in this country. All you hear about are arguments among the authorities over what they think are the best methods, as if their beliefs are the important thing, rather than the children the system is designed to help in the first place. League tables and results are all that matter. It's a short step from that to focusing all your attention on the high-flyers to the exclusion of those who struggle. But it's the ones who struggle who need the help. The high-flyers are going to do fine. I have come across special-needs teachers who have had just one day's training. That's ridiculous and sums up as much as anything society's attitude to the ones who can't keep up.

When I finally learnt to read and write properly it did so much for my self-esteem, even at the age of thirty, even when I'd played rugby nearly sixty times for my country. It was an exciting time for me, but it threw me into the middle of controversy. I'd taken an unconventional course, which cost nearly three grand, it is true – and I was lucky to be able to afford it – but it was also based on emerging research not recognised by the authorities. That meant it was continually dealing with hostility from the establishment, rather than support and development.

Inspired by what it had done for me, I did a lot of promotional work for the company that ran the programme and then became a director when I opened up a new branch relating to sport. Unfortunately, the company went into liquidation in 2008. I found the conflict between the programme and the official dyslexia associations of Great Britain depressing. These are people who should all be working together. If the programme I took can work for even one other person as well as it worked for me (and I know it has done so for many more than that), then it has to be worth investment and acceptance.

I wonder how much dyslexia has made me who I am and how much it has stood in my way. That desperate need to prove myself that pushed me on throughout my rugby career might not have been so strong had I found things easier at school. Then again, some of my weaknesses as a rugby player were classic symptoms of dyslexia. My lack of concentration was number one among those. When I was good on the rugby field, I was good; when I was bad, I was bad. I could do the impossible things better than anyone; it was the basic, simple ones that caused me problems. I know I would have been more consistent had it not been for dyslexia. The last two-and-a-half years of my career, after the programme, felt very different from what had gone before.

Now that I think about it, my whole life has been about learning things on the hoof, doing everything the wrong way round. I learnt how to read and write fifteen years after leaving school; I saw my beloved cousin Hamish die suddenly when I was eighteen; my father died two years after that, and I was suddenly left to run his farm; and four years after that I was heading down to London for a new career, with the golden girl of Scottish television on my arm. And I was an illiterate farmer. I had to adapt very quickly at each stage.

Having never been exceptional as a kid, at the age of twenty I suddenly found myself good enough at rugby to play for Scotland. Stirling County was where I had learnt the game, a humble little club down the road who rose up the leagues from nowhere – and suddenly in 1995 we were Scottish champions. Then it was to Wasps in London, to join up with a group of like-minded kids, led by a twenty-four-year-old called Lawrence Dallaglio – and suddenly in 1997 we were English champions. It took us a while to get to grips with that tag, but when we grew up we got to grips with it with a vengeance. It was always about growing up, making do, finding a way.

In 1999 Scotland won the last Five Nations, and that was the season I suddenly became goal-kicker for club and country, basically because no one else wanted to do it. At Wasps I received the kind of support from a close family of players and coaches that I had never received in the classroom, and I thrived on it. With Scotland I often felt like I was treated as the naughty schoolboy again – a naughty schoolboy who had to kick vital goals in front of 70,000 people. On a couple of occasions the results were as bad as my results in the classroom. Despite seventy caps that took in some incredible highs and lows I will no doubt be remembered for some of those misses.

Jonny Wilkinson said to me once that the kicks I was missing were the kind he'd been able to get out of his system at school. 'You've just started goal-kicking,' he said, 'and suddenly you're kicking for your country. I've been kicking since I was a kid. You're twenty-eight. You're doing it the wrong way round.'

Doing it the wrong way round – they should write that on my gravestone. God knows, they wrote it on my school reports often enough. And, when I went to that celebrity dance school they call *Strictly Come Dancing*, doing it the wrong way round was the least of the criticisms that came my way from the judges.

What made that show so important to me was the way I started at such a low point but then got better and better. It helped me finally to leave behind the ghosts of my schooldays, when there was no chance of ever moving on from that lowest of low points I started at. I suppose I'd known through my rugby what it was like to get better at something, but the difference was that I was always good at rugby. *Strictly* was the first time, other than when I learnt my vowels only a few years earlier, that I started off not being able to do something at all and then went on to learn.

A little thing, but it's amazing the difference it makes. Now I look forward to the next part of my life with far more confidence than I did the first. Since I retired from rugby my sports marketing business has grown from being a little sideline to keep me off the streets in my free time to a company of six of us. We act as agents in sponsorship deals, we organise events and offer advice. We are what they call a niche company, and we wouldn't want to get much bigger than we are, or we'd lose that.

Do I want to make lots of money? I wouldn't say no to it, obviously, but not if it meant spoiling my quality of life and the balance I have between work and family. To be happy is what I want above all. It should really be all any of us want. Making money, excelling at sport, working hard on a farm, learning to dance, learning to read and write – they may all seem like goals in themselves, but in truth they're only ways of getting to happiness, even if they so often get ideas above their station.

Am I a successful person? I reckon so. I don't care that it took me to the age of thirty to read and write. I don't care about all the tries and the trophies. I'm a happy man now. That means I've made it.

# Career Statistics

Compiled by John Griffiths

## KENNY LOGAN

- In his 70 Test appearances he started 63 times and appeared off the bench on seven occasions.
- 68 of his caps were won as a wing and he is Scotland's most-capped player in this position. His other two caps were as a full-back (first appearance and third appearance, when he was a blood sub for Gavin Hastings).
- He stands seventh on the list of all-time Scotland cap-winners behind Chris Paterson, Scott Murray, Gregor Townsend, Gordon Bulloch, Jason White and Stuart Grimes.
- He scored 220 Test points for Scotland comprising 13 tries, 34 conversions and 29 penalty goals.
- Only Chris Paterson, Gavin Hastings and Andy Irvine have scored more Tests points for Scotland.
- He stands eighth on Scotland's list of all-time Test try-scorers.
- He was the first player capped by Scotland from the Stirling County club.

# SCOTLAND

## CAP 1

LOST 13–37 v AUSTRALIA, 21 June 1992, Brisbane

SCOTLAND: **K M Logan**; A G Stanger, S Hastings, S R P Lineen, I Tukalo; C M Chalmers, A D Nicol; D M B Sole (*captain*), M W Scott, P H Wright, D F Cronin, G W Weir, C D Hogg, R I Wainwright, I R Smith

SCOTLAND SCORERS: *Tries:* Lineen, Sole *Conversion:* Chalmers *Penalty Goal:* Chalmers

## CAP 2

LOST 12–26 v ENGLAND, 6 March 1993, Twickenham

SCOTLAND: A G Hastings (*captain*); A G Stanger, S Hastings (rep **K M Logan**), A G Shiel, D A Stark; C M Chalmers (rep G P J Townsend), G Armstrong; P H Wright, K S Milne, A P Burnell, A I Reed, D F Cronin, D J Turnbull, G W Weir, I R Morrison

SCOTLAND SCORERS: *Penalty Goals:* A G Hastings 3 *Dropped Goal:* Chalmers

## CAP 3

LOST 15–51 v NEW ZEALAND, 20 November 1993, Murrayfield

SCOTLAND: A G Hastings (*captain*) (temp rep **K M Logan**); A G Stanger, I C Jardine, A G Shiel, S Hastings; C M Chalmers (rep D S Wyllie), A D Nicol (temp rep B W Redpath); A G J Watt, K S Milne, A P Burnell, D F Cronin (rep C D Hogg), A E D Macdonald, D J McIvor, G W Weir, R I Wainwright

SCOTLAND SCORERS: *Penalty Goals:* A G Hastings 4, Chalmers

## CAP 4

LOST 6–29 v WALES, 15 January 1994, Cardiff

SCOTLAND: A G Hastings (*captain*); A G Stanger, G P J Townsend, I C Jardine, **K M Logan**; C M Chalmers (rep D S Wyllie), A D Nicol; P H Wright, K S Milne, A P Burnell, N G B Edwards, D S Munro, D J Turnbull, R I Wainwright, I R Morrison (rep G W Weir)

SCOTLAND SCORER: *Penalty Goals:* A G Hastings 2

## CAP 5

LOST 14–15 v ENGLAND, 5 February 1994, Murrayfield

SCOTLAND: A G Hastings (*captain*); A G Stanger, S Hastings (rep I C Jardine), D S Wyllie, **K M Logan**; G P J Townsend,

G Armstrong (temp rep B W Redpath); A V Sharp, K S Milne, A P Burnell, D S Munro, A I Reed, P Walton, G W Weir, R I Wainwright (rep I R Smith)

SCOTLAND SCORERS: *Try:* Wainwright *Penalty Goals:* A G Hastings 2 *Dropped Goal:* Townsend

## CAP 6

DRAWN 6–6 v IRELAND, 5 March 1994,
Lansdowne Road, Dublin

SCOTLAND: A G Hastings (*captain*) (temp rep M Dods); A G Stanger, S Hastings, D S Wyllie, **K M Logan**; G P J Townsend, G Armstrong; A V Sharp, K S Milne, A P Burnell, D S Munro, A I Reed, P Walton, G W Weir, I R Smith

SCOTLAND SCORER: *Penalty Goals:* A G Hastings 2

## CAP 7

LOST 12–20 v FRANCE, 19 March 1994, Murrayfield

SCOTLAND: A G Hastings (*captain*); A G Stanger, S Hastings, D S Wyllie, **K M Logan**; G P J Townsend, B W Redpath; A V Sharp, K S Milne, A P Burnell, D S Munro, A I Reed, P Walton, G W Weir, I R Smith

SCOTLAND SCORER: *Penalty Goals:* A G Hastings 4

## CAP 8

LOST 15–16 v ARGENTINA, 4 June 1994,
Buenos Aires

SCOTLAND: M Dods; C A Joiner, I C Jardine, A G Shiel, **K M Logan**; G P J Townsend, B W Redpath; A V Sharp, K D McKenzie, A P Burnell, D S Munro, A I Reed (*captain*), P Walton, C D Hogg, I R Smith

SCOTLAND SCORER: *Penalty Goals:* Dods 5

## CAP 9

LOST 17–19 v ARGENTINA, 11 June 1994, Buenos Aires

SCOTLAND: M Dods; C A Joiner, I C Jardine, A G Shiel, **K M Logan** (rep S A Nichol); G P J Townsend, B W Redpath; A V Sharp (rep A G J Watt), K D McKenzie, A P Burnell, D S Munro (temp rep A G J Watt), A I Reed (*captain*), P Walton, C D Hogg, I R Smith

SCOTLAND SCORERS: *Try:* **Logan** *Penalty Goals:* Shiel 2, Dods *Dropped Goal:* Townsend

## CAP 10

LOST 10–34 v SOUTH AFRICA, 19 November 1994, Murrayfield

SCOTLAND: A G Hastings (*captain*); A G Stanger, S Hastings, A G Shiel, **K M Logan**; C M Chalmers, D W Patterson; A V

Sharp, K S Milne, A P Burnell, J F Richardson, A I Reed, D J McIvor, G W Weir, I R Morrison

SCOTLAND SCORERS: *Try:* Stanger *Conversion:* A G Hastings *Penalty Goal:* A G Hastings

## CAP 11

WON 22–6 v CANADA, 21 January 1995, Murrayfield

SCOTLAND: A G Hastings (*captain*); C A Joiner, G P J Townsend, I C Jardine, **K M Logan**; C M Chalmers, B W Redpath; D I W Hilton, K S Milne, P H Wright, D F Cronin, S J Campbell, R I Wainwright, E W Peters, I R Morrison

SCOTLAND SCORERS: *Try:* Cronin *Conversion:* A G Hastings *Penalty Goals:* A G Hastings 5

## CAP 12

WON 26–13 v IRELAND, 4 February 1995, Murrayfield

SCOTLAND: A G Hastings (*captain*); C A Joiner, G P J Townsend, I C Jardine, **K M Logan**; C M Chalmers, B W Redpath; D I W Hilton, K S Milne, P H Wright, D F Cronin, S J Campbell, R I Wainwright, E W Peters, I R Morrison

SCOTLAND SCORERS: *Tries:* Cronin, Joiner *Conversions:* A G Hastings 2 *Penalty Goals:* A G Hastings 4

## CAP 13

WON 23–21 v FRANCE, 18 February 1995,
Parc des Princes, Paris

SCOTLAND: A G Hastings (*captain*); C A Joiner, G P J
Townsend, I C Jardine, **K M Logan**; C M Chalmers, B W
Redpath; D I W Hilton, K S Milne, P H Wright, D F Cronin
(rep G W Weir), S J Campbell, R I Wainwright, E W Peters,
I R Morrison

SCOTLAND SCORERS: *Tries:* A G Hastings, Townsend
*Conversions:* A G Hastings 2 *Penalty Goals:* A G Hastings 3

## CAP 14

WON 26–13 v WALES, 4 March 1995, Murrayfield

SCOTLAND: A G Hastings (*captain*); C A Joiner, G P J
Townsend, S Hastings, **K M Logan**; C M Chalmers, B W
Redpath; D I W Hilton, K S Milne, P H Wright, G W Weir,
S J Campbell, R I Wainwright, E W Peters, I R Morrison

SCOTLAND SCORERS: *Tries:* Hilton, Peters *Conversions:* A G
Hastings 2 *Penalty Goals:* A G Hastings 4

## CAP 15

LOST 12–24 v ENGLAND, 18 March 1995, Twickenham

SCOTLAND: A G Hastings (*captain*); C A Joiner, G P J
Townsend, S Hastings, **K M Logan**; C M Chalmers, B W

Redpath; D I W Hilton (rep J J Manson), K S Milne, P H Wright, G W Weir, S J Campbell, R I Wainwright, E W Peters, I R Morrison

SCOTLAND SCORERS: *Penalty Goals:* A G Hastings 2 *Dropped Goals:* Chalmers 2

## CAP 16

WON 49–16 v ROMANIA, 22 April 1995, Murrayfield

SCOTLAND: A G Hastings (*captain*) (rep S Hastings); C A Joiner, A G Stanger, A G Shiel, **K M Logan**; C M Chalmers, B W Redpath; D I W Hilton, K D McKenzie, P H Wright, G W Weir, S J Campbell, R I Wainwright, E W Peters, I R Morrison

SCOTLAND SCORERS: *Tries:* Stanger 2, A G Hastings, Joiner, Shiel, **Logan,** Peters *Conversions:* A G Hastings 4 *Penalty Goals:* A G Hastings 2

## CAP 17

WON 89–0 v IVORY COAST, 26 May 1995, Rustenburg

SCOTLAND: A G Hastings (*captain*); C A Joiner, A G Stanger, A G Shiel, **K M Logan**; C M Chalmers, B W Redpath; A P Burnell, K D McKenzie, P H Wright, G W Weir, S J Campbell, P Walton, R I Wainwright, I R Smith

SCOTLAND SCORERS: *Tries:* A G Hastings 4, **Logan 2,** Walton 2, Stanger, Shiel, Chalmers, Burnell, Wright *Conversions:* A G Hastings 9 *Penalty Goals:* A G Hastings 2

## CAP 18

WON 41–5 v TONGA, 30 May 1995, Pretoria

SCOTLAND: A G Hastings (*captain*); C A Joiner, S Hastings, I C Jardine, **K M Logan**; C M Chalmers, D W Patterson; D I W Hilton, K S Milne, P H Wright (rep A P Burnell), D F Cronin, G W Weir, R I Wainwright, E W Peters, I R Morrison

SCOTLAND SCORERS: *Tries:* A G Hastings, S Hastings, Peters *Conversion:* A G Hastings *Penalty Goals:* A G Hastings 8

## CAP 19

LOST 19–22 v FRANCE, 3 June 1995, Pretoria

SCOTLAND: A G Hastings (*captain*); C A Joiner, S Hastings, A G Shiel (rep I C Jardine), **K M Logan**; C M Chalmers, B W Redpath; D I W Hilton, K S Milne, P H Wright (rep A P Burnell), D F Cronin, G W Weir, R I Wainwright, E W Peters, I R Morrison

SCOTLAND SCORERS: *Try:* Wainwright *Conversion:* A G Hastings *Penalty Goals:* A G Hastings 4

## CAP 20

LOST 30–48 v NEW ZEALAND, 11 June 1995, Pretoria

SCOTLAND: A G Hastings (*captain*); C A Joiner, S Hastings, A G Shiel, **K M Logan**; C M Chalmers (rep I C Jardine), B W Redpath; D I W Hilton, K S Milne, P H Wright, D F

Cronin (rep S J Campbell), G W Weir, R I Wainwright, E W Peters, I R Morrison

SCOTLAND SCORERS: *Tries:* Weir 2, S Hastings *Conversions:* A G Hastings 3 *Penalty Goals:* A G Hastings 3

## CAP 21

DRAWN 15–15 v WESTERN SAMOA, 18 November 1995, Murrayfield

SCOTLAND: R J S Shepherd; M Dods, G P J Townsend, A G Shiel, **K M Logan**; C M Chalmers, B W Redpath; D I W Hilton, J A Hay, A P Burnell, G W Weir, D F Cronin. R I Wainwright (*captain*), S J Reid, I R Smith (temp rep S J Campbell)

SCOTLAND SCORER: *Penalty Goals:* Dods 5

## CAP 22

WON 16–14 v WALES, 17 February 1996, Cardiff

SCOTLAND: R J S Shepherd; C A Joiner (**rep K M Logan**), S Hastings, I C Jardine, M Dods; G P J Townsend, B W Redpath; D I W Hilton, K D McKenzie, P H Wright, S J Campbell, G W Weir, R I Wainwright (*captain*), E W Peters, I R Smith

SCOTLAND SCORERS: *Try:* Townsend *Conversion:* Dods *Penalty Goals:* Dods 3

## CAP 23

LOST 31–62 v NEW ZEALAND, 15 June 1996, Carisbrook, Dunedin

SCOTLAND: R J S Shepherd; C A Joiner, I C Jardine, B R S Eriksson, **K M Logan**; G P J Townsend, G Armstrong; D I W Hilton, K D McKenzie, P H Wright, G W Weir, D F Cronin, R I Wainwright (*captain*), E W Peters, I R Smith

SCOTLAND SCORERS: *Tries:* Townsend, Peters, Joiner *Conversions:* Shepherd 2 *Penalty Goals:* Shepherd 3 *Dropped Goal:* Townsend

## CAP 24

LOST 12–36 v NEW ZEALAND, 22 June 1996, Eden Park, Auckland

SCOTLAND: R J S Shepherd; A G Stanger, S Hastings, I C Jardine (rep D A Stark), **K M Logan**; G P J Townsend, G Armstrong; D I W Hilton, K D McKenzie, B D Stewart, G W Weir, D F Cronin, R I Wainwright (*captain*), E W Peters, I R Smith

SCOTLAND SCORERS: *Tries:* Shepherd, Peters *Conversion:* Shepherd

## CAP 25

LOST 19–29 v AUSTRALIA, 9 November 1996, Murrayfield

SCOTLAND: R J S Shepherd; A G Stanger, G P J Townsend (*captain*), B R S Eriksson, **K M Logan**; C M Chalmers, G Armstrong (rep B W Redpath); D I W Hilton, K D McKenzie, B D Stewart, G W Weir, D F Cronin, M I Wallace, E W Peters, I R Smith

SCOTLAND SCORERS: *Tries:* Stanger, **Logan** *Penalty Goals:* Shepherd 3

## CAP 26

WON 29–22 v ITALY, 14 December 1996, Murrayfield

SCOTLAND: R J S Shepherd (rep D A Stark); A G Stanger, S Hastings, G P J Townsend (*captain*), **K M Logan**; C M Chalmers, B W Redpath; D I W Hilton, K D McKenzie, M J Stewart, D F Cronin (rep G W Weir), A I Reed, M I Wallace, E W Peters, I R Smith

SCOTLAND SCORERS: *Tries:* **Logan 2**, Stark, Stanger *Conversions:* Chalmers 3 *Penalty Goal:* Shepherd

## CAP 27

LOST 19–34 v WALES, 18 January 1997, Murrayfield

SCOTLAND: R J S Shepherd; A G Stanger, S Hastings, G P J Townsend, **K M Logan**; C M Chalmers (rep D A Stark), G Armstrong; D I W Hilton, D G Ellis, M J Stewart, G W Weir, A I Reed (rep D S Munro), P Walton, R I Wainwright (*captain*), M I Wallace

SCOTLAND SCORERS: *Try:* S Hastings *Conversion:* Shepherd *Penalty Goals:* Shepherd 3 *Dropped Goal:* Chalmers

## CAP 28

LOST 13–41 v ENGLAND, 1 February 1997, Twickenham

SCOTLAND: R J S Shepherd; D A Stark, A G Stanger, B R S Eriksson (rep S Hastings), **K M Logan**; G P J Townsend, B W Redpath; T J Smith, D G Ellis, M J Stewart, G W Weir, A I Reed, P Walton, R I Wainwright (*captain*), I R Smith

SCOTLAND SCORERS: *Try:* Eriksson *Conversion:* Shepherd *Penalty Goals:* Shepherd 2

## CAP 29

WON 38–10 v IRELAND, 1 March 1997, Murrayfield

SCOTLAND: R J S Shepherd; A G Stanger, A V Tait, G P J Townsend, **K M Logan**; C M Chalmers, B W Redpath; T J Smith, D G Ellis, M J Stewart, G W Weir, A I Reed, R I Wainwright (*captain*), P Walton, I R Smith

SCOTLAND SCORERS: *Tries:* Stanger, Townsend, Walton, Tait, Weir *Conversions:* Shepherd 5 *Penalty Goal:* Shepherd

## CAP 30

LOST 20–47 v FRANCE, 15 March 1997, Parc des Princes, Paris

SCOTLAND: R J S Shepherd; A G Stanger, A V Tait (rep I C Glasgow), G P J Townsend, **K M Logan**; C M Chalmers (rep D W Hodge), B W Redpath; T J Smith, D G Ellis, M J Stewart, G W Weir, A I Reed, R I Wainwright (*captain*), P Walton (rep D F Cronin), I R Smith

SCOTLAND SCORERS: *Tries:* Tait 2 *Conversions:* Shepherd 2 *Penalty Goals:* Shepherd 2

## CAP 31

LOST 8–37 v AUSTRALIA, 22 November 1997, Murrayfield

SCOTLAND: D W Hodge; J M Craig, A G Stanger (rep C M Chalmers), A V Tait, **K M Logan**; G P J Townsend, A D Nicol (*captain*); D I W Hilton (rep M J Stewart), G McKelvey, M J Stewart (rep G Graham), S J Campbell, S Murray, A J Roxburgh (rep by S B Grimes), E W Peters, I R Smith (temp rep S B Grimes)

SCOTLAND SCORERS: *Try:* Murray *Penalty Goal:* Hodge

## CAP 32

WON 17–16 v IRELAND, 7 February 1998, Lansdowne Road, Dublin

SCOTLAND: R J S Shepherd (rep D J Lee); C A Joiner (rep A G Stanger), A V Tait, G P J Townsend, **K M Logan**; C M Chalmers, G Armstrong (*captain*); G Graham (rep D I W

Hilton), G C Bulloch, M J Stewart, D F Cronin (rep S B Grimes), G W Weir, R I Wainwright, P Walton, S D Holmes

SCOTLAND SCORERS: *Try:* Tait *Penalty Goals:* Shepherd 2, Chalmers 2

## CAP 33

LOST 16–51 v FRANCE, 21 February 1998, Murrayfield

SCOTLAND: D J Lee; A G Stanger, A V Tait, G P J Townsend, **K M Logan**; C M Chalmers (rep S L Longstaff), G Armstrong (*captain*); D I W Hilton (rep G Graham), G C Bulloch, M J Stewart, D F Cronin (rep S B Grimes), G W Weir, R I Wainwright, P Walton (rep A J Roxburgh), S D Holmes

SCOTLAND SCORERS: *Try:* Stanger *Conversion:* Chalmers *Penalty Goals:* Chalmers 3

## CAP 34

LOST 10–35 v SOUTH AFRICA, 21 November 1998, Murrayfield

SCOTLAND: D J Lee (rep G P J Townsend); A V Tait (rep **K M Logan**), M J M Mayer, J A Leslie, C A Murray; D W Hodge, B W Redpath (*captain*) (rep G Armstrong); T J Smith, G C Bulloch, A P Burnell (rep D I W Hilton), S Murray, G W Weir, P Walton (rep M D Leslie), E W Peters, A C Pountney

SCOTLAND SCORER: *Try:* Hodge *Conversion:* Hodge *Penalty Goal:* Hodge

## CAP 35

WON 33–20 v WALES, 6 February 1999, Murrayfield

SCOTLAND: G H Metcalfe; C A Murray, G P J Townsend, J A Leslie, **K M Logan**; D W Hodge (rep A V Tait), G Armstrong (*captain*); T J Smith, G C Bulloch, A P Burnell (rep D I W Hilton), S Murray, G W Weir (rep S B Grimes), P Walton (rep A C Pountney), E W Peters, M D Leslie (temp rep A C Pountney)

SCOTLAND SCORERS: *Tries:* J Leslie, Townsend, S Murray, Tait *Conversions:* **Logan 2** *Penalty Goals:* **Logan 2**, Hodge

## CAP 36

LOST 21–24 v ENGLAND, 20 February 1999, Twickenham

SCOTLAND: G H Metcalfe; C A Murray, A V Tait, J A Leslie, **K M Logan**; G P J Townsend, G Armstrong (*captain*); T J Smith, G C Bulloch, A P Burnell (rep D I W Hilton), S Murray, S B Grimes, P Walton (rep A C Pountney), E W Peters, M D Leslie

SCOTLAND SCORERS: *Tries:* Tait 2, Townsend *Conversions:* **Logan 3**

## CAP 37

WON 30–12 v ITALY, 6 March 1999, Murrayfield

SCOTLAND: G H Metcalfe; C A Murray, A V Tait (rep S L

Longstaff), J A Leslie, **K M Logan**; G P J Townsend, I T
Fairley (rep G G Burns); T J Smith (rep D I W Hilton), G
C Bulloch, A P Burnell, S Murray, S B Grimes (rep A I Reed),
P Walton, E W Peters (*captain*) (rep A C Pountney), M D
Leslie (temp rep A C Pountney)

SCOTLAND SCORERS: *Tries:* C Murray, Townsend, **Logan**
*Conversions:* **Logan** 3 *Penalty Goals:* **Logan** 3

## CAP 38

WON 30–12 v IRELAND, 20 March 1999, Murrayfield

SCOTLAND: G H Metcalfe; C A Murray (rep S L Longstaff),
A V Tait, J A Leslie, **K M Logan**; G P J Townsend, G Armstrong
(*captain*) (rep I T Fairley); T J Smith (rep D I W Hilton),
G C Bulloch (rep S J Brotherstone), A P Burnell S Murray,
S B Grimes, P Walton (rep A C Pountney), E W Peters, M
D Leslie

SCOTLAND SCORERS: *Tries:* C Murray 2, Townsend, Grimes
*Conversions:* **Logan** 2 *Penalty Goals:* **Logan** 2

## CAP 39

WON 36–22 v FRANCE, 10 April 1999,
Stade de France, Paris

SCOTLAND: G H Metcalfe; C A Murray, A V Tait, J A Leslie,
**K M Logan**; G P J Townsend, G Armstrong (*captain*); D I W
Hilton (rep G Graham), G C Bulloch, A P Burnell, S Murray

(rep A I Reed), S B Grimes, A C Pountney (rep P Walton), S J Reid, M D Leslie

SCOTLAND SCORERS: *Tries:* Tait 2, M Leslie 2, Townsend *Conversions:* **Logan** 4 *Penalty Goal:* **Logan**

## CAP 40

LOST 22–31 v ARGENTINA, 21 August 1999, Murrayfield

SCOTLAND: G H Metcalfe; C A Murray (rep S L Longstaff), A V Tait, J G McLaren (rep C M Chalmers), **K M Logan**; D W Hodge, G Armstrong (*captain*); T J Smith, G C Bulloch, A P Burnell (rep G Graham), S Murray, S B Grimes (rep G W Weir), P Walton (rep G L Simpson), S J Reid, A C Pountney

SCOTLAND SCORERS: *Tries:* Tait, Metcalfe, Walton *Conversions:* **Logan** 2 *Penalty Goal:* **Logan**

## CAP 41

WON 60–19 v ROMANIA, 28 August 1999, Hampden Park, Glasgow

SCOTLAND: G H Metcalfe; S L Longstaff, A V Tait, J G McLaren, **K M Logan** (rep C A Joiner); D W Hodge, G Armstrong (*captain*) (rep B W Redpath); T J Smith, R R Russell, G Graham (rep D I W Hilton), S Murray, S B Grimes, P Walton (rep C G Mather), G L Simpson (rep G W Weir), M D Leslie

SCOTLAND SCORERS: *Tries:* **Logan** 2, McLaren, Tait, Smith,

Grimes, M Leslie, pen try *Conversions:* **Logan 5,** Hodge 2 *Penalty Goals:* **Logan 2**

## CAP 42

LOST 29–46 v SOUTH AFRICA, 3 October 1999, Murrayfield

SCOTLAND: G H Metcalfe; C A Murray, A V Tait, J A Leslie (rep M J M Mayer), **K M Logan**; G P J Townsend, G Armstrong (*captain*); T J Smith, G C Bulloch, G Graham (rep D I W Hilton), S Murray (rep G W Weir), S B Grimes, M D Leslie, G L Simpson (rep P Walton), A C Pountney

SCOTLAND SCORERS: *Tries:* Tait, M Leslie *Conversions:* **Logan 2** *Penalty Goals:* **Logan 4** *Dropped Goal:* Townsend

## CAP 43

WON 43–12 v URUGUAY, 8 October 1999, Murrayfield

SCOTLAND: G H Metcalfe; C A Murray (rep S L Longstaff), A V Tait, M J M Mayer, **K M Logan**; G P J Townsend, G Armstrong (*captain*); T J Smith, G C Bulloch (rep R R Russell), G Graham (rep D I W Hilton), S Murray, S B Grimes, M D Leslie (rep P Walton), G L Simpson, A C Pountney

SCOTLAND SCORERS: *Tries:* Metcalfe, Townsend, M Leslie, Armstrong, Russell, Simpson *Conversions:* **Logan 5** *Penalty Goal:* **Logan**

## CAP 44

WON 35–20 v SAMOA, 20 October 1999, Murrayfield

SCOTLAND: G H Metcalfe; C A Murray, M J M Mayer, J G McLaren, **K M Logan**; G P J Townsend (rep D W Hodge), G Armstrong (*captain*); T J Smith, G C Bulloch, G Graham (rep A P Burnell), S Murray (rep S B Grimes), G W Weir, M D Leslie (rep R R Russell), G L Simpson, A C Pountney (rep C G Mather)

SCOTLAND SCORERS: *Tries:* pen try, C Murray, M Leslie *Conversion:* **Logan** *Penalty Goals:* **Logan** 5 *Dropped Goal:* Townsend

## CAP 45

LOST 18–30 v NEW ZEALAND, 24 October 1999, Murrayfield

SCOTLAND: G H Metcalfe; C A Murray, A V Tait, M J M Mayer, **K M Logan**; G P J Townsend, G Armstrong (*captain*); T J Smith, G C Bulloch (rep R R Russell), A P Burnell (rep G Graham), S Murray, G W Weir (rep S B Grimes), M D Leslie, G L Simpson, A C Pountney

SCOTLAND SCORERS: *Tries:* Pountney, C Murray *Conversion:* **Logan** *Penalty Goal:* **Logan** *Dropped Goal:* Townsend

## CAP 46

LOST 20–34 v ITALY, 5 February 2000, Stadio Flaminio, Rome

SCOTLAND: G H Metcalfe; S L Longstaff, M J M Mayer, J A Leslie (*captain*) (rep J G McLaren), **K M Logan**; G P J Townsend, B W Redpath; T J Smith, G C Bulloch, M J Stewart (rep D I W Hilton), S Murray (rep G W Weir), S B Grimes, M D Leslie, G L Simpson (temp rep S J Reid), A C Pountney

SCOTLAND SCORERS: *Tries:* Bulloch, M Leslie *Conversions:* **Logan**, Townsend *Penalty Goal:* Townsend *Dropped Goal:* Townsend

## CAP 47

LOST 22–44 v IRELAND, 19 February 2000, Lansdowne Road, Dublin

SCOTLAND: G H Metcalfe; S L Longstaff, M J M Mayer, A G Shiel, **K M Logan**; G P J Townsend, B W Redpath (*captain*) (rep A D Nicol); T J Smith, G C Bulloch (rep R R Russell), M J Stewart (rep G Graham), S Murray (rep G W Weir), S B Grimes, M D Leslie, G L Simpson, A C Pountney

SCOTLAND SCORERS: *Tries:* Metcalfe, **Logan**, Graham *Conversions:* **Logan** 2 *Penalty Goal:* **Logan**

## CAP 48

LOST 16–28 v FRANCE, 4 March 2000, Murrayfield

SCOTLAND: C D Paterson; G H Metcalfe, J G McLaren (rep D W Hodge), J A Leslie (*captain*), **K M Logan**; G P J Townsend, A D Nicol; T J Smith, S J Brotherstone, M J Stewart (rep D I W Hilton), S Murray, G W Weir (rep S B Grimes), M D Leslie, S J Reid (temp rep C G Mather), A C Pountney

SCOTLAND SCORERS: *Try:* Nicol *Conversion:* Paterson *Penalty Goals:* Paterson 2, **Logan**

## CAP 49

WON 31–8 v SAMOA, 18 November 2000, Murrayfield

SCOTLAND: C D Paterson; C A Murray, A J Bulloch (rep D W Hodge), J A Leslie, **K M Logan**; G P J Townsend, B W Redpath (rep G Beveridge); T J Smith, S J Brotherstone (rep G C Bulloch), G Graham (rep G R McIlwham), S Murray, R Metcalfe (rep S B Grimes), J P R White (rep R S Beattie), J M Petrie, A C Pountney (*captain*)

SCOTLAND SCORERS: *Tries:* A Bulloch, Smith, Petrie, **Logan** *Conversion:* Townsend *Penalty Goals:* Townsend 3

## CAP 50

LOST 6–16 v FRANCE, 4 February 2001, Stade de France, Paris

SCOTLAND: C D Paterson; C A Murray, J G McLaren (rep A J Bulloch), J A Leslie (temp rep A J Bulloch), **K M Logan**; G P J Townsend (rep D W Hodge), A D Nicol (*captain*) (rep B W Redpath); T J Smith, G C Bulloch (rep R R Russell), M J Stewart (rep G R McIlwham), S Murray, R Metcalfe (rep S B Grimes), M D Leslie, J M Petrie (rep J P R White), A C Pountney

SCOTLAND SCORER: *Penalty Goals:* **Logan 2**

## CAP 51

DRAWN 28–28 v WALES, 17 February 2001, Murrayfield

SCOTLAND: C D Paterson; C A Murray (rep J M Craig), J G McLaren, J A Leslie, **K M Logan**; D W Hodge, A D Nicol (*captain*); T J Smith, G C Bulloch, M J Stewart (rep G R McIlwham), S Murray, R Metcalfe (rep S B Grimes), M D Leslie, J M Petrie, A C Pountney

SCOTLAND SCORERS: *Tries:* Paterson, McLaren, Smith *Conversions:* Hodge, **Logan** *Penalty Goals:* **Logan 3**

## CAP 52

LOST 3–43 v ENGLAND, 3 March 2001, Twickenham

SCOTLAND: C D Paterson; C A Murray (rep J M Craig), A J Bulloch (rep J G McLaren), J A Leslie, **K M Logan**; D W Hodge, A D Nicol (*captain*) (rep B W Redpath); T J Smith, G C Bulloch, M J Stewart (rep G R McIlwham), S Murray,

R Metcalfe (rep S B Grimes), M D Leslie, S M Taylor, A C Pountney

SCOTLAND SCORER: *Penalty Goal:* Hodge

## CAP 53

WON 23–19 v ITALY, 17 March 2001, Murrayfield

SCOTLAND: C D Paterson; J M Craig (rep C A Murray), G P J Townsend, J A Leslie, **K M Logan**; D W Hodge, B W Redpath; T J Smith, G C Bulloch (rep S Scott), M J Stewart (rep G R McIlwham), S Murray, S B Grimes, M D Leslie, S M Taylor (rep J M Petrie), A C Pountney (*captain*)

SCOTLAND SCORERS: *Try:* Smith *Penalty Goals:* Hodge 5 *Dropped Goal:* Hodge

## CAP 54

LOST 22–43 v IRELAND, 2 March 2002, Lansdowne Road, Dublin

SCOTLAND: B J Laney; G H Metcalfe (rep **K M Logan**), J G McLaren, A R Henderson, C D Paterson; G P J Townsend, B W Redpath (*captain*); T J Smith, G C Bulloch, M J Stewart (rep G Graham), S Murray, S B Grimes, J P R White (rep M D Leslie), S M Taylor, A C Pountney

SCOTLAND SCORERS: *Try:* M Leslie *Conversion:* Laney *Penalty Goals:* Laney 5

## CAP 55

LOST 10–22 v FRANCE, 23 March 2002, Murrayfield

SCOTLAND: B J Laney; G H Metcalfe, J G McLaren (rep **K M Logan**), J A Leslie, C D Paterson; G P J Townsend, B W Redpath (*captain*); T J Smith, G C Bulloch (rep R R Russell), M J Stewart (rep G Graham), S Murray (rep S B Grimes), J P R White, M D Leslie (temp rep J M Petrie), S M Taylor, A C Pountney

SCOTLAND SCORERS: *Try:* Redpath *Conversion:* Laney *Penalty Goal:* Laney

## CAP 56

WON 27–22 v WALES, 6 April 2002, Cardiff

SCOTLAND: B J Laney (rep D W Hodge); **K M Logan** (rep G H Metcalfe), J G McLaren, J A Leslie, C D Paterson; G P J Townsend, B W Redpath (*captain*); T J Smith, G C Bulloch (rep R R Russell), M J Stewart (rep G Graham), S Murray, J P R White (rep S B Grimes), M D Leslie (rep J M Petrie), S M Taylor, A C Pountney

SCOTLAND SCORERS: *Tries:* Bulloch 2 *Conversion:* Laney *Penalty Goals:* Laney 4, Hodge

## CAP 57

LOST 6–36 v IRELAND, 16 February 2003, Murrayfield

SCOTLAND: G H Metcalfe; **K M Logan**, A Craig, B J Laney, C D Paterson; G Ross (rep G P J Townsend), B W Redpath (*captain*); T J Smith, G C Bulloch, B A F Douglas (rep G Kerr), S Murray, S B Grimes, M D Leslie, S M Taylor, A L Mower

SCOTLAND SCORER: *Penalty Goals:* Ross 2

## CAP 58

LOST 3–38 v FRANCE, 23 February 2003, Stade de France, Paris

SCOTLAND: G H Metcalfe; C D Paterson, G P J Townsend, K N Utterson, **K M Logan**; B J Laney (rep A Craig), B W Redpath (*captain*) (rep M R L Blair); T J Smith, G C Bulloch, B A F Douglas (rep G Kerr), S Murray (rep J P R White), S B Grimes, M D Leslie, S M Taylor, A L Mower (rep J M Petrie)

SCOTLAND SCORER: *Penalty Goal:* Paterson

## CAP 59

WON 30–22 v WALES, 8 March 2003, Murrayfield

SCOTLAND: G H Metcalfe; C D Paterson, J G McLaren, K N Utterson (rep A Craig), **K M Logan**; G P J Townsend (rep G

Ross), B W Redpath (*captain*) (rep M R L Blair); T J Smith, G C Bulloch (rep R R Russell), B A F Douglas (rep G Kerr), S Murray, S B Grimes (rep N J Hines), J P R White (rep J M Petrie), S M Taylor, A L Mower

SCOTLAND SCORERS: *Tries:* Paterson, Douglas, Taylor *Conversions:* Paterson 3 *Penalty Goals:* Paterson 3

## CAP 60

LOST 9–40 v ENGLAND, 22 March 2003, Twickenham

SCOTLAND: G H Metcalfe; C D Paterson, J G McLaren (rep K N Utterson), A Craig, **K M Logan**; G P J Townsend, B W Redpath (*captain*); T J Smith, G C Bulloch, B A F Douglas (rep G Kerr), S Murray (rep S B Grimes), N J Hines, J P R White, S M Taylor, A L Mower (rep R S Beattie)

SCOTLAND SCORER: *Penalty Goals:* Paterson 3

## CAP 61

WON 33–25 v ITALY, 29 March 2003, Murrayfield

SCOTLAND: G H Metcalfe; C D Paterson, J G McLaren, A Craig, **K M Logan**; G P J Townsend, B W Redpath (*captain*); T J Smith, G C Bulloch (rep R R Russell), B A F Douglas, S Murray (rep S B Grimes), N J Hines, J P R White (rep R S Beattie), S M Taylor, A L Mower

SCOTLAND SCORERS: *Tries:* Paterson, McLaren, **Logan**, White *Conversions:* Paterson 2 *Penalty Goals:* Paterson 3

## CAP 62

LOST 25–29 v SOUTH AFRICA, 7 June 2003, Durban

SCOTLAND: G H Metcalfe; C D Paterson, A Craig, A R Henderson (rep J G McLaren), **K M Logan**; G P J Townsend, B W Redpath (*captain*); G Kerr, G C Bulloch (rep R R Russell), B A F Douglas, S Murray, N J Hines, J P R White (rep M D Leslie), S M Taylor, A L Mower (rep J M Petrie)

SCOTLAND SCORERS: *Tries:* Paterson, Craig, White *Conversions:* Paterson 2 *Penalty Goals:* Paterson 2

## CAP 63

LOST 19–28 v SOUTH AFRICA, 14 June 2003, Johannesburg

SCOTLAND: G H Metcalfe; C D Paterson, A Craig, A R Henderson (rep B J Laney), **K M Logan**; G P J Townsend (rep G Ross), B W Redpath (*captain*) (rep M R L Blair); G Kerr (rep G R McIlwham), G C Bulloch (rep R R Russell), B A F Douglas, S Murray, N J Hines (rep M D Leslie), J P R White, S M Taylor, A L Mower (rep J M Petrie)

SCOTLAND SCORERS: *Try:* Craig *Conversion:* Paterson *Penalty Goals:* Paterson 4

## CAP 64

WON 47–15 v ITALY, 23 August 2003, Murrayfield

SCOTLAND: B G Hinshelwood; S C J Danielli, J G McLaren, A R Henderson (rep B J Laney), **K M Logan** (rep C D Paterson); G Ross, M R L Blair; T J Smith, R R Russell (rep G C Bulloch), B A F Douglas (rep G R McIlwham), S Murray (*captain*), N J Hines (rep I A Fullarton), J P R White (rep M D Leslie), S M Taylor, J M Petrie

SCOTLAND SCORERS: *Tries:* Danielli, McLaren, Ross, Blair, White, Laney *Conversions:* Paterson 2, Ross 2 *Penalty Goals:* Ross 3

## CAP 65

LOST 10–29 v IRELAND, 6 September 2003, Murrayfield

SCOTLAND: G H Metcalfe (rep S L Webster); C D Paterson, A Craig, A R Henderson (rep J G McLaren), **K M Logan**; G Ross, M R L Blair; A F Jacobsen, G C Bulloch (*captain*) (rep R R Russell), G R McIlwham (rep M C Proudfoot), S B Grimes (temp rep I A Fullarton), N J Hines, R S Beattie (rep J M Petrie), S M Taylor, A L Mower

SCOTLAND SCORERS: *Try:* Webster *Conversion:* Paterson *Penalty Goal:* Paterson

## CAP 66

WON 32–11 v JAPAN, 12 October 2003, Townsville

SCOTLAND: B G Hinshelwood; C D Paterson (rep S C J Danielli), A Craig, J G McLaren, **K M Logan**; G Ross (rep G

P J Townsend), B W Redpath (*captain*); T J Smith, R R Russell, B A F Douglas (rep G Kerr), S Murray (rep R S Beattie), S B Grimes, J P R White, S M Taylor, J M Petrie (rep M D Leslie)

SCOTLAND SCORERS: *Tries:* Paterson 2, Grimes, Taylor, Danielli *Conversions:* Paterson, Townsend *Penalty Goal:* Paterson

## CAP 67

WON 39–15 v UNITED STATES, 20 October 2003, Brisbane

SCOTLAND: G H Metcalfe; S C J Danielli, A Craig (rep B G Hinshelwood), A R Henderson, C D Paterson; G P J Townsend (rep **K M Logan**), M R L Blair (rep B W Redpath); T J Smith (rep B A F Douglas), G C Bulloch (*captain*), G Kerr, N J Hines, S B Grimes, R S Beattie (temp rep B A F Douglas and rep by J P R White), S M Taylor, J M Petrie (rep M D Leslie)

SCOTLAND SCORERS: *Tries:* Danielli 2, Paterson, Townsend, Kerr *Conversions:* Paterson 4 *Penalty Goals* Paterson 2

## CAP 68

LOST 9–51 v FRANCE, 25 October 2003, Sydney

SCOTLAND: G H Metcalfe; C D Paterson, A Craig, A R Henderson (rep J G McLaren), **K M Logan**; G P J Townsend, B W Redpath (*captain*); T J Smith, G C Bulloch (rep R R Russell), G Kerr (rep B A F Douglas), S Murray (rep N J

Hines), S B Grimes, J P R White, S M Taylor (rep J M Petrie),
C G Mather (temp rep J M Petrie)

SCOTLAND SCORER: *Penalty Goals:* Paterson 3

## CAP 69

WON 22–20 v FIJI, I November 2003, Sydney

SCOTLAND: G H Metcalfe (rep B G Hinshelwood); S C J
Danielli (rep J G McLaren), G P J Townsend, A R Henderson,
**K M Logan**; C D Paterson, B W Redpath (*captain*); T J Smith,
G C Bulloch (temp rep R R Russell), B A F Douglas, N J
Hines, S B Grimes, R S Beattie (rep J P R White), S M Taylor,
C G Mather

SCOTLAND SCORERS: *Try:* Smith *Conversion:* Paterson *Penalty Goals* Paterson 5

## CAP 70

LOST 16–33 v AUSTRALIA, 8 November 2003, Brisbane

SCOTLAND: G H Metcalfe (rep B G Hinshelwood); S C J
Danielli, G P J Townsend, (rep J G McLaren), A R Henderson,
**K M Logan**; C D Paterson, B W Redpath (*captain*); T J Smith,
G C Bulloch (rep R R Russell), B A F Douglas (rep G R
McIlwham), N J Hines, S B Grimes (rep S Murray), J P R
White (rep J M Petrie), S M Taylor, C G Mather

SCOTLAND SCORERS: *Try:* Russell *Conversion:* Paterson *Penalty Goals* Paterson 2 *Dropped Goal:* Paterson

# SCOTLAND XV APPEARANCES

- In 21 non-Test appearances he was on the winning side a dozen times, lost seven and twice appeared in drawn matches.
- He scored 85 points from 17 tries.
- His five tries against Spain in 1998 would have equalled the national record (set in 1887) had the SRU followed the other Home Unions and awarded caps for World Cup qualifying matches that autumn.

| Date | Opponents | Result | Position |
|---|---|---|---|
| 28 May 1992 | v Northern Territory XV | Lost 16–17 | W |
| 31 May 1992 | v Queensland | Drawn 15–15 | Rep |
| 3 June 1992 | v Emerging Wallabies | Drawn 24–24 | W |
| 6 June 1992 | v New South Wales | Lost 15–35 | FB |
| 9 June 1992 | v NSW Country Origin XV | Won 26–10 | Rep |
| 22 May 1993 | v Fiji B | Won 14–7 | FB |
| 29 May 1993 | v Fiji (scored one try) | Won 21–10 | FB |
| 2 June 1993 | v Tongan President's XV | Won 21–5 | Rep |
| 5 June 1993 | v Tonga (scored one try) | Won 23–5 | W |
| 12 June 1993 | v Western Samoans | Lost 11–28 | W |
| 28 May 1994 | v Cuyo | Won 25–11 | FB |
| 31 May 1994 | v Cordoba (scored one try) | Won 40–14 | W |
| 7 June 1994 | v Rosario (scored one try) | Lost 16–27 | W |
| 6 May 1995 | v Spain (scored one try) | Won 62–7 | W |
| 31 May 1996 | v Northland (scored one try) | Lost 10–15 | W |
| 5 June 1996 | v Waikato (scored one try) | Lost 35–39 | Rep |
| 8 June 1996 | v Southland (scored one try) | Won 31–21 | W |
| 11 June 1996 | v South Island XV (scored two tries) | Won 63–21 | W |
| 17 August 1996 | v Barbarians | Lost 45–48 | W |
| 28 November 1998 | v Portugal (scored two tries) | Won 85–11 | W |
| 5 December 1998 | v Spain (scored five tries) | Won 85–3 | W |

# SCOTLAND A APPEARANCES

- In eight appearances he finished with a 50/50 win/loss record.
- He scored 20 points from four tries.

| Date | Opponents | Result | Position |
|------|-----------|--------|----------|
| 12 September 1992 | v Spain (scored one try) | Won 35–14 | FB |
| 28 December 1992 | v Ireland A (scored one try) | Won 22–13 | FB |
| 20 March 1993 | v France A (scored one try) | Lost 19–29 | FB |
| 13 November 1993 | v New Zealanders | Lost 9–20 | W |
| 18 December 1993 | v Italy | Lost 15–18 | W |
| 28 December 1993 | v Ireland A | Won 24–9 | FB |
| 6 January 1996 | v Italy A | Lost 17–29 | W |
| 6 March 1998 | v Wales A (scored one try) | Won 18–10 | W |

# TOP-FLIGHT DOMESTIC
# RUGBY SEASON BY SEASON

1989–90    Helps Stirling County to finish fifth in the SRU Division One in the club's first season in the top-flight.

1990–91    Stirling County finish seventh in the SRU Division One. Scores tries against Stewart's Melville FP and Edinburgh Wands in the league.

1991–92    Stirling County finish joint-fifth in the SRU Division One. Scores a try in the match against Watsonians. Debut as left-wing for Glasgow District (v North & Midlands on 21 September 1991) at Bridgehaugh, Stirling. Glasgow win 16–3. Plays later the same season at full-back for Glasgow in the Inter-City match (v Edinburgh) scoring a try in Glasgow's 16–12 win at Hughenden.

1992–93    Stirling County finish joint-eighth in the SRU Division One. Scores tries in three of the last four league games of the season and kicks penalties in two of those games. Ever-present as a wing for Glasgow in the District Championship, scoring tries in the 13-all draw against Edinburgh and the defeat by North & Midlands.

1993–94    Stirling County finish joint-sixth in the SRU Division One. Scores three tries, a conversion and three penalties in league games. Plays full-back in both of Glasgow's District matches.

1994–95    Stirling County win the SRU Division One Championship title. Scores seven league tries, including a hat-trick against Watsonians, and kicks three penalties and a conversion. Ever-present as a wing for Glasgow in the District Championship, scoring a try in the match against Edinburgh. Makes Barbarians debut against Leicester on 27 December 1994.

1995–96    Stirling County are runners-up (on inferior points difference) to Melrose in the SRU Premiership. Scores five league tries. Plays on the left-wing for Glasgow in the Inter-City match at Murrayfield.

1996–97    Stirling County finish eighth in the SRU Premiership. Scores 36 league points (including three tries). Ever-present as full-back for Glasgow in the Inter-District Championship scoring three tries and three conversions, and plays twice (scoring two tries) for them in the European Challenge Cup before crossing the border to join Wasps. Plays first game for Wasps, against Gloucester, on 9 March

1997. He scores five tries, a then record for the English top-flight, a fortnight later in the league game against Orrell. Plays nine games scoring 11 tries (55 points) as Wasps become the Courage League champions.

1997–98    Wasps finish ninth in the Allied Dunbar Division One, runners-up in the Tetley's Bitter Cup and reach the quarter-finals of the Heineken Cup. Plays 25 games for the side scoring 62 points including twelve tries.

1998–99    Wasps win the Tetley's Bitter Cup and finish fifth in the Allied Dunbar Division One. (English clubs do not compete in Europe this season.) Plays 25 games scoring 319 points comprising 12 tries, 44 conversions and 57 penalty goals.

1999–2000    Wasps win the Tetley's Bitter Cup, finish seventh in the Premiership and reach the quarter-finals of the Heineken European Cup. Plays 29 games scoring 285 points comprising 15 tries, 33 conversions and 48 penalty goals.

2000–01    Wasps are runners-up in the Premiership. Plays 26 games scoring 407 points comprising 14 tries, 62 conversions and 71 penalty goals to finish as the season's leading scorer in the English top-flight.

2001–02    Wasps finish seventh in the Premiership. Plays 22 times scoring 153 points made up of four tries, five conversions and 41 penalty goals.

2002–03    Wasps are Premiership Champions and winners of the European Challenge Cup. Makes 31 appearances scoring 60 points from four tries, two conversions, eleven penalty goals and a dropped goal.

2003–04    His final season in London. Wasps retain the Premiership Champions title and win the Heineken Cup. Scores seven tries in his eight appearances bringing his career record in all games for Wasps to 1,376 points (79 tries, 147 conversions, 228 penalty goals and a dropped goal) from his 175 club appearances.

2004–05    Final season. Plays with Glasgow making five appearances in the Heineken Cup and 12 (with three as a sub) in the Celtic League (scoring 25 points from five tries), Glasgow finishing sixth. Bows out of competitive rugby with an appearance as a sub for the Barbarians in their 38–7 defeat by a Scotland XV at Pittodrie on 24 May 2005.

# Index

Note: KL denotes Kenny Logan. Names of countries, cities, towns, etc., refer to teams unless otherwise indicated.

# Picture Credits

Credits are listed according to the order the pictures appear on each page, left to right, top to bottom. 'KL' denotes photographs that are courtesy of Kenny Logan.

## Section 1

Page 1: KL, KL, KL, Whyler Photos; Page 2: KL, T Scott Roxbrough, Stirling Observer; Page 3: KL, KL, KL, KL; Page 4: KL, David Gibson/Fotosport, KL, PA Photos; Page 5: Whyler Photos, Whyler Photos, Action Images, PA Photos, PA Photos, Colorsport; Page 6: PA Photos, Offside, Colorsport, KL; Page 7: Colorsport, Action Images, Action Images, Colorsport, PA Photos; Page 8: Getty Images, KL, Colorsport

## Section 2

Page 1: PA Photos, KL, Getty Images, Colorsport; Page 2: Colorsport, Getty Images, Colorsport, Action Images; Page 3: Rex Features, PA Photos, PA Photos, PA Photos; Page 4: PA Photos, KL, KL; Page 5: Getty Images, Getty Images, Colorsport; Page 6: snspix.com, Topfoto, Getty Images, KL; Page 7: KL, KL, BBC, BBC, PA Photos; Page 8: KL, PA Photos, KL, KL